MARKETING

MARKETING

M VIDHYA
Lecturer
Department of Commerce
KSR College of Arts and Science
Tiruchengode
Tamil Nadu

MJP Publishers

Cataloguing-in-Publication Data

Vidhya, M. (1976 –)
  Marketing / by
M. Vidhya. – Chennai : MJP Publishers, 2010
  xxii, 396p. ; 21 cm.
  Includes Glossary, references and index.
  ISBN 978-81-8094-021-7 (pbk.)
  1. Marketing I. Title
  381 dc22 VID MJP 0077

ISBN 978-81-8094-021-7   **MJP PUBLISHERS**
    © Publishers, 2010   47, Nallathambi Street
    All rights reserved   Triplicane
Printed and bound in India   Chennai 600 005

            Publisher : J.C. Pillai
    Managing Editor : C. Sajeesh Kumar
  Marketing Manager : S.Y. Sekar
      Project Editor : P. Parvath Radha
  Acquisitions Editor : C. Janarthanan
      Editorial Team : N. Yamuna Devi, Lissy John,
                M. Gnanasoundari, N. Thilagavathi
          CIP Data : Prof. K. Hariharan, Librarian
                RKM Vivekananda College, Chennai.

This book has been published in good faith that the work of the author is original. All efforts have been taken to make the material error-free. However, the author and publisher disclaim responsibility for any inadvertent errors.

To

My husband, Mr. S. Arumugam
and
my daughter, A. Theekshana

PREFACE

Marketing is the task of creating, promoting and delivering goods and services to customers and business. It involves marketing of ten types of entities: goods, services, experiences, events, persons, places, properties, organization, information and ideas. The study of all these ten types of entities constitutes the backbone of marketing.

An effective study and analysis of market and marketing functions helps one to achieve success in business. So, the students who are pursuing their commerce and management courses have to study marketing as a core subject. To meet their needs, this book provides all the aspects of marketing in a comprehensive and self-explanatory style and details them in 22 chapters.

Though there exist numerous books on marketing that are voluminous and exhaustive, this book is designed in a unique fashion so that the topics are arranged sequentially and coherently to be helpful to students. To help self-study, review questions are provided for every chapter.

Valuable suggestions to improve the contents of the book in further editions are most welcome.

M. VIDHYA

ACKNOWLEDGEMENT

I express my heartful thanks to the God almighty for having bestowed the power and strength on me to complete this task successfully. I am grateful to the authors of various text books, journals and periodicals.

I extend my thanks to the management of KSR College of Arts and Science for their endless support and for giving me the opportunity to write this book. I am deeply indebted to Dr. N. Kannan, the Principal, KSR College of Arts and Science, for his constant encouragement and valuable guidance throughout the writing of this book. I express my deepest and sincere thanks to my guide Dr. V. Renugadevi, Lecturer, Vellalar College for Women, for her valuable suggestions and guidance towards the successful completion of the book. I also thank my colleagues, friends and other well wishers who have been behind this task.

This task will not be complete without the support of the MJP Publishers. Hence, I express my deepest sense of gratitude to MJP Publishers; particularly I owe much thanks to Mr. C. Sajeesh Kumar, the Managing Editor and the editorial team of MJP Publishers for their continuous suggestions and assistance.

Finally, I wish to express my gratitude to my husband for his sincere efforts to bring out this textbook and to my daughter, my mother and my sister for their cooperation, support and encouragement throughout my writing.

M. VIDHYA

CONTENTS

1

INTRODUCTION

Human beings have many desires, wants and needs. All human activities are directed towards one ultimate purpose or aim, that is, the satisfaction of wants. Needs and wants are satisfied by the use of goods and services. Hence, goods and services must be moved from the manufacturers and brought into the hands of the ultimate consumer; otherwise, production of goods has no value. This movement involves a series of problems like shortage of raw materials, shortage of labour supply, lack of advertisement, financial problems etc. These problems can be solved by marketing. In short, we can say that all activities which involve the physical movement of goods and services from one person to another can be collectively termed as marketing.

Marketing is typically seen as the task of creating, promoting and delivering goods and services to consumers and business. It involves marketing of ten types of entities: goods, services, experiences, events, persons, places, properties, organization, information and ideas.

MARKET

The term market is derived from the latin word, *Mercatus*, meaning merchandise, wares, traffic or trade. A market, may be described as a place or geographical area where buyers and sellers meet and function, goods or services are offered for sale, and transfers of title of ownership occur. In its most common usage the word "market" means a place where goods are bought or sold.

Classification of Market

Markets may be classified into various types according to:

1. *Nature and volume of selling* According to the nature and volume of selling, market may be a wholesale market or retail market. When goods are sold in large quantities to dealers, it is called a wholesale market. When goods are sold in small quantities to consumers, it is known as a retail market.

2. *The product sold in the market* The market is distinguished on the basis of the product itself, for example, jute market, cotton market, share market, money market, etc.

3. *The nature of dealings* According to the nature of dealing, market may be spot market or forward/future market. In spot market, goods are bought and sold immediately, while in future market, the actual purchasing and selling may take place at some future time as agreed by the buyer and seller.

4. *Regulated markets* Markets may be owned and controlled by associations or institutions. If an association controls the market, it is known as a regulated market. If the municipality owns and controls the market, it is called a municipal market.

5. *Areas covered* According to the area covered, the market may be international market, national market and home market or local market.

6. *Time-interval* On the basis of time-interval the market may be short-period market or long-period market. Money market is a short-term market and capital market is a long-term market.

7. *Economic concept* On the basis of economics, the market may be perfect market or imperfect market. Perfect market refers to perfect competition and imperfect

market refers to absence of perfect competition and existence of monopoly.

8. *Seller's position* On the basis of seller's position, the market may be primary or local market, secondary or central market, or terminal market. In the case of primary or local market, producers, for example, farmers, sell their surplus produce to the traders in the village; in the case of secondary or central market, wholesalers sell to retailers and in the case of terminal market, consumers buy from retailers or local dealers.

MARKETING

In the most simple and non-technical language, marketing may be explained as a business function entrusted with the creation and satisfaction of customers to achieve the aims of business itself. Thus, the term may be logically broken down as follows:

- Business aims at profit.
- To realize profit, a sale has to be made.
- To make the sale, a customer has to be identified.
- To retain the customer, he has to be satisfied.
- To satisfy the customer, his needs have to be met.
- To meet his needs, the product should conform to his requirements.

This leads us to the conclusion that the process of marketing begins with the conceiving of a business idea itself or sometimes even earlier than that.

Definition

The following are the some of the definitions given by different authors:

According to Clark and Clark, market is "an area in which the forces leading to exchange of title to a particular product operate, and towards which and from which the actual goods tend or travel".

In the words of Pyle, "Market includes both place and region in which buyers and sellers are in free competition with one another".

According to Mitchell, "Market, for most commodities, may be thought of not as a geographical meeting place but as getting together of buyers and sellers in person, by mail, telephone, telegraph or any other means of communication."

More definitions have emerged for the term marketing. Few of the best and important definitions have been listed below.

    i. The official definition for the term marketing by the American Marketing Association (AMA) is as follows: " Marketing is the process of planning and executing the conception, pricing, promotion, and distribution of ideas, goods, and services to create exchanges that satisfy individual and organizational objectives."

   ii. According to E.F.L. Brech, "Marketing is the process of determining consumer demand for a product or service, motivating its sales, and distributing it to the ultimate consumer at a profit."

  iii. A more precise statement is the one given by Philip Kotler—"Marketing is specifically concerned with how transactions are created, stimulated, facilitated and valued."

The Chartered Institute of Marketing defines marketing as:

"Marketing is the management process for identifying, anticipating and satisfying customer requirements profitably."

In Peter Drucker's (1973) words, "Marketing is so basic that it cannot be considered as a separate function on par with others such as manufacturing and personnel. It is first a central dimension of the entire business. It is the whole business seen from the point of view of its final results, that is, from the customers' point of view."

One can assume that there will always be need for some selling. But the aim of marketing is to make selling superfluous. The aim is to know and understand the customers well so that the product or service fits him and sells itself. Ideally, marketing should result in a customer who is ready to buy. All that should be needed then is to make the product or service available.

Nature of Marketing

1. *Marketing is consumer-oriented* It means "what is offered for sale should be determined by the buyer rather than by the seller."

2. *Marketing starts and ends with customers* It is essential to know what the customers really want and this is possible only when information is collected from the customers. A mechanism is required to keep in touch with customers. Marketing research and information systems provide clues about customer needs.

MARKETING VERSUS SELLING

The basic difference between marketing and selling lies in the attitude towards business. The selling concept takes an inside-out perspective. It starts with the factory, focuses on the company's existing products, and calls for heavy selling and promoting to produce profitable sales. The marketing concept takes an outside-in perspective. It starts with a well-defined market, focuses on customer needs, coordinates all the activities that will affect customers, and produces profits through creating customer satisfaction(Table 1.1).

In marketing, the focus is on customer's needs and the customer enjoys supreme importance. The customer's needs are converted into products and profits are obtained through customer satisfaction. An integrated approach is practiced and the principle of "caveat vendor" (let the seller beware) is followed.

Table 1.1 The concepts of selling and marketing

	Starting point	Focus	Means	Ends
Selling concept	Factory	Products	Selling and promoting	Profit through sales volume
Marketing concept	Market	Customer needs	Integrated marketing	Profit through customer satisfaction

Table 1.2 Marketing vs. selling

Marketing	Selling
Marketing starts with the buyer and focuses mainly on the needs of the buyer.	Selling starts with the seller and focuses mainly on the needs of the seller.
Emphasizes on identification of a market opportunity; seeks to convert customer "needs" into "products"; emphasizes on fulfilling the needs of the customers.	Emphasises on saleable surpluses available within the company; seeks to quickly convert "products" into "cash"; focuses on selling the products to customers.
Views business as "customer satisfying process".	Views business as a "goods producing process".
Buyer determines the shape that the marketing mix should take.	Seller's convenience dominates the formulation of the marketing mix.
Product is determined by the customer. The firm makes a product that would match and satisfy the needs of the customers.	The firm makes the product first and then figures out how to sell it and make profit.
Customer determines price; price determines costs.	Costs determine price.
The customer occupies the pride of place in any marketing scheme.	The product occupies the pride of place in any selling scheme.
Marketing is concerned with planning and development of products to match the market requirements.	Selling is concerned with selling the goods and services which have already been produced.
Represents an integrated approach to achieve long-term goals.	Represents a piecemeal approach to achieve short-term goals.
Emphasises on innovation in every sphere; on producing better value to the customer by adopting the most innovative technology.	Emphasises on following existing technology and reducing the cost of production.

In selling, the emphasis is on product planning and development to match the products with the market. The focus is on seller's needs. The product enjoys supreme importance and the product is converted into cash and profits are earned through sales volume. The emphasis is placed on the sale of products already produced. A fragmented approach is practiced in selling. The principle of "caveat emptor" (let the buyer beware) is followed.

Selling comes to an end with the delivery of the product to the customer. But marketing continues even after sale so as to provide after-sales service.

Thus marketing is a much wider term embracing selling which merely involves promotional activities. The other differences between marketing and selling is given in Table 1.2.

MARKETING PROCESS

Marketing has been viewed as an ongoing or dynamic process involving a set of interactive activities dealing with a market offered by producers to consumers on the basis of reliable marketing anticipation (sales or demand forecasts). Marketing is a matching process by which a producer provides a marketing mix (product, price, promotion and place) that meets consumer demand of a target market within the limits of society. The process is based on corporate goals and corporate capabilities. Marketing process brings together producers and consumers, the two main participants, in exchange. Each producer or seller has certain goals and capabilities in making and marketing his products.

He uses marketing research as a tool to anticipate market demand. Then he provides a marketing mix (product, services, promotion, advertising, pricing, distribution etc.) in order to capitalize a marketing opportunity. An exchange or a transaction takes place when market offering is acceptable to the customer who is prepared to give something of value (money) in return against the product so bought.

In the process of exchange both give up something and both gain something in return. The producer gets the surplus value in the form of profit which is a reward for delivering customer satisfaction. The consumer gets the surplus value in the form of utility or individual satisfaction. Market mechanism brings together a willing seller and a willing and informed buyer for mutual gain. The marketing process is influenced by competition, government rules and policies, mass media of communication, consumer advocates etc. Marketing environment affects both producer and consumer. The business enterprise engaged in the marketing process itself is influenced by social environment. It consists of political, economic, social, cultural and technological forces. Marketers have to adapt to these ever-changing environmental forces and fulfil the needs and desires of the society or community. Thus, marketing is an economic as well as social activity, in the long run; society must approve the marketing process and control its effectiveness. Marketing process must reflect social awareness and social responsiveness, and we must have a judicial combination of productivity and social responsibility in all business enterprises. Only then we will have assured survival, growth and prosperity of our units. In essence, marketing is the business function charged with responsibility of directing the firm's response to an ever-changing market environment and orienting all parts of the business towards the sole purpose of the business, viz. the creation of satisfied customers at a profit.

COST OF MARKETING

Marketing is blamed for its high cost. Nowadays it has attracted the attention of different sections of the society like government, producers and educational institutions. It is almost impossible to estimate accurately the overall cost of marketing functions and services. However, many marketing experts have tried to calculate the marketing cost and have found that it accounts for about 50% of the price paid by consumers. The study of marketing of wheat, rice and cotton in India indicated that marketing costs accounted for 50% to 60% of the total cost.

Reasons for the High Cost

There are many reasons to support the fact that marketing cost is high, which are as follows:

1. Large-scale production has brought down the cost of production, improved the quality and multiplied varieties, and these have become the main causes for increase in the cost of marketing. There is a big gap between the points of production and consumption. This gap is bridged by an army of middlemen, that is, production must be matched by mass marketing. This results in high cost because mass marketing is possible only by providing varied services to consumers.

2. Society has also accepted to pay high prices in view of the valuable services that it is getting in return from the marketing system.

3. Further, the inefficiency that creeps into various marketing functions and segments due to presence of inefficient and incompetent personnel, results in higher costs of marketing.

How to Reduce Marketing Costs

To reduce the marketing costs, greater attention is now being paid by all—marketing personnel as well as outsiders like the government, producers and educational institutions. The development of chain stores, multiple shops, and departmental stores are the innovative measures taken to avoid middlemen. Cooperatives are developed to provide better services to consumers. Educational institutions are helping by turning out able and highly qualified marketing experts. At the same time governments are trying to give superfine infrastructure like communication system, railways, waterways, airways etc.

MARKET INFORMATION

The success of marketing depends on correct and timely decisions. These decisions are based on market information or market intelligence. Informations such as size, location, characteristics of markets, etc. are available. The customer's wants, habits, purchasing power etc., are to be considered; the strength or weakness of competitors, trend in market, supply and demand etc. are also to be taken into account. Marketing conditions are dynamic and affect the industry immensely. Market information includes all facts, estimates, opinions and other information used in making decisions, which affect the marketing of products or services. Major decisions of business firms are based on the interpretation, of the available data. Plans and programmes of marketing are based on the information acquired through market research and marketing intelligence services.

BENEFITS OF MARKETING

Marketing gives benefits to both society and business and its importance to each has been growing rapidly since 1950.

Importance to Society

Undoubtedly, marketing plays a vital role in society as explained below:

1. *Delivery of Standard of living* In a society, there are different standards of living. There is a small class of people that enjoys highest standard of living. It is in this class that people have everything in abundance. On the contrary, there is another class namely, poor class, which forms a vast majority with subsistence level of living. In between these two extreme classes of rich and poor, there exists the middle class. In fact, it is considered as the backbone of the nation. Unfortunately, this middle class is below the upper class, thus leading a middle standard of living.

Despite such differences in their level of living, every member of the society depends—for each and every need—on this huge interlinked system, that is, marketing. Marketing is the means through which production and purchasing power are converted into consumption. Hence Paul Mazur states that marketing is the delivery of standard of living. Prof. Malcolm Nair improved Mazur's statement and has said that, marketing is the creation and delivery of standard of living to the society.

Moreover, marketing process brings new varieties of useful and quality goods to consumers. This raises the standard of living. Better marketing gives room for mass production. Thus cost of production will be low and hence price of the article will be low, Hence, people can buy more goods for their money. This will result in a higher standard of living.

2. *Employment opportunities* Marketing process increases employment opportunities. Just as every industry provides employment opportunities to thousands of skilled and unskilled labourers in various capacities, marketing also provides employment to millions of people. Marketing is a complex mechanism involving a number of functions and sub-functions which call for different specialized persons for employment. The major marketing functions are buying, selling, transport, warehousing, financing, risk-bearing, market information and standardization. In each such function, different activities are to be performed by a large number of individuals or institutions. It is said that roughly 30 to 40% of the population depends directly or indirectly on marketing.

3. *National income* The nation's income is composed of goods and services which money can buy. An efficient system of marketing reduces the cost to the minimum, this in turn it lowers the prices and increases the consumer's purchasing power. This will automatically increase the national income.

4. *Economic stability and economic development* Economic stability is the sign of an efficient and dynamic economy. Economic stability is maintained only when there is a balance of supply and demand. If production is more than demand, the excess goods cannot be sold at acceptable prices. Then the stocks of goods would pile up and there would be glut in the market, resulting in fall in price, and depression creeps in. Similarly if production is less than demand, prices shoot up resulting in inflation. In such situations, marketing maintains the economic stability by balancing the two aspects—production and consumption.

5. *Link between the consumer and the producer* The marketing process brings new items to retail shops on a continuous basis from where the consumers can have them.

6. *Remove the imbalances of supply* This is done by transferring the surplus to deficit areas, through better transport facilities.

7. *Create utilities* Marketing as an economic activity, creates place, time, possession, firm and information utilities. Exchange creates ownership and possession utilities. Transport creates place utility. Storage creates time utility. Promotional activities create information utility. Product development, packaging, branding and standardization creates firm utility.

Importance to Individual Business Firms

The following benefits accrue to individual firms through marketing:

1. *As a source of revenue generation* Profit is the core on which the whole super-structure of business is built. Functions of marketing develop and widen the markets. When markets are widened, sales increases and thus profit to the firm increases.

2. *As the basis for making decisions* The problems of the entrepreneur are what, how, when, how much and for whom to produce. In the past, the producer was in direct contact with consumers. Hence, the problems of the product were tackled very easily. However, today the producer does not have any direct contact with the consumers. Therefore the problems of the producer become very acute and complicated. These problems

are solved by the marketing department. The marketing department collects all information regarding what, how, when, how much and for whom to produce and this information is passed on to the top management who use it for decision-making.

3. *Helps to manage innovations and changes* Marketing and innovation are the two basic functions of any business. We are living in a dynamic world. There is nothing permanent except change. Change is the essence of life and change means progress. Today, the minds of the consumers are not firm, but fluctuating or changing very often. The behaviour and demand of consumers keep on changing. Hence, in order to run a business successfully, a businessman should adapt himself to the changing preferences, changing styles, changing fashions, etc. and being innovate in producing new customers, new products, new markets, new methods and procedures. Marketing helps to adopt change and innovate. Retailers communicate to the wholesalers about consumers' needs. Wholesalers, in turn, communicate to manufacturers about market demand. Market research also acts as a source of marketing information on consumer behaviour and market trends. Salesmen of a marketing concern are its ears and eyes for information and feedback.

MARKETING MANAGEMENT

The process of planning, executing and controlling marketing activities to attain marketing goals and objectives effectively and efficiently is marketing management.

Marketing management can be seen as the art and science of choosing target markets and getting, keeping and growing customers through creating, delivering and communicating superior customer value.

REVIEW QUESTIONS

I. Short-answer questions:

1. What is marketing?
2. Define marketing.
3. What is regulated market?
4. What is share market?
5. What is spot market?
6. What is forward or future market?
7. What do you mean by wholesale market?
8. What do you mean by retail market?
9. What is marketing process?

II. Essay-type questions:

1. Explain the difference between marketing and selling.
2. What are the different types of market?
3. Explain the benefits of marketing.
4. Explain the importance of marketing.
5. Explain the reasons for high cost of marketing and how to reduce the cost of marketing.
6. What are the merits of marketing?
7. Explain the marketing process.
8. Explain the nature of marketing.
9. Discuss the nature and scope of marketing.

2

EVOLUTION OF MARKETING CONCEPT

The evolution of marketing is quite akin to any discipline that is innately dynamic. Since inception, marketing has been growing as a multidimensional and multidisciplinary concept. Moreover, marketing has permeated into each and every functional aspect of business. All these have contributed to the confusion of precisely defining the term marketing.

An analysis of contemporary literature reveals vividly the conceptual variations in the use of the term "marketing". They describe it as a "function", "an orientation", "an approach or attitude", "a philosophy of business" and "a management science or technique". A closer analysis would reveal that marketing, in fact, conveys all of these and often more. An attempt is made here to trace the evolution of marketing from all the following possible perspectives:

1. Historical perspective
2. Conceptual perspective
3. Functional perspective
4. Managerial perspective

Historical Perspective

The traditional objective of marketing was to make goods available at places whereever they are in need. This idea was later on changed by shifting the emphasis from exchange to satisfaction of human wants. As human needs and wants multiplied and technological progress supplemented such developments, the scope of marketing function had to be enlarged. Almost simultaneously, new dimensions for marketing were incorporated due to changes in the organizational patterns of business and increase in their size of operation. The developments are easily recognizable along with the growth of civilization—culturally, socially and economically. Each stage is explained in the following paragraphs:

i. *Self-sufficient stage*   After the nomadic stage, people started setting at the banks of rivers and started doing agriculture and allied activities. But each family then was a self-sufficient unit as far as production and consumption function was concerned. They produced what they wanted to consume and practically no surplus was available to initiate the process of exchange. Hence, it may be stated that the concept of marketing was absent in this stage.

ii. *Exchange-oriented stage*   When nomads chose to live permanently along the river banks and continuously engaged in agricultural and allied operations, the problem of surplus production arose. This necessitated exchange of surplus products with others. Gradually commerce and trade evolved, emphasizing the need for exchange. In order to smoothen out exchange "Barter system" came into vogue, though the latent inconveniences of such a system were felt only a little later. It was gradually realized that the double coincidence of wants could be attained only if the products are brought to a central location so that exchange will take place smoothly.

iii. *Production-oriented stage (1869–1930)*   ("Make what you know how to make") The next stage came with the dawn of the Industrial Revolution. Adam Smith in his book *Wealth of Nations* said, "Consumption is the sole end and purpose of all production, and the interest of the producer ought to be attempted to, only so far as it may be necessary for promoting that of the consumer." But under the mercantile system, the interest of the consumer was virtually sacrificed to that of the producer. It was believed that if the product is of good quality and priced reasonably, nothing would prevent the producers from achieving satisfactory sales and a profit.

iv. *Sales-oriented stage (1930–1950)* ("Get rid of what you have") The ripple effect of Industrial Revolution did not stop with the technological changes in industrial activities alone. It caused major social changes; there was a shift from agriculture to industry, increase in the living standards, etc. Consequently, drastic changes were reflected in the buying patterns and behaviour of consumers. There was also a revolutionary change in the growth of transport and communications. This stage witnessed the emergence of corporate form of organizations as a means to reap economies of large-scale operations.

v. *Marketing-oriented stage (1950–1960)* ("Have what you can get rid off") As the demand from consumers and the production capacity of the manufacturers came into equilibrium, the producers were forced to rethink the philosophy of marketing. Further, the evil effect of competition made the producers to realize that the product could not be sold without an effective sales force. Customer's importance was further realized but only as a means of disposing off the goods produced. Essentially, this stage did not go a long way from production orientation, though for the sake of differentiation, it is termed as marketing-oriented stage.

vi. *Consumer-oriented stage (1960s to present)* ("Have what you can get rid off with responsibility") Chronologically this stage may be recognized with the second half of the 20th century. It witnessed a changed outlook of producers towards marketing. During this period competition became keen and production was far in excess of demand. Rapid changes in consumer demands drove many organizations into turmoil.

vii. *Management-oriented stage*   This is the present stage of the evolution of the marketing concept. As consumer orientation became an accepted marketing philosophy, the entire business philosophy underwent a subtle change. Today, marketing considerations are most crucial in business planning and decision making. The National Association of Manufacturers said that in this exciting age of change, marketing is the beating heart of many operations; it must be considered a principal reason for corporate existence. The modern concept of marketing recognizes its role as a direct contribution to profits as well as sales volume.

Conceptual Perspective

In the previous section, it was shown how marketing evolved and developed into a full-fledged business philosophy. In the course of development, marketing underwent radical changes and its emphasis shifted from one concept to the other. This was mainly due to the rapidly changing business environment. But the marketing concept still suffers without the clarification and definition essential for understanding, perceptive adoption and substantial implementation.

Functional Perspective

Though marketing was originally brought out as an adjunct of total business functions, its functional area was limited to selling. But in course of time, the growth of the selling department surpassed all expectations and enrolled under it a number of specialized functions. From a theoretical point of view, the process of marketing could be split down to certain major economic activities that are inherent in the marketing processes like buying, selling, etc. Through a continuous division of labour these functions became specialized. Although, these functions are independent, when the marketing process is considered as a total system, each function forms only a part of it.

Managerial Perspective

As explained earlier, the concept of marketing has much deviated from its original concepts and had undergone radical changes in recent years. Marketing has reached a stage where it does not mean simply matching any product with the market. Fundamentally, modern marketing concept rests on the fact that marketing activities start and end with consumer. Further, the thread of marketing begins as early as in the pre-production stage and passes through the production and post-production stage. The cardinal principle of marketing therefore, is that, first of all, firms should seek to determine the differing nature of customer's demand.

Marketing Management vs. Sales Management

Four points of differences between marketing management and sales management are:

i. *Scope*   The scope of marketing management is wider than the scope of sales management. Marketing management includes all the activities from the beginning of ascertaining the needs and requirements of the consumers to the fulfilment and satisfaction of the wants of the actual users. Whereas sales management includes activities concerned with the transfer of ownership of goods and services from the seller to the buyer and deals with the problems of seller.

ii. *Concept*   Marketing management is a modern concept while sales management is a traditional one.

iii. *Object*   The object of marketing management is the satisfaction of the consumers or users in utilizing the available resources in the best possible way so as to maximize profitability. The object of sales management is to maximize sales. The emphasis is on volume and not on the satisfaction of the consumers.

iv. *Performance of activities* The activities of marketing management are superior and the activities of sales management come under the jurisdiction of marketing management. In fact, sales management is only a part of a wider marketing management. In the opinion of E.F.L Brech, "The overall management of sales" refers to only a specialized application of the process of management as a whole."

APPROACHES TO THE STUDY OF MARKETING

1. Product or Commodity Approach

This approach undertakes the study of marketing on the basis of a commodity. For example, when studying the marketing of cotton, one will begin with examining the sources of supply, nature and volume of demand, the purpose for which it is required, how it is transported, the problem of storage, standardization, packing, branding, etc.

This approach is termed as "descriptive approach". In this method, the commodity serves as a focus around which the organizational and managerial aspects of marketing are studied.

This approach is criticized for being repetitive and time consuming since the emphasis is on products. The classification of products tends to create another problem.

2. Institutional Approach

Under this approach, analysis of different institutions engaged in marketing is undertaken. The activities performed by each institution form a part of the entire marketing process. Under this approach marketing process is split up into three institutional functions namely, concentration, equalization and dispersion.

This approach has failed to bring out effectively the interrelations of all the institutions.

3. Functional Approach

Functional approach splits down the field of marketing into a few functions. The purpose is to enable one to separate the essential from the non-essential elements.

According to this approach (designed by A.W. Shaw), middlemen perform the following functions—sharing the risk, transporting the goods and financing the operations.

4. Managerial Approach

This approach combines certain features of the other three approaches. This approach lays emphasis on the application aspects of marketing problems. The changes in marketing are mainly due to two factors—controllable and non-controllable. The controllable factors mean those marketing forces which are well under the control of the firm, for example, personal selling, advertising, etc. The non-controllable factors include economic, sociological and political forces.

5. Societal Approach

In the societal approach to the study of marketing, the entire marketing process is regarded not as a means by which business meets the needs of consumers but as a means by which society meets its own consumption needs. This approach mainly focuses on the environmental factors like sociological, cultural, political, legal, etc. and marketing decisions and their impact on the society. It gives importance to the society and not to the customer.

6. Systems Approach

Marketing has different sub-systems such as product planning, pricing, promotion, distribution, etc. This approach would help the management to plan the activities of each small group in detail and implement them effectively.

Marketing process is not a bundle of isolated functions as was thought in the past. Each function has a profound influence on the other. Moreover, all marketing activities are performed in an ever-changing atmosphere. The above two reasons necessitate the introduction of the systems approach.

Companies are also realizing that losing a customer means more than losing a single sale, that is, losing the entire stream of purchases that the customer would make over a lifetime of patronage. Thus, working to retain customers makes good economic sense.

7. Scientific Approach

In recent years considerable progress has been made in the study of marketing because of the scientific approach. This approach is otherwise known as interdisciplinary approach. It refers to the uses of all disciplines—social, physical, quantitative and business—to develop marketing insights, concepts and theories, investigate and solve marketing problems. It includes the application and integration of pertinent material to advance marketing.

With the application of behavioural sciences, many new concepts on perception, attitude, opinion, leadership, communication and consumer behaviour have been developed which are of vital importance to the marketers. The field of statistics, mathematics and electronics has developed many new analytical tools which are applied to identify and solve marketing problems.

NEW HORIZONS IN MODERN MARKETING

1. Social Marketing

Marketing must develop a social consciousness and provide important public services. Marketing technique must be used for achieving society's satisfaction as a whole, for example, selling clean water, housing facilities, marketing of family planning concept, etc.

Business must be assessed not only from the profitability aspect but also based on its overall effect on the society.

2. Demarketing

According to Kotler and Levy, the new concept of "demarketing" is a situation, which may come about as a result of temporary shortage, occasionally by short-term excess demand for a company's products.

Demarketing has become the declared policy of an increasing number of oil exporting countries to preserve resource and earn greater revenues.

3. Remarketing

Remarketing takes the form of finding or creating new uses or users for an existing product. Remarketing creates new bundles of satisfaction for the consumer. For example, nylon had an end use for making ropes and threads. But later it was remarketed for making cloth and hosiery. Similarly, Baking soda now finds use as cleaning and deodorizing agent. Thus in the real sense, remarketing is a method by which new type of utilities are created for old products.

4. Over-marketing

Over-marketing constitutes striving by a firm to generate increased sales while neglecting quality control and production efficiency. An example of over-marketing is found in the US auto industry. Since the advent of Japanese imported cars, American auto companies escalated advertisements to protect themselves from the foreign competition.

5. Meta-marketing

The word "meta" is used to mean "beyond", in metaphysics. This concept is developed as marketing appears to be moving towards the broader horizons. The concept of meta-marketing is to bring the whole of scientific, social, ethical and managerial experience to have a bearing on marketing.

6. Macromarketing

Macromarketing means "the study of marketing within the context of the entire economic system with special emphasis on its aggregate performance". It studies the aggregate of the different components of the marketing mix employed by different marketers operating within the economic system and the manner in which they interact with the socio-economic life of a society.

7. Micromarketing

Micromarketing is described as the process of formulating and implementing such policies by a firm (viz., product development, pricing, promoting and distributing) that ensures flow of need-satisfying goods which, in return, accomplish the objectives of the firm, viz. profit.

The concept of micromarketing reveals two aspects:

i. It has to ensure need-satisfying goods; this indicates that marketing should begin with the customer and not with the production process.

ii. Marketing should determine what products are to be made.

These two aspects implies that consumer is the centre of all marketing activities. This is exactly consumer orientation on which modern marketing is built.

REVIEW QUESTIONS

I. Short-answer questions:

1. What is sales-oriented marketing?
2. What is customer-oriented marketing?
3. What is product approach of marketing?

4. What do you mean by systems approach of marketing?
5. Define social marketing.
6. What is demarketing?
7. What is over-marketing?
8. What is remarketing?
9. What is
    i. macromarketing
    ii. micromarketing
    iii. metamarketing

II. Essay-type questions:

1. How marketing concepts evolved?
2. Explain the various perspectives of marketing.
3. What are the different stages in the historical perspective?
4. Distinguish between marketing management and sales management.
5. Explain the various approaches to the study of marketing.
6. Explain the recent innovations in modern marketing.

3

MODERN
MARKETING CONCEPT

The new managerial awareness and desire, reflected in the consumer orientation for an all-out commitment to the market consideration and to dovetail all marketing operations to the consumer needs, has given birth to a new operational notion called the "marketing concept". This concept has been in vogue in the free economies for quite sometime and especially in the US since 1950.

The importance of this concept is being realized by Indian business houses owing to the fast changing environment characterized by sectoral supply abundance, consumer resistance, government interest and participation in the marketing operation.

Marketing concept means developing a strategy to get the products in front of customers so that they have the opportunity to buy it, ... and determining scientifically what products or services to make and how best to market them to meet customer needs".

Planning, developing strategy systematically and scientifically, selecting among available alternatives and controlling the operation in order to provide customer satisfaction are relatively new implications in the marketing concept.

Marketing concept also involves a systems approach to marketing. Under it, "Marketing is a total system of interacting business activities designed to plan, price, promote and distribute want-satisfying products and services to present to potential customers".

The marketing concept holds that the key to achieving organizational goals consists of determining the needs and wants of target markets and delivering the desired satisfactions more effectively and efficiently than competitors. Here, the emphasis is on customer satisfaction and not merely on selling the product. The consumer is the pivot point and all marketing activities operate around this central point. It is, therefore, essential that the entrepreneurs identify the customers, establish a rapport with them, identify their needs and deliver the goods and services that would meet their requirements.

Definitions

According to Kotler, "The marketing concept is customer-oriented backed by integrated marketing aimed at generating customer satisfaction as the key to satisfying the organizational goals".

According to Cundiff and Still, "Marketing is the business process by which products are matched with the markets and through which transfer of ownership is effected".

Modern marketing is thus the integrated process of identification, assessment and satisfaction of human wants. The focus is on the customer and his wants.

Marketing concept has been defined as a way of life in which all resources of an organization are mobilized to create, stimulate and satisfy the customer at a profit.

According to Felton, "It is a corporate state of mind that insists on the integration and coordination of all marketing functions which, in turn, are welded with all other corporate functions, for the basic objective of producing maximum range of corporate profits".

COMPONENTS OF MARKETING CONCEPT

The components of marketing concept are:

1. *Satisfaction of customers* In the modern era, the customer is the focus of the organization. The organization should aim at producing those goods and services, which will lead to satisfaction of customers.

2. *Integrated marketing* The functions of production, finance and marketing should be integrated to satisfy the needs and expectations of customers.

3. *Profitable sales volume* Marketing is successful only when it is capable of maximizing profitable sales and achieves long-run customer satisfaction.

IMPORTANCE OF MARKETING CONCEPT

Since marketing is consumer-oriented, it has a positive impact on the business firms. It enables the entrepreneurs to improve the quality of their goods and services. Marketing helps in improving the standard of living of the people by offering a wide variety of goods and services with freedom of choice, and by treating the customer as the most important person. Concern for customers' needs and wants increases the acceptability of the products. The chances of the firm becoming a sick unit are also reduced due to continuous patronage of customers.

Marketing generates employment both in production and in distribution areas. Since a business firm generates revenue and earns profits by carrying out marketing functions, it will engage in exploiting more and more economic resources of the country to earn more profits.

The business firm pursuing the marketing concept can respond effectively to change in its environment. The firm can very well face the pressures of competition and environmental changes.

A large-scale business can have its own formal marketing network, media campaigns, and sales force, but a small unit may have to depend totally on personal efforts and resources, making it informal and flexible. Marketing makes or breaks a small enterprise. An enterprise grows, stagnates, or perishes with the success or failure, as the case may be, of marketing. "Nirma" is an appropriate example of the success of small-scale enterprise.

However, marketing concept is not free from limitations. It focuses attention solely upon satisfying customers and ignores other stake holders like employees, investors, supplier, the state and the public at large. Consequently, the concept may lead managers to commit actions that are harmful to various groups, for example, polluting air or water in the manufacturing operations.

OTHER KEY MARKETING CONCEPTS

The five alternative concepts under which organizations conduct their marketing activities are production, product, selling, marketing and societal marketing concepts.

Production Concept

The production concept holds that consumers will favour products that are available and highly affordable. Therefore, management should focus on improving production and distributing efficiently.

The production concept is still a useful philosophy in two types of situations. The first occurs when the demand for a product exceeds the supply. Here, management should look for ways to increase production. The second situation occurs when the product's cost is too high and improved productivity is needed to bring it down.

Product Concept

Another major concept guiding sellers is the product concept. It holds that consumers will favour products that offer good quality, performance and innovative features. Thus, an organization should devote energy for making continuous product improvements.

Selling Concept

Many organizations follow the selling concept, which holds that customers will not buy organization's products unless it undertakes a large-scale selling and promotion effort.

Most firms practice the selling concept when they have over capacity. Their aim is to sell what they make rather than make what the market wants. Such marketing carries high risks. It focuses on creating sales transactions rather than on building long-term profitable relationships with customers. This approach assumes that customers will forget their dissatisfaction with the product and buy it again later. But studies show that dissatisfied customers do not buy again. While an average satisfied customers tell a few people about this good experience, a dissatisfied customers would tell many people about their bad experiences.

Marketing Concept

Under the marketing concept, companies produce what consumers want, thereby satisfying consumers and making profits. The firm using marketing concepts satisfies its customers more effectively and efficiently than the competitors do.

The selling concept and marketing concept are sometimes confused. Selling concept focuses on company's products, and calls for heavy selling and promotion to obtain profitable sales. It focuses heavily on getting short-term sales with little concern about who buys or why. In contrast, the marketing concept focuses on customer needs, and makes profit by creating long-term customer relationship based on customer value and satisfaction.

Several years of hard work are needed to turn a sales-oriented company into a market-oriented company. The goal is to build customer satisfaction into the very fabric of the firm.

Societal Marketing Concept

The societal marketing concept is the newest of the five marketing management philosophies.

The societal marketing concept questions whether the pure marketing concept is adequate in an age of environmental problems, resource shortages, rapid population growth, and whether it reflected social services.

According to the societal marketing concept, the pure marketing concept overlooks possible conflicts between customer's short-run wants and consumer's long-run welfare.

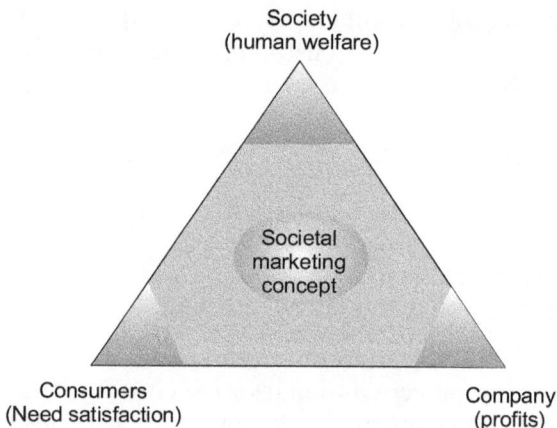

Society
(human welfare)

Societal
marketing
concept

Consumers
(Need satisfaction)

Company
(profits)

Figure 3.1   Societal marketing concept

Consider the fast-food industry. Today's giant fast-food chains are offering tasty and convenient food at reasonable prices. Yet, many consumer and environment groups have voiced concerns and health critics point out that fried chicken, french fries, etc. sold by fast-food restaurants are high in fat and salt. The products are wrapped in convenient packaging, but this leads to pollution.

Such concerns and conflicts led to the societal marketing concept. The societal marketing concept calls on marketers to balance three considerations in setting their marketing policies —company profits, consumer needs and society's interests (Figure 3.1).

The failure to be truly consumer-oriented results in several undesirable consequences. In many of the centrally planned economies, consumers have no choice at all. But the economic situation in such countries is also changing rapidly. Poland is a good example in this regard, where government planners have started investigating customer tastes and preferences and advertising is being used to stimulate demand.

OBJECTIVES OF
MODERN MARKETING CONCEPT

The marketing concept refers to the philosophy of marketing as adopted by a firm. The present fashion of many units is to pronounce that their philosophy of marketing stresses on "consumer orientation". But in reality, converting an organization into a consumer-oriented firm is not that simple. For instance, Lazer and Kelly list the following criteria to consider a firm as consumer-oriented:

1. The firm appreciates and understands the strategic position of the consumers.
2. The marketing system is designed to serve consumer needs.
3. The marketing system is integrated and well coordinated.
4. The marketing research is a continuous process.
5. Product innovation and product planning is recognized and emphasized.

6. There is continuous reshaping of company's products and services to meet the changing demands of the consumers.

The objectives of the modern marketing concept are discussed below:

1. *Modern marketing is consumer-oriented* Modern marketing is a dynamic field of business activity and is becoming more and more complex. This is evident from the analysis of the growth of marketing over two centuries.

Years ago, the village craftsmen made wagons or shoes with their hands as per the requirements of their customers, whom they knew personally. In the simplest form, it contained three elements as shown in Figure 3.2. Such a village craftsman had his shop in front of his house, made his products, sold them, and collected the money all by himself. He was in close contact with his customers. Misjudgment of consumer demand was known to him directly and almost instantaneously. He was also in a position to make changes in his product to bring it in line with the demands of his customers. And this was possible only because of the instant flow of information about the customers needs and desires.

2. *Modern marketing starts and ends with the consumer* Historically, production activities in free enterprise economies were meant to make the maximum profit (a profit possible within the legal and moral constraints of the system). But this idea has undergone an orientation along with changes in values that took place in the industrial society. Production orientation paved the way for financial orientation which later on changed into sales orientation. This change is much evident in the words of Theodore Levitt, who said, "Instead of trying to market what is easiest for us to make, we must find out much more about what the consumer is willing to buy. In other words, we must apply our creativeness more intelligently to people, and their wants and needs, rather than to products."

The concept of marketing, that was concerned only with the flow of goods from the producer to the consumer, has changed, to include also the flow of information from the consumer to the producer. In other words, to achieve maximum efficiency in marketing, there must also be a flow of information vis-à-vis, the flow of goods. This information, for practical purposes, has to be collected even before a product is planned. Subsequent information would also enable the manufacturer to assess periodical changes that are required. That is why it is very often remarked that "marketing starts and ends with the consumer, with information flowing from the consumer to the producer and goods flowing back to the consumer from the producer."

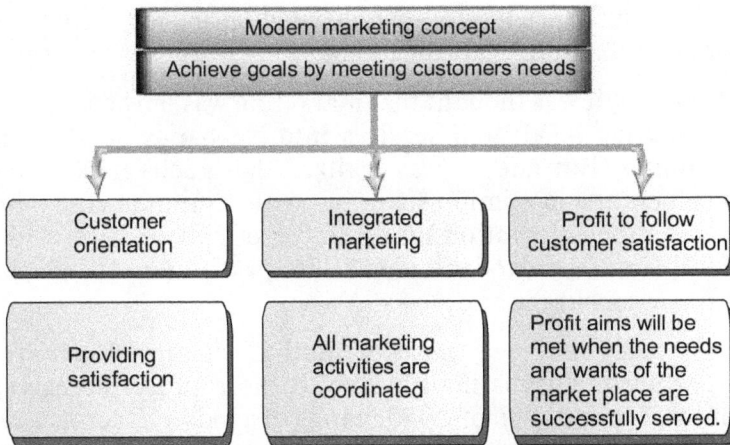

Figure 3.2   Modern marketing concept

3. *Modern marketing precedes and succeeds production* A market transaction takes place when there is a successful matching of a buyer and a seller. The power of either party to influence a transaction is basically dependent upon the competitive strength. The seller has the bargaining power over the features of the product, its price, competitiveness, etc. The buyer, on the other hand, acquires his bargaining power from the usefulness and acceptability of a product to him. This evidently is a conflicting and contradictory state which cannot be reconciled with ease.

For the earliest management, marketing was a peripheral problem in the same class as that of accounting. Firms tried to sell products that were successful in the past. They never made any effort to adapt themselves to the changing consumer needs. Some of them even underrated the critical importance of the customers and their behaviour. Rapid changes in consumer demands, however, left the manufacturing organization in turmoil.

4. *Modern marketing is the guiding element of business* It would be clear now that marketing has become a pervasive force capable of guiding and even controlling production. In fact, it is the market potential and not production resources that guide a business today.

In past, it was thought that marketing was only concerned with getting goods and services into the hands of ultimate consumers. But later it was realized that goods must reach customers at a maximum speed but with minimum cost. This involves the integration of a number of activities from the conception of a product idea to its profitable selling and ultimate consumption.

In recent years marketing has assumed greater importance. This is mainly due to the rapidly increasing tempo of production of a wide range of goods and services. It is an undiscounted fact that sustained economic growth depends, to a large extent, on the performance of marketing activities, because it is only through marketing that the demands for goods and services are stimulated. This stimulation leads to the multiplication of products and ultimately to higher production. Marketing, therefore, is at the heart of all industrial activity.

REVIEW QUESTIONS

I. Short-answer questions:

1. What is marketing concept?
2. What are the components of marketing concept?
3. What are the different philosophies of marketing concept?
4. What is modern concept of marketing?
5. Define marketing concept.

II. Essay-type questions:

1. Explain the various components of marketing concept.
2. Explain the various philosophies of marketing concept.
3. Explain the features of marketing.
4. What are the objectives of marketing concept?
5. Explain the importance of marketing in small business.

4

MARKETING
FUNCTIONS

INTRODUCTION

The mission of marketing is to satisfy customer needs. That takes place in a social context. In developed societies, marketing is needed in order to satisfy the needs of the society. Industry is a tool to produce products for the satisfaction of needs of society.

Marketing has a connective function in society. It connects supply and demand or production and consumption. At microlevel, marketing builds and maintains the relationship between producer and consumer.

At business unit level, marketing has an integrative function. It integrates all the functions and parts of a company to serve the markets.

Marketing is a function of a business enterprise between production and markets taking care that products move smoothly from production to customers.

The scope of marketing is very wide. It may be analysed in terms of marketing functions. Marketing functions are interconnected in every marketing process and these functions may have to be repeated during marketing of a given product.

SOCIETAL FUNCTION OF MARKETING

In modern society, production and consumption remain apart. Marketing connects them. From the societal point of view, marketing is a philosophy which shows how to create effective production systems and consequently, prosperity.

Business is a subsystem of society, which has both a social and an economic role. Thus, a company must operate in a way that will make possible the production of benefits for society and, at the same time, produce profits for the company itself (Davis, K. *et al.* 1980). The role of marketing in society means also responsibilities. In addition to economic and social responsibility, ecological responsibility is nowadays emphasized. Beyond doubt, environmental responsibility is part of social responsibility. Improvement of marketing is related to the changing emphases of economic, social and environmental responsibility. Three patterns of thought can be distinguished for a company's social responsibility. They are:

1. *The invisible hand view*   This view was promoted by Milton Friedman. It concludes that the only social responsibility of business organizations is to make profits and obey laws. Free and competitive marketplace will ensure the moral behaviour of companies. The common good is best served when individuals and organizations pursue competitive advantage.

2. *The hand of government view*   This view was promoted by John Kenneth Galbraith. It concludes that companies are to pursue rational and purely economic objectives. It is the regulatory hand of the law and political process which guides these objectives towards common good.

3. *The hand of management view*   This view was presented by Goodpaster and Matthews. It puts the responsibility of a company's actions into the hands of the company itself. It is concluded that the moral responsibilities of an individual may be projected into an organization, and

that the concepts of an individual's responsibility and a company's responsibility are largely parallel. Therefore, organizations should be no less or no more responsible than ordinary persons.

The development of marketing is clearly related to adopted values which may be seen in the patterns of the thoughts mentioned above.

TRADITIONAL AND INTEGRATING FUNCTIONS OF MARKETING

Traditionally, marketing was seen as a link between production and customer. The situation could be captured better by using the term selling. Selling is associated to the so-called "Production and Sales Eras of Marketing".

Slogans such as "Make what you can make" and "Get rid of what you have made" describe the traditional view of marketing/selling.

Figure 4.1 shows the role of traditionally oriented marketing in management.

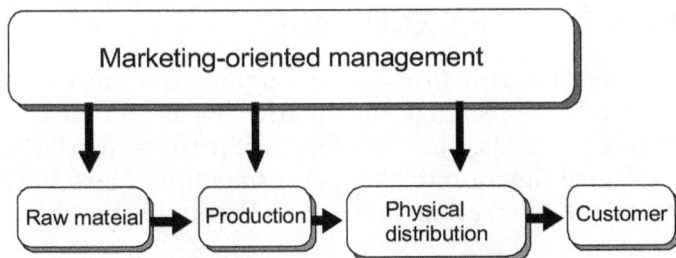

Figure 4.1   The Traditional Function of Marketing

Marketing was born out of a need to take into better consideration, the demand factors in production planning. The function of marketing is to channel information of consumer needs to the production and satisfaction of needs to consumers. The basic power of marketing is the aspiration to produce and sell only that kind of products which have demand. Marketing integrates the whole company to serve this demand aims at effective production systems, where information is transmitted effectively between production and consumption.

The functions of marketing can be classified into three mains categories as shown in Figure 4.2.

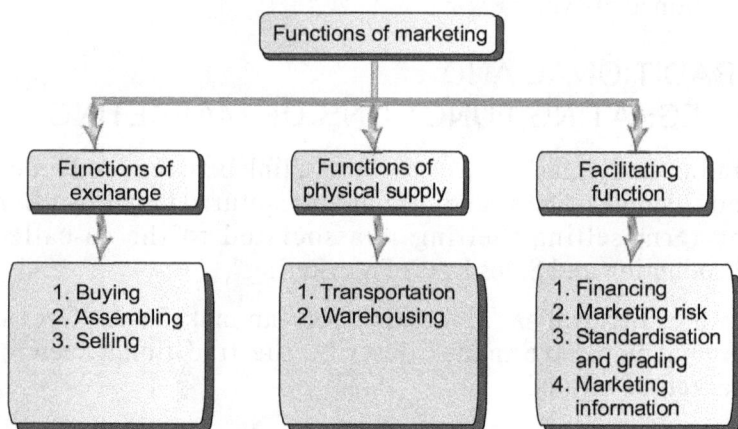

Figure 4.2   Functions of marketing

FUNCTIONS OF EXCHANGE

Despite the changing thrusts of different marketing concepts, one can easily recognize that marketing is composed of a number of functions. These functions are performed to facilitate the exchange function to take place smoothly. Thus, the core factor of the marketing process is definitely the exchange function.

The exchange function consists of three different functions. In logical sequence these functions are:

1. Buying
2. Assembling
3. Selling

All these functions have a common feature in one respect that they are directly concerned with the change in the ownership of goods. They effect transfer of title and hence create possession utilities. These functions are intimately bonded and unitization is only a theoretical exercise. For every sale there has to be a purchase and vice versa and, assembling is the unifying function of sale and purchase.

Buying

Buying is a basic marketing activity. Often it is not considered as an important function. Sometimes, quite erroneously, this function is treated as a passive one. Many consider it as merely the opposite of selling. But it is an active "concentration function" and its impact is felt whenever retailing is reduced. For instance, today buying does not create any problem to anyone. This is because for every manufacturer there is a wide network of retailing arrangement which helps the easy outflow of goods into the market. Thus choosing is not a problem since goods are made available within consumer's reach. If such an arrangement was not there, the buyer would have to go in search of the producer or would have to be satisfied with whatever was available in the market.

The ordinary purpose of buying is to bring commodities together, upon demand, for use in production or for personal consumption. Buying is the result of demand satisfaction. Due to the activities of members of the marketing channels, goods move from producers to intermediaries and to ultimate consumers. Buying involves ownership control and not necessarily physical concentration of goods and services. Thus buying involves careful planning, and needs setting up of policies and procedures. Even in the ordinary course of buying, the following points are considered before a particular product is bought:

    i. What to buy?

    ii. When and how much to buy?

    iii. From where and how to buy?

    iv. On what terms and conditions and prices?

Buying Objectives   Finding out proper answers for these questions may be termed as "buying decisions". Irrational buying always leads to problems such as high prices, inferior quality, etc. Hence, proper buying objectives are to be set-up whether buying is for production or consumption.

The purposes for setting buying objectives are:

- To support production schedules by maintaining suppliers
- To avoid duplication and wastage of materials
- To maintain standards of quality
- To buy materials at lowest cost

The following factors are to be considered in buying:

- Quality
- Quantity
- Timing
- Price
- Source of supply

Elements of Buying (Buying Process)   The following are the individual elements involved in the buying function:

1. *Estimating the demand*   This is also referred to as "quantity decision" in buying. The quantity to be bought is dependent on the purpose of buying.

2. *Assembling*   Assembling, according to Holtz Claw, means "seeking out sources of supply, buying wisely as to quantity, quality and variety, and making commodities available when and where they are wanted." Since the goods are collected at one place, it is treated as a "concentration" function. The major purpose of concentrating goods at one point is to bring them together in a lot, very near to places of production or consumption. The process is not automatic but is done

consciously and is the result of efforts made by businessmen, manufacturers and final users. This function is described as post-buying function, because assembling is possible only after the goods are bought.

3. *Merchandising* It has been defined earlier as "product planning". Merchandising is loosely related to several aspects of buying and stock management. It is the barometer of efficiency in buying and selling. The success of any firm depends on the speed with which the stocks are sold out.

4. *Locating source of supply* This is also known as "contractual function" of buying. It is concerned with searching for and determining the sources of supply, and establishing and maintaining contact with them. With the development of communications and with the emergence of trade magazines and directories, locating the course of supply of products is no longer difficult.

5. *Market news* The buyers must always have the knowledge of markets especially with regard to supply positions, demand position and price variations. The past experience forms a main guideline in this matter. In developed countries, there are government, semi-government and even private agencies which provide sufficient and advance information.

6. *Negotiation of terms* After considering the foregoing factors, the buyer has to finalize buying. Buying takes place between two individuals who may or may not have a prior relationship. The buyer actually invests his money when he is buying.

7. *Transfer of title* The buying function ends when the seller transfers his title over the goods to the buyer. Though the buying function seems to be a simple affair, it has a legal veil restricting or preventing certain actions.

Kinds of buying The various kinds of buying are described as follows:

1. *Hand-to-mouth buying* As the name suggests, it is a kind of buying in small quantities. Housewives preferably adopt this

method of buying. Wholesalers and retailers of fashionable goods follow this method when abrupt downward price changes are expected. They maintain only minimum stock on such occasions. It is also called "current need" buying. This policy is adopted in the case of goods that are seldom used.

2. *Forward buying*   It is also known as "speculative buying". This is practiced usually by the retailers, when the prices move up. They try to accumulate inventories to gain from the price increase. This kind of buying is the opposite of hand-to-mouth buying.

3. *Buying by inspection*   This is the simplest method in buying. Before the buying decision is taken the buyer examines a whole lot of goods to be purchased. This method is adopted when goods are purchased locally. For goods which are not of uniform quality, the buyer will have to insist on prior inspection.

4. *Buying by samples or grades*   In certain cases goods may be of uniform quality. In certain other cases goods could be graded into different lots in spite of differing qualities. This provides ease in buying and eliminates the labour of examining the whole quantity of goods to be purchased. In contrast to the method of buying by inspection, this method is invariably used where the distance involved is greater.

5. *Buying by description*   Where samples cannot be provided and where the seller cannot take with him the goods to be sold to all the places, this is the most suitable method. An example is the case of huge machineries that cannot be easily sent to the buyer for inspection before selling. Under such conditions, the goods are to be bought with the help of descriptions furnished by the supplier.

6. *Contract buying*   Manufacturers as a group require sufficient flow of raw materials for smooth production. They cannot waste time in locating the sources of supply or verifying the quality of materials to be purchased. So, they resort to contract buying.

7. *Scheduled buying*   It is an another type of contract buying. The buyer, however, does not enter into a long-term agreement but indicates the estimated quantity that would be needed over a period. This agreement is done between two units where the end product of one unit becomes the raw material for the other. This enables the former unit to plan its production with greater confidence, for example, arrangement between a spinning mill and a weaving mill.

8. *Period buying*   When buying is made at regular and fixed intervals, it is known as period buying. Usually month-to-month requirements are bought in a lot. This method is adopted by retailers.

9. *Buying by requirement*   In certain firms their production has to be increased to meet the demands of special seasons. This happens only occasionally and purchases are made on a "need" basis.

10. *Open-market buying*   When buying is done by buyers who are solely attracted to the reduction in prices, it is called open-market buying. Though goods might not be necessary at that moment, the buyers may try to stock goods when prices are low. This method is suitable only when prices are very low and products are not perishable in nature.

11. *Reciprocal buying*   It is a method of buying as agreed upon by two parties to mutually buy and sell their own products. For example, an oil refinery may enter into an agreement for shipping its products with a shipping company. The shipping company also will agree, in turn, to buy its requirements of oil from the refinery. This method has both disadvantages and advantages.

12. *Concentrated buying*   When the sources of supply are limited to the minimum it is referred to as concentrated buying.

13. *Scattered buying*   This is the opposite of concentrated buying method. It means buying from any source that is profitable and convenient. Accordingly, purchase is made from quite a large number of sources depending on the advantages in price, quality, transportation cost, etc.

Assembling

Goods are collected from small and big towns and villages at a central place for their further movement to the factory, mill, consumer, etc.

Assembling is different from buying. In assembling goods of the same type, goods scattered in small lots are brought together. Here, the goods already purchased from different sources are collected at a common point. Whereas, buying is the purchase of a variety of goods and involves determination of requirements, finding sources of supply, placing orders and receiving goods.

The following types of goods need assembling

1. A number of small producers produce goods, which are scattered over a vast area. Such types of goods need assembling.
2. Non-standardized goods and goods which are of different qualities.
3. Seasonal availability of goods.

Advantages of Assembling

1. *Economy in the cost of transportation*   Goods are assembled in one place by gathering them from different places. When large quantities of goods are brought from different places to one place, it is natural that the transportation cost will be less.

2. *Helps in standardization and grading*   The aim of grading and standardization is to give higher prices to the dealers and producers and provide standard quality to the consumers. When the total production is brought together, grading can be done.

3. *Helps in bulk sale*   Large orders can also be easily delivered to the consumers as goods are assembled in bulk.

4. *Wider markets are possible*   Wider markets for the commodities are possible only in the assembling centres.

Wholesalers and retailers can have their large and small requirements met at the assembling places.

5. *Cheaper warehousing*   Storing and warehousing becomes easy as the products are assembled in one centre. The cost of warehousing is also less.

6. *Economic processing*   If there is a large quantity, economic processing is possible. Economic processing leads to lower price. This is desired by people at all levels.

7. *Stable and regular supply*   Assembling can ensure stable and regular supply. Some products are seasonal in supply. Such a type of product is stored in one centre in large quantities during the season. The products can be supplied regularly throughout the year and even during the period of shortage.

Problems in Assembling

1. *Need of special skill*   There are number of producers and a number of small units of supply, which are scattered over a wide area. The products are seasonal and irregular in character. To remove all these problems, special skill is required.

2. *Lack of transportation*   Assembling needs a developed means of transport. But there is lack of proper transportation. There is no proper road connecting the villages and the market.

3. *Absence of properly regulated markets*   In India, properly regulated markets are very few and they also do not function well. This leads the producers to sell their products in the private market, at a lower price.

4. *Lack of standardization and grading*   This leads to the danger of adulteration, which leads to many problems.

Selling

Selling is the other side of exchange function. Selling is the heart of the marketing task. Selling in business means the transfer of ownership of goods or services to a buyer in exchange for money. According to Cundiff and Still, "Selling, in its broad sense, aims not just at making sales but also finding buyers, stimulating demand, and the providing of advice and services to buyers." According to Pyle, "Selling comprises of all those personal and impersonal activities involved in finding, securing and developing a demand for a given product or service, and in consummating the sale of it."

American Marketing Association defines it as, "Selling is the personal or impersonal process of assisting and persuading a prospective customer to buy a commodity or service and to act favourably upon an idea that has commercial significance to the seller." Demand is created for a product by selling. Only through selling, demand can be developed. Hence, selling function plays an important role in the process of marketing.

Elements of Selling   Following are the five elements of the selling function:

1. *Product planning and development*   The product planning function, also called merchandising function, is very important in marketing. The starting point of marketing is a satisfactory product through which consumer's satisfaction is aimed. It also aims at disposing off the products at a satisfactory price. The producers earn profit. Satisfactory product with satisfactory price helps the consumers also. Selling function is a consumer-oriented function. The production of commodities must suit the needs of the consumers. Hence, the production of commodities must be carefully analysed according to the needs, requirements and desire of the consumers.

Product planning is a process, which covers the technical knowledge of the product as to its cost and profit consideration available from sale. It is a continuous process, from the starting of the new idea of one product till the day it goes out of the market. The nature of the product is decided by product planning. It must investigate the problems of production from the point of view of the consumer.

Product development acts according to plan, that is, it makes the goods available to the customer as per the plan in connection with the quality, quantity, price, place and time. In planning and development, the following decisions are made.

i. *Decision regarding variety* The producer must decide wisely about the variety of products to be produced. Decision regarding variety must cater to the choice and satisfaction of the consumers. He must decide about the limited or larger varieties to produce, based on size, colour, shape, etc.

ii. *Decision regarding quality* The producer must decide whether he has to produce a single quality of the product. Higher quality goods fetch higher price. The policies of trading up and trading down must be known.

A firm trades up when it adds high-priced and better items to improve sales of a presently low-priced article. A firm trades down, when it adds or introduces low-priced articles along with the existing high-priced products.

iii. *Decision regarding diversification or simplification of product lines* Diversification of product line refers to finding of new products falling in the same line of the product. For example, if a radio dealer adds to his product the television set, he is said to have diversified his product line.

Diversification takes place for the following reasons:

- to take advantage of the existing reputation
- to increase sales
- to meet customers' demand
- to increase profitability of the firm
- to avoid inevitable obsolescence of the present product
- to minimize risks of fashion changes
- to utilize the existing capacity of plant and manpower

Simplification refers to the practice of limiting the product line. It is the opposite of diversification. It reduces the number of products a seller deals in and it claims to:

- reduce capital locked up in the products.
- minimize the confusion among consumers regarding products.
- specialize

iv. *Decision regarding branding* Branding the product is one of the devices of product differentiation. Product differentiation is the feature of manufactured goods. A brand is a name, a mark, a colour, or a symbol. Brand is the value and quality of a product. Consumers give preference to branded products.

It aims at controlling the price of the commodities. The purpose is to provide product identification for assistance in buying and selling. The producer must select the name, mark or symbol that is easy to remember. It must be short, sweet and attractive and appealing to the eyes, ears and brain.

v. *Packaging of products* The fundamental function of packaging is to preserve the products till they are sold to the consumers. It also helps in product differentiation and sales promotion. Hence it plays a very important role in marketing.

The producer must select the best material for packaging. It must attract the attention of the consumers. It must be durable, have a good colour and an appeal. Sometimes consumers buy things, not because of the contents but for the containers. Nowadays, plastic packages are widely used to attract customers.

Thus, product planning and development plays a vital role in selling the products.

2. *Contactual function* If the customers are prepared to buy the products, the aim of selling will be fulfilled. Only if there is contact between buyers and sellers, selling function will be completed. For the establishment of contact with the world, the following steps must be taken into account:

i. *Choosing between limited or wide markets* The nature of markets must be decided first. Markets are local market, state-level market, national market and international market.

It depends on the nature of the product, that is, durable or perishable, quality, price of the product, and financial position of the producer. The producer must make the choice to maximize his sales.

ii. *Choosing of large versus small buyers*   It is another important decision of the producer. There are a large number of small buyers and small number of large buyers. If the seller has many product lines, he must prefer large number of small buyers and vice versa.

iii. *Finding out or locating the customers*   After deciding the nature of market and the number of buyers, the seller must find out the customers for his product. The seller must know the answer for the following questions:

Where are they located?

What do they want?

At what price do they want?

When do they want?

iv. *Establishing contacts*   This is the function of establishing business relationship with the consumers. Establishment of contact must be widened and the buyers must act as the chain of communication.

3. *Demand creation*   Demand creation may be defined as all special efforts to stimulate a desire for goods with the ultimate objective of sale at a profit. Conversion of a desire into a demand is demand creation. It is a process that is designed to stimulate the existing desire to take the shape of demand.

There is a variety of promotion tools to capture and maintain demand against competition. The important ones are: personal selling, advertising and sales promotion.

i. *Personal selling*   Salesmanship is of paramount importance. It means that "ability to persuade people to buy goods or services at a profit to the seller and with benefit to the buyer." The salesman, in order to effect a sale, must persuade the customers to buy his products by applying AIDAS formula

(Attention, Interest, Desire, Action and Satisfaction). By applying this formula, a prospective buyer can be converted into a customer.

ii. *Advertising* It is an impersonal approach. It means "all the activities involved in presenting to a group of persons a non-personal, oral or visual, openly sponsored message regarding a product. The message is called an advertisement. It is a relatively less costly method of demand creation, because it conveys the message to a large number of customers at a time.

iii. *Sales promotion* Sales promotion are those activities which supplement and coordinate the personal sales and advertisements. It refers to a group of activities such as displays, demonstrations, samples, exhibitions, setting of showrooms, etc.

4. *Negotiation* It is the discussion between the buyer and seller to determine the terms and conditions of sale. They exchange their ideas of the product in relation to price, quantity, delivery date, terms of payment, discount if any, mode of transport, etc. The period of settlement depends upon the nature of transaction.

5. *Contractual function* Functions of selling come to an end at this stage. The terms and conditions are agreed upon by the buyer and the seller and bind both the parties. If there is any dispute, the parties can proceed to the court of law to get redressed.

Kinds of sales The different kinds of sales are discussed below:

1. *Sale by inspection* Under this, the buyer inspects the goods before he makes the purchase. This is a very old method. The rule "caveat emptor" (let the buyer beware) is implied on the purchaser.

2. *Sale by sample* A sample is a specimen or representation of the goods stocked. When goods are supplied by sample, it is guaranteed by the seller that the supplied goods will correspond with the sample. When goods are bulky and are in different qualities, sale by sample is better. It is unnecessary to carry the whole goods before the sales take place. The buyer has the right to reject the goods, if the supplied goods do not match to the sample shown.

3. *Sale by description* Under this, the seller gives a description of the goods through a catalogue, brochure, etc. Where standardization is possible, this type of sales is easy. Huge type of plants, machines, etc. cannot be shown as samples or sent for inspection. In such cases, only sale by description is possible.

4. *Agricultural sales* In agricultural marketing, usually sales are effected in the following manner:

i. *Under cover* In this method, the buyer intimates the price by clasping the hand of the seller, under a cover. Sometimes, the buyer or his representative indicates the price by pressing or manipulating the fingers of the seller under cover. At the end, the highest bidder is announced. This method is practiced in many parts of India.

ii. *By open auction* All those who take part in the auction sales, can inspect the goods. Open prices are offered during the scheduled time, that is, the time fixed for transactions. The sale will be made to the highest bidder.

iii. *By private agreement* Under this system the buyers at their convenience announce their prices, individually. The prices may or may not be accepted by the seller. At the closing of the transaction time, the decision about the price will be disclosed by the seller.

iv. *Closed tender system* Under this system, the buyers have to write the price, place it in a cover and submit. At a fixed time, the tenders are opened and whoever has quoted the highest price, will become the buyer, that is, sales is made to the highest bidder.

v. *Maghum sale* This type of sales takes place without mentioning the sales rate. Generally, cultivators borrow finance from traders or if the market place is far away from the place of the seller then the product is given to the trader. The trader pays the amount to the cultivator on the basis of the price, at which it has been sold in the market.

vi. *Dara sales*   Large heaps of produces of different quantities are sold at a flat rate under this system. Thus large amount of sales can be made within a short span of time.

FUNCTIONS OF PHYSICAL DISTRIBUTION

In the early times, marketing had two different but related functions. One was demand creation and the other was distribution of goods. When competition increased, more emphasis was laid on demand creation. The physical distribution was then viewed only as subsidiary service. This function is now recognized as the "key line" between production and marketing functions. Proper planning and designing of physical distribution would not only save cost of distribution but also would stimulate and create demand. This is achieved by certain "place" and "time" utilities to the products. Perhaps, these may be the reasons by which physical distribution management has established itself as one of the principal branches of marketing management.

Peter F. Drucker has described the physical distribution function as the "Industry's Dark Continent", because this function seldom received attention in strategic marketing planning. In fact, it is the distribution function that includes all the activities necessary in getting a product from the manufacturer to the final consumer. In between the producer and the user, there exist certain "gaps" on account of the following reasons:

1. Production is concentrated whereas customers are scattered.

2. Production is continuous but consumption is infrequent.

3. Production is on a large-scale but consumers buy in small quantities.

4. Knowledge gap exists between producers and consumers.

By performing physical distribution function, these gaps could be closed effectively. This function is concerned with the material aspects of the flow of goods to the customer.

Physical distribution management may be divided into the following broad areas of managerial responsibility.

1. Physical distribution management consisting of transportation and storage

2. Logistical coordination

3. Materials management

The first aspect is concerned with arranging a proper mode of transportation and storing locations (warehouses) at convenient places.

Logistical coordination is a critical element of effective physical distribution management. It is a process that harmoniously combines physical distribution and materials management. The coordination effort depends heavily on forecasting to develop plans for incoming items, production scheduling and the monitoring of materials and finished goods inventories.

Materials management is concerned with finding sources of supply and acquiring raw materials to keep the production process going smoothly. It is closely related to the buying function also.

From the flow concept, physical distribution activities may be classified into three distinct flows:

1. The flow of materials to the factory

2. The flow of semi-finished products within the plant and between plants

3. The flow of finished goods to the consumer

Transportation

Transportation is a necessary function of marketing because most of the markets are geographically separated from the areas of production. Majority of manufacturing plants are far away from their most important markets because of various factors. All goods are not utilized at the place of their origin. They require some kind of transportation to create place utility. Holtz Claw vividly puts the importance of transportation in the following lines: "Minerals or other raw materials are to be transported from the place of extraction or production to the factory; crops are to be carried from the farm to the local market or primary market and from there to the places of consumption. Finished products are to be transported from the warehouse to the wholesale warehouse, from the warehouse to the retail dealer and from the dealer to the ultimate consumer".

Functions of transport   Transport performs a large number of functions. It diffuses knowledge, removes prejudices and destroys ignorance. But its contributions in the field of marketing alone are considered here. Some of the important functions of transport are as follows:

1. It helps in the growth of industries whose products require quick marketing.
2. It increases the demand for goods.
3. It creates place utility by bridging the gap between production and consumption centres.
4. By virtue of improvements in the speed of transport, it offers time utility to products.
5. Transport helps to stabilize prices of several commodities.
6. It ensures even flow of commodities into the hands of the consumers.
7. It enables the consumers to enjoy the benefits of many goods not produced locally.
8. Transport intensifies competition which, in turn, reduces prices.

Classification of transport Broadly, the various modes of transport fall under the three categories—land, water and air. These are further classified on the basis of the vehicle used. The following paragraphs discuss the various modes of transport.

Land transport It includes roadways, railways and tramways.

Road transport This is an ancient form of transport. Even today it remains the commonest form of transport.

Rail transport The railways occupy a premier place among the various modes of modern transportation methods. Rail transport is a principal system of the world transport and plays a crucial role in fulfilling the economic aspirations of nations. The rapid industrialization in the world took place only after the development of rail transport.

Water transport Water transport is one of the primitive modes of transport. In the past this was the only means of transport available for moving bulky goods. In fact, world trade and industry was developed through the medium of waterways.

Air transport With the advent of airways, distance nowadays is measured not in miles but in hours. For instance, one may say that any two places on the globe are not more than twenty-four hours apart. Besides the political, military, social and cultural aspects, the contribution of air transport in commercial field is highly significant. It has created "time utility" even in international markets.

In the recent years, a lot of improvement has taken place in the field of transportation. These include introduction of containers, pipelines, piggy-backs, etc.

Warehousing

The function of storage is performed through housing or storing the products properly. The place where the goods are stored is known as a warehouse. The term "ware" means article or merchandise collectively and warehouse is a building or room for storing goods. Thus, storage is one of the physical distribution functions of marketing and warehouse is the tool with which this function is performed.

Kinds of warehouse   Broadly, warehouses can be divided into three groups on the basis of place of necessity, ownership and special provisions (Figure 4.3).

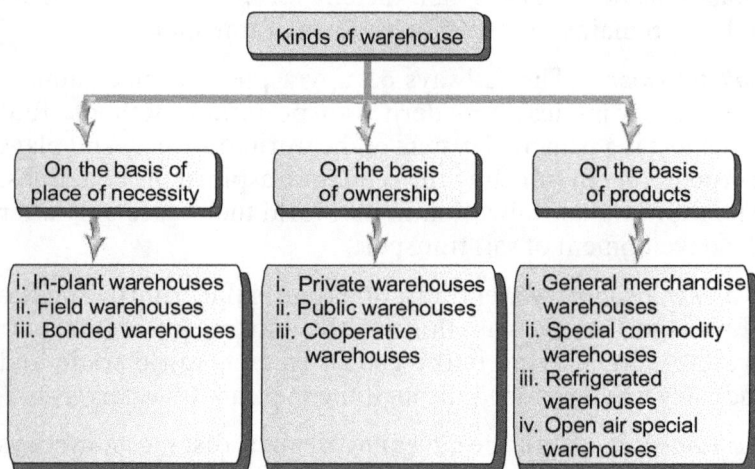

Figure 4.3   Kinds of warehouse

1. *On the basis of place of necessity*

i. *In-plant warehouses*   Most manufacturers have their own warehouses though the size may be small. In any case it is impossible for the manufacturers to "slug-load" all the production. Simply stated, the entire production is not immediately sent to the market. In most cases, the manufactured products have to wait for some time. In-plant warehouses are located within the premises—raw materials in separate warehouses and finished goods in different warehouses.

ii. *Field warehouses*   These are centrally located warehouses from where distribution is done to wholesalers and retailers.

This is necessary where products from different plants are to be mixed together. It is otherwise known as custodian warehouses. Goods are in field warehouses till they are shifted to wholesalers or retailers. It is suitable when the company has a wide market for goods, because they reduce the time to supply goods. Repacking is done in the field warehouses to reduce the work at the factories.

iii. *Bonded warehouses*   These warehouses are located near ports. They enable the unloading of commodities from a ship safely into a place until the owner of the goods takes delivery of them. The importer normally has to take the goods after paying customs and other duties due to the shipping and port authorities.

Ships can unload goods into these warehouses and the owners can take delivery after payment of the dues. Similarly, exportable goods are stored by manufacturers in bonded warehouses till they can be loaded in a ship.

An importer can release goods in smaller lots by paying proportionate duties and dues. Till the time the dues are paid, the goods are kept in the warehouse. The importer may show the goods to prospective buyers even without releasing them. Importer is permitted to grade, pack and mix the goods for marketing purpose without releasing them. It is an acceptable security for getting loan from the bank.

2. On the basis of ownership

i. *Private warehouses*   A warehouse operated by a firm, or a manufacturer or a trader exclusively for his own purpose is called a private warehouse. In-plant warehouses and field warehouses in most cases are private warehouses.

ii. *Public warehouses*   The best known and the most widely accepted services are offered by public warehouses. Products can be stockpiled in appropriate physical condition and in strategic locations until the seller wishes to distribute them to the consumers.

Advantages of public warehouses are:

- ● Traders need not maintain their warehouses.
- ● Distribution risks are reduced.
- ● Repacking facility is available in the warehouse.

iii. *Cooperative warehouses*   The ownership of these houses is vested in the hands of a primary cooperative society. This has not been a popular method so far but if properly organized it will be a boon to agriculturists in villages.

3. *On the basis of products*

Certain products, like explosives, have to be stored under special conditions. To meet this need specialized warehouses came into operation.

i. *General merchandise warehouses*   All kinds of commodities are stored here.

ii. *Special commodity warehouses*   These warehouses are specially constructed to store certain commodities, which require special treatment. Warehouse specializes in storing a particular commodity, for example, crude oil which needs large containers.

iii. *Refrigerated warehouses*   This is the latest contribution of technology which made the storing function really capable of giving time utility to any product. This is otherwise called as cold storage warehouse. This is useful to extend the life of perishable goods. They prevent the spoilage of the product.

iv. *Open air special warehouses*   Products which are non-perishable, are stored in vast open yards, for example, granite, wood, iron, etc.

FACILITATING FUNCTIONS

MARKETING FINANCE

Finance plays an important role in every economic activity which involves buying and selling. It holds the key to all human activities.

Finance is to be systematically controlled and regulated so that it may contribute to the different functions of business administration such as purchasing, production, marketing and so on. Thus, according to Pyle "Finance is to facilitate operation of marketing machine, money or credit is the lubricant". Producers, wholesalers, retailers and customers all require finance to produce, sell and purchase goods.

Need for Marketing Finance

1. There is a time gap between purchases and sales. During this period, the marketer has to meet some expenses connected with selling process. To bridge the gap, finance is required.

2. Goods cannot be sold on cash basis at all times. Sometimes, the marketer sells goods on credit. For that purpose, the marketer needs finance and this enables to increase the sales volume.

3. Finance is required to meet some capital and revenue expenditure in the process of marketing.

4. Finance is also important to increase the credit worthiness of the firm.

Kinds of Marketing Finance

1. *Fixed capital* The term fixed capital or permanent capital refers to the investment in land, building, machinery and other assets that have permanent existence. It is more or less fixed. It is required for long term and so it is also called as long-term capital.

Fixed capital is raised from issuing shares, debentures and borrowings from special institutions providing long-term capital. Fixed capital may be from own resources also.

2. *Working capital* The term working capital is also described as current working capital. Working capital is generally required for running the business and to meet day-to-day expenses. It is used for investment in raw material, holding stock of partly finished and wholly finished products, for paying wages etc. Working capital is generally financed by own as well as borrowed sources.

Working capital is raised from short-term borrowings from various institutions and banks like trade credit, mercantile credit, retail credit, instalment system and hire purchase system, accounts receivable financing, customer advance, etc.

MARKETING RISK

Marketing risk may be defined as the danger of loss from unforeseen circumstances in future. It implies an element of uncertainty or possibility of loss. The uncertainty or risk is assumed by participants who are in marketing and more particularly by those who take the title of goods. Market operations are based more on future conditions than on the present conditions. Exposure of business to the danger of financial losses, which are caused by multiplicity of reasons, in a nutshell, can be termed as marketing risks.

Causes of Marketing Risks

The risk is the result or effect of happening of any unforeseen event. The business world is dynamic and full of risks or uncertainties. The future is unpredictable and full of uncertainties and planning alone cannot solve or protect against it. In modern business, which has become the stage for severe competition, the element of risk is inherent in the marketing transactions. Modern business is usually conducted on a large-scale basis and is based on anticipation of demand. Thereby risks are involved till the moment the product reaches the consumers. The producers and customers are separated by distance. The risks in market conditions may be classified as:

1. Risks resulting from changes in market conditions.
2. Risks arising mainly or wholly out of natural causes.
3. Risks resulting from human behaviour.

Risk from market conditions Marketing risks are mainly due to price fluctuations which are in turn due to market conditions. The price changes are chiefly responsible for the loss of expected profits. For example, there is a fall in the demand for electrical fans in the cold season and fans remain unsold are to be sold at a marked-down price.

This type of risk is generally of three kinds: time risks, place risks, and competition risks.

i. *Time risk* The present stage is one of mass production, which is in anticipation of demand. Products have been bought in the hope of selling them at a good price, which will realize a profit but sometimes, the anticipated price is not realized. The wholesalers and retailers face such risks. Generally the wholesalers purchase goods from producers for selling them to the retailers, who sell them at a profit to the consumers.

Time factor is an important cause of market risk. Change in price is seen with the passage of time. Improved products are being offered for sale by the competitors; change in the weather conditions, new inventions as a result of scientific research, change in the size of population, changes in fashion, etc. are the causes for this.

ii. *Place risk* The changes in price are caused by the passage of time, which involves time risks. But place risk is different. The prices of a product are different in different markets at the same time. The demand and supply pattern differs from one market to another. This is because of price, which is based on demand and supply of the product. When businessmen purchase products from a market, they aim to sell it at a higher price.

iii. *Competition risk* Competition is normally witnessed in the market. Mass production is followed by mass selling, which is again followed by keen competition among sellers. A producer or a market must always be alert to the attitude of competition. A competitor may change the method of production in order to improve the quality and durability of goods, or lower the prices, or adopt better methods of selling, or offer special guarantee, etc., to maintain his position in the market.

Natural risks   Natural risks such as earthquakes, fire, storm, rain, heat, cold, etc., are not under the control of human beings. Pests, rats, etc., cause physical damage to grains. Extreme cold or heat may deteriorate the quality of products. A farmer may not be able to raise his crops because of drought, flood, plant disease, etc. Normal precautions only limit the losses but total avoidance is not possible.

Risks from human behaviour   Some uncertainties arise out of human behaviour, which are perhaps the major source of risks. These risks are:

i.   Dishonesty, carelessness, incompetence, etc., of the employees. Death of responsible officers is disastrous to the firm as a whole.

ii.   Strike, war, riots, theft, burglary, etc.

iii.   Loss from bad debts because of dishonesty of the customers.

iv.   Arrival of new products at lower prices, better service facilities, attractive terms, etc.

v.   Legal liability under Workmen's Compensation Act.

vi.   Changes in taxation policy of the government or freight.

vii.   Careless handling of materials.

Other business risks

i.   Price risks are difficult to avoid. In a free and competitive market, prices always fluctuate.

ii.   Credit sales will increase the sales as also bad debts. To a certain extent bad debts can be avoided with the help of factors, del credere agents, etc.

iii.   Supply of raw materials to the producer must be regular. The irregularities in supply of materials will affect the production. This can be overcome by vertical combination.

iv. Consumer's preference is dynamic and it should be satisfied otherwise the produced goods cannot be sold. To overcome this, marketing research is a good guide.

v. Commodities exposed to open air may deteriorate and this will affect the quality of products. Airtight packing and cold storage will maintain the quality.

vi. Substitutes can divert the sales, thus leading to low sales. Devices like branding and packaging will solve this to some extent.

vii. The actions of the government in the country and foreign countries affect the profitability of a business. Price hikes of oil, petrol, levy of new taxes, imposition of tariffs, etc. are examples.

viii. Physical losses that may happen due to fire, flood, storm, earthquake, burglary, etc. can be avoided through insurance.

ix. Fluctuations in the rate of exchange may constitute losses in foreign trade. This risk can be reduced with foreign exchange contracts.

x. Market conditions greatly affect the sales. Over-stocking is profitable in rising market but fatal in falling market. One must know the latest market conditions.

Methods of Handling Risks

Although marketing risks are inevitable, precautions are to be adopted in protecting against unforeseen risks. To minimize the losses certain methods are practiced to control risks. They are:

1. *Prevention of risks* "Prevention is better than cure." Preventive measures are designed to eliminate the risks or the causes of risks. It is not possible to find out a formula to avoid the risks completely, but to a great extent the risks can be reduced. The following steps are generally used in preventing the risks:

i. Losses from theft, shop-lifting, etc. can be minimized by giving effective training to the employees of the firm and by appointing watchmen. Apart from this, burglar alarms, safety vaults, etc. can also be used.

ii. Losses from bad debts can be prevented if credibility of the party is known before granting credit. The help from factors and del credere agents can be utilized.

iii. Loss from fire, weather change, etc. can be completely avoided by constructing fire-proof buildings for stocking products.

iv. To avoid the non-availability of raw materials, it is advisable to adopt vertical integration, in which full control, from the supply of raw materials to the distribution of final goods, can be exercised.

v. Loss from overstocking or understocking should be avoided by producing the products to meet the orders. Overstocking will block the capital and understocking will result in the loss of profits. This can be avoided by producing to orders.

vi. Reduced demand for the products can be regulated by effective sales efforts through trademarks and brands. This will overcome the loss through bogus sales.

vii. To reduce the market risk, the pulse of the changes in the market has to be known at the proper time. The prices of the raw materials may be low or high in the future, and this information must be obtained from the market.

viii. The marketing risk is mainly due to price fluctuations, and the changes in demand and supply. These risks must be overcome by obtaining proper and accurate knowledge of the market by the management.

2. *Reduction of risks* Many risks are neither transferable nor avoidable. But market risks are reduced by the concentrated efforts of the producers. In this modern period, it is difficult to predict the market conditions.

Suggestions to overcome loss are as follows:

i. Loss on sale on account of change in fashion and improved products can be overcome by stock clearance sales at discount prices.

ii. Loss on account of market change may be minimized by market research.

iii. Innovation invites risks and at the same time changes may lead to progress. Business cannot progress without innovations. At the same time we are unable to forecast changes in the future, which are beyond our control.

iv. Reorganization of firms, amalgamation, conversion to company, etc. greatly help in improving the managerial ability, financial strength, etc.

3. *Shifting of risks*   Some types of risks involving loss can be shifted to other's shoulders. The professional agencies accept the risks as their responsibility.

i. In the business world, there are many risks, uncertainties or losses. Generally business people are unwilling to bear such risks, which create losses to the firm and so want to transfer them. Many natural risks or losses can be avoided through insurance. The importance of insurance in marketing lies in the fact that it helps in eliminating uncertainty. Insurance companies cover many risks for the payment of a sum, known as premium. For instance, marine insurance, fire insurance, credit insurance, burglary insurance, etc. are some types of insurance. A businessman can easily transfer the risk to the insurer. Insurance is a contract by which the insurer (insurance company) in consideration of the payment of a sum (premium), agrees to pay a specified sum to the insured when certain event occurs. The insurer undertakes to indemnify the assured for the loss due to the unforeseen event.

ii. The loss on account of price changes can be shifted through hedging by means of future contracts. The marketing risks, generally found in agricultural marketing, due to price changes are shifted effectively by entering into contracts of sales and purchase at a future date.

iii. Government also plays its role. Government places tariff on imports of products and thereby, demand for home products arises. Restriction on import of goods is favourable to internal traders.

STANDARDIZATION

Standardization and grading are very helpful to the customer to identify the product. Product identification by consumers is essential for repeat sales.

It is the process by which a standard, already decided, is attained. Broadly stated, standardization involves the determination of basic measures to which products must conform and includes the process of conforming to such standards. Standardization is considered to be a facilitating or ancillary function of marketing because it helps in the efficient performance of the various marketing functions, particularly buying and selling.

Types of standards   Standard is a measure that is generally accepted as having a fixed value. Standards are determined on the basis of scientific studies and practical studies. Standard products must be as good as the others. Standards can be positive or negative and general or private.

1. *Positive standards*   Positive standards mention what attributes must be there in a product to conform to the standard.

2. *Negative standards*   They mention the characteristics absent in a product. A standard product will not possess

certain features. For example, Odourless cooking oil means cooking oil without any unpleasant odours.

3. *General standards* They specify characteristics of products to be present to conform to a standard, whoever is the producer.

4. *Private standards* They are the standards used by individual producers for their own products.

Standards may be determined for a product. Then the production is streamlined to produce the product as per the predetermined standards.

Standardized products may need standardized processes, machines, production methods and tools. Standardization is usually applied to manufactured products.

GRADING

Grading is the process of grouping the products on the basis of common characteristics or standards.

Standardization, in the case of manufactured goods and for most of the industrial goods, is a function of production. Once a standard is set up there will be no difficulty in maintaining it. Because in manufacturing operations, not only the finished products are standardized, but materials, processes, and performances are also standardized. The case is, however, different with regard to the products of agriculture and extractive industries. There is a lack of uniformity or standards in the variety of natural products available from the soil. The features of these products vary from one firm to the other and from season to season. The production process itself is largely beyond the control of the producer. Thus, there will be variations between two or more products of the same variety. In short, natural products can never be standardized. But such products afford one facility that they are capable of being divided, assorted, grouped or classified into certain common lots that show same similarities. This process is known as "grading". In other words, "grading is the process of sorting individual specimens of a given product to the standard grades or classes to which they belong." Grades may be fixed or variable grades. Grades are fixed if the required characteristics are determined in advance but are variable if available products are sorted out on the basis of characteristics present in that lot. They are not permanent and vary from time to time and lot to lot.

Advantages of Standardization and Grading

The introduction of standards for weights and measures is an evidence for the ethical advancement of the human race. As long as no objective standard prevails there is opportunity for the stronger to take advantage of the weaker. Besides, standardization and grading offer a number of advantages:

1. It helps to protect products in transit from damage and reduces the cost of marketing by achieving economy in freight and handling.
2. Standardized goods require less storage area.
3. Sale by description or sample is possible.
4. The comparison of values of different qualities of a product in a single market and the differences in prices of the same grade in different markets can be made.
5. It helps to reduce risks and aids financing.
6. It helps to remove the elements of speculation.
7. Standardization and grading enable the manufacturers to use the brand names effectively.
8. Advertisements backed by standards are more effective.

Standardized products actually enjoy a wide reputation and they are capable of capturing new markets. The problem is only to maintain the standard and prevent imitation goods. But standardization is effective only when it is legalized, because where custom plays an important part in the production of a commodity, standardization has no effect. Ignorance on the part of the consumer is another obstacle.

In India, many of the manufactured goods are being brought under standardization with the establishment of the Indian Standards Institutions (ISI).

Distinction Between Standardization and Grading

1. Standardization is the process of establishing certain standards based upon qualities and then conforming to these in the process of output. Grading is the sorting out of available products in different lots.
2. Standardization precedes production. So, production starts after standards are fixed. Grading succeeds production. So, grading takes place after production.
3. Standards determine quality. Grading uses these standards. So, it is said, "where standardization ends, grading begins".
4. Standardization is widely applied in manufacturing activities. Grading is applied mostly for natural and agricultural products.

Methods of Standardization and Grading

1. *Weights and measures*   Introduction of standard weights and measures has revolutionized retail and wholesale trade. Cheating in weighing and measuring is minimized.
2. *Storing and packaging*   It is easier to pack and stock standard and graded products than mixed products.
3. *Price comparisons*   Prices of standardized and graded products can be compared in the same market or in different markets. Buying for price advantage is possible.
4. *Financing*   Evaluating standardized products is easier. So, financing can be obtained on the security of such goods.
5. *Branding*   Branding can be effective only for standard and graded products. Manufacturers can establish brand loyalty among customers for their standardized products.

6. *Advertising and demand creation*   It is easier to advertise for standard products and graded items. Specific qualities of products can be emphasized. Demand creation becomes effective.

Examples of Standardizations

1. *AG mark*   The agricultural produce (Grading and Marketing) Act 1937 was passed for grading of agricultural produce in India. AG mark is a standardized grade name for agricultural products. To get AG mark it is necessary to fulfill the requirements of the Act.

A central quality control laboratory, called "The Central AG Mark Laboratory", was set-up at Nagpur with 16 regional control laboratories all over India.

These labs undertake two specific programmes:

1. Compulsory grading for export and
2. Voluntary grading for internal consumption.

The labs conduct frequent analysis and testing to ensure quality.

2. *ISI*   The Indian Standards Institution (Certification) Marks Act was passed in 1952 and the Indian Standards Institution was created. ISI is affiliated to Asian Standards Advisory Committee (ASAC). Indian Standards Institution was renamed as "Bureau of Indian Standards".

3. *BIS*   Bureau of Indian Standards is regarded as the "National Standards Organization". Its main aim is to lay down standards for commodities, materials, processes and practices.

It promotes standardization, quality control and simplification in industry and technology. It also imparts training in standardization methods and techniques for company officials.

It interacts with the international organizations for standardization.

Every producer interested in obtaining ISI mark for his product must obtain a licence from BIS under its marketing scheme. The licence prescribes certain procedures to be followed for quality control and testing. Constant checks by BIS inspectors ensure quality. Samples may be drawn from open market for this purpose.

Benefits of BIS are:

1. It creates quality awareness among consumers and quality consciousness among producers.
2. Wastage in production process can be eliminated.
3. Superfluous varieties can be eliminated because of standardized products.
4. Increase in productivity and cost cutting are facilitated.

MARKETING INFORMATION

The information needed for effective marketing is obtained from the data collected from various sources. These functions are discussed in chapter 21.

REVIEW QUESTIONS

I. Short-answers questions:

1. What is buying?
2. What is selling?
3. What is assembling?
4. What is reciprocal buying?
5. What is forward buying?
6. What is Hand-to-mouth buying?
7. What is sale by inspection?
8. What is closed tender system?
9. What is magnum sale?

10. What is a Dara sale?
11. What are called exchange functions?
12. What are called functions of physical supply?
13. What are called facilitating functions?
14. What are the different modes of transport?
15. What is warehousing?
16. What is standardization and grading?
17. What is meant by AGMARK?
18. What is meant by ISI, BIS?
19. What is marketing finance?
20. Define marketing finance.
21. What is fixed capital?
22. What is working capital?
23. What is marketing risk?
24. What are the types of marketing risk?
25. What is BIS?

II. Essay-type questions:

1. What are the functions of marketing?
2. What are the characteristics of good marketing information?
3. Distinguish between marketing information system (MIS) and marketing research.
4. What are the types of buying?
5. Explain the elements of buying.
6. What are the objectives of buying?
7. What are the advantages of assembling?
8. Explain the problems in assembling.
9. What are the types of selling?
10. Explain the elements of selling.

11. Explain the functions of exchange of marketing.
12. Explain the functions of physical supply.
13. Explain the facilitating functions.
14. What are the benefits of transportation?
15. What are the functions of transportation?
16. What are the modes of transportation?
17. What are the types of warehousing?
18. What is marketing finance?
19. Why finance is required?
20. What are the types of marketing finance?
21. What are the sources of marketing finance?
22. Explain the causes of marketing risk.
23. What are the methods of handling marketing risk?
24. What are the types of marketing risk?
25. Distinguish between standardization and grading.
26. What are the benefits of standardization and grading?
27. Write short notes on ISI, BIS and AGMARK.

5

MARKETING MIX

Marketing mix represents the total marketing programme of a firm. It involves decisions with regard to product, price, place and promotion. These four elements differ from firm to firm and every firm must determine its own mix keeping in view its own marketing environment. Marketing mix serves as the link between a business firm and its customers.

Philip Kotler has defined the term "marketing mix" as "The set of controllable variables that the firm can use to influence the buyer's response."

In other words, the concept of marketing mix is useful in designing a marketing strategy either to meet the "non-controllable variables" or to nullify its effects.

Examples of non-controllable variables are:

- Consumer's buying behaviour
- Trader's behaviour
- Competitor's behaviour
- Government behaviour

ELEMENTS OF MARKETING MIX

The four major ingredients of the marketing mix are described as follows:

1. *Product* A product is any good or service that consumers want. It is a bundle of utilities or a cluster of tangible and intangible attributes. It involves planning, developing and producing the right type of products and services. It deals with the dimension of product line, durability and other qualities. Product policy of a firm also deals with proper branding, right packaging, appropriate colour and other product features.

2. *Price* Pricing decisions and policies have a direct influence on sales volume and profits of the business. In practice, it is very difficult to fix the right price. Right price can be determined through pricing research and test marketing. Demand, cost, competition, government regulations, etc. are the vital factors that must be taken into consideration in the determination of price. Price mix involves decisions regarding base price, discounts, allowances, freight payment, credit, etc.

3. *Place* This element of the marketing mix involves choice of the place where products are to be displayed and made available to the consumers. It is concerned with decisions relating to the channels of distribution.

A manufacturer may distribute his goods through his own outlets or he may employ wholesalers and retailers for this purpose. Irrespective of the channel used, management should continuously evaluate channel performance and make changes whenever performance falls short of expected targets. Management must develop a physical distribution system for handling and transporting the goods through the selected channels.

4. *Promotion* Promotion component of the marketing mix is concerned with bringing products to the knowledge of customers and persuading them to buy. It involves decisions with respect to advertising, personal selling and sales promotion.

All these techniques help to promote the sale of products and fight competition in the market. No single method of promotion is alone effective and therefore a promotional campaign involves a combination of two or more promotional methods.

There is no one ideal promotional mix that fits all situations. While devising a promotional mix, nature of the product, type of customers, promotion budget and the stage of demand should be taken into consideration.

Determination of the Marketing Mix

The following are the steps involved is determining the marketing mix:

1. Identification of the present and potential customers to whom the sales are to be made.
2. Analysis of customer needs and desires.
3. Obtaining information on the number, location, buying power, market share, strengths and weaknesses of rival firms, etc., since marketing research is used in locating and analysing the target market.

On the basis of the knowledge obtained through identification and analysis, an appropriate mix of product, price, promotion and channel is designed. Moreover, there must be proper integration of individual variables so that they reinforce each other. It is desirable to make a test run of the marketing mix designed by the marketing department on a small group of customers. The reaction of customers will indicate the adjustments required in the mix.

ADOPTION OF MARKETING MIX

After the necessary modifications, the marketing mix is adopted and put into use. The adopted mix should be evaluated from time to time and it must be adapted to changes in the marketing environment of the firm.

Every market segment may require a different marketing mix. This is so because the needs and requirements vary between segments. The same marketing mix may not appeal to all segments or target group of customers.

MARKETING MIX UNDER VARIOUS CONDITIONS

Marketing mix may be changed during various economic conditions. Following are the conditions prevailing in the economy and the corresponding adjustments that are to be made.

Recession

It is a period of decrease in the rate of growth of the economy. Credit becomes less available, the money supply decreases and production goes down so that demand for raw materials and labour is reduced and the purchasing power of people also becomes less during this period.

The marketing mix is adjusted as follows to suit the condition:

Product

- Reduce product line.
- Offer cheaper and functional products.
- Use few raw materials.
- Offer discounts.

Price

- Lower the prices wherever possible.
- Change the price to increase the demand.
- Offer price discounts.
- Price decisions can be centralized.

Place

- Increase distribution outlets.
- Motivate intermediaries to increase the sale of the company's products.
- Reduce the channels, and offer products directly to customers.

Promotion

- Increase demand through promotional measures.
- Increase promotional measures so as to stimulate demand.
- Motivate sales force to sell more.
- Select consumer groups with best sales potential.

Inflation

During inflation, money circulation increases, prices rise when the demand exceeds supply and purchasing power is greater than the goods in the market. Under such conditions, prices rise abruptly. People purchase only necessary products during this period.

Adjustments in marketing mix are made as follows:

Product

- Adopt narrow product line.
- Offer cheap products.
- Use less expensive materials for production.
- Conduct and invest in research regarding substitute materials.
- Avoid discounts.

Price

- Increase price.
- Adjust price frequently in the upward direction.
- Stop price-discounting practices.
- Tighten grant of credit to customers.

Place

- Limit quantity per customer.
- Reduce distribution channels to make product less available.
- Fix higher price to achieve product differentiation.

Promotion

- Discourage demand through promotion.
- Decrease advertising and personal selling.
- Make sale of more profitable products.
- Encourage customer loyalty.

Scarcity

It refers to the condition of shortage of essential goods like cement, edible oil, sugar, onions, petroleum or gas, etc. Their scarcity increases the price for that product and people go for substitutes.

In marketing, it has two effects:

i. In order to increase the demand, prices may be reduced in short period.
ii. Substitutes may be found for scarce products in long term.

The following adjustments are made in the marketing mix during this period.

Product

- Narrow the product line.
- Offer cheaper products to increase the demand.
- Buy materials in short supply.
- Make investment in research regarding substitute materials.
- Introduce substitute products.
- Avoid discounts.

Price

- Increase prices.
- Adjust price in the upward directions periodically.
- Stop price-discounting process.

- Limit credit granting to customers.
- Centralize price decisions.

Place

- Limit quantity per customer.
- Encourage customer loyalty.
- Limit distribution to make products less available.
- Drop marginal accounts whenever possible.

Promotion

- Increase promotion of more readily available products.
- Discourage demand.
- Decrease promotion of goods in short supply.

Stagflation

It represents a combination of stagnation and inflation. During this period, marketing strategy has to be prepared with great caution so that demand neither increases nor decreases excessively.

During stagflation, the marketing mix is adjusted as follows:

Product

- Reduce product line.
- Increase investment in research and development.
- Develop alternative new materials.

Price

- Adjust price frequently.
- Increase profit margin heavily.
- Maintain competitive pricing.
- Grant credit more strictly.

Place

- Re-examine distribution channels.

Promotion

- Provide discount for slow-moving products.
- Increase use of coupons.
- Increase promotion budget.
- Increase the responsibilities of sales force.

DYNAMICS OF MARKETING MIX

In designing a marketing programme, it is necessary to understand the changing nature of consumer demand. This can be known from the product. The product life cycle has the following stages: 1. Introduction, 2. Growth, 3. Maturity and 4. Decline. These stages require changes in the marketing mix. This is explained as follows:

1. *Introduction stage* Before the introduction of a new product, consumers have little idea about the product and may not know the need of the product also. Marketer's job is to educate the consumer regarding "need" and "product or service availability to fulfill the need". This requires advertising and selling expenditure on technical service.

The appropriate marketing mix normally seem to be the one calling for " relatively high prices per unit, with margins for technical service, personal sales effort, advertising and close coordination with selective distributors or dealers in order to focus attention on the end-user".

2. *Growth stage* At this stage, demand for product is accelerated, because satisfied customers act as the weapon of spreading the news about the usefulness of the product. Competition may begin to enter at the producing level and prices may begin to decline.

The marketing programme gives emphasis on increasing demand and the tendency towards enlarging distribution channel. Sales may decline, but advertising plays important role in increasing demand.

3. *Maturity stage*   In this stage, new competitors enter the production activity. Being attracted by high profits earned by the original producers, the consumer market gets widened. Products are accepted by the customers. Major influencing factors are price, quality and reputation of the producer.

More emphasis is placed on volume of sales, and service and personal selling decline.

4. *Decline stage*   During this stage, new substitutes are placed in the market, quality of the product is improved; margins become light, advertising and selling expenditure decline and main focus is on distribution at lower cost.

The appropriate marketing mix is to reduce expenses on advertising, selling, service and distribution to the lowest possible level, and to market the product by adopting competitive prices.

REVIEW QUESTIONS

I. Short-answer questions:

1. What is marketing mix?
2. What are the elements of marketing mix?

II. Essay type questions:

1. Explain the elements or ingredients of marketing mix.
2. Describe the steps involved in determining the marketing mix.
3. Explain the adoption of marketing mix.
4. What are the 4 P's in marketing? Explain.
5. What are the ways to adjust the marketing mix under various economic conditions?
6. Explain the dynamics in marketing mix.

6

MARKETING ENVIRONMENT

INTRODUCTION

Marketing activities are influenced by several factors inside and outside a business firm. These factors or forces influencing marketing decision making are collectively called marketing environment. It comprises all those forces which have an impact on market and marketing efforts of the enterprise. According to Philip Kotler, marketing environment refers to "external factors and forces that affect the company's ability to develop and maintain successful transactions and relationships with its target customers". Marketing environment includes both controllable and uncontrollable forces.

The marketing environment may be broadly divided into two types (Figure 6.1):

1. Microenvironment
2. Macroenvironment

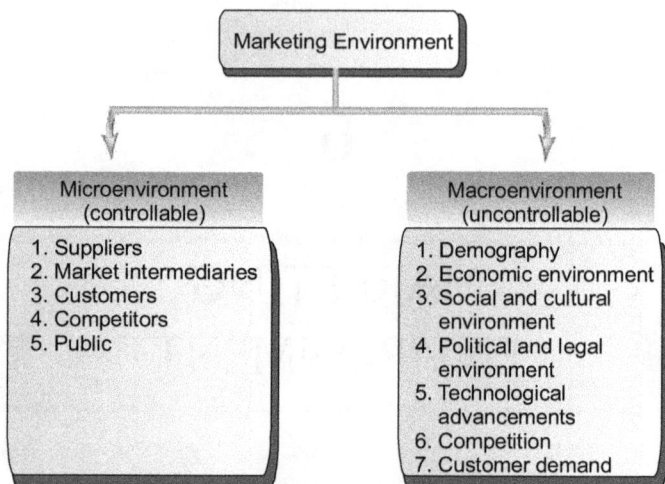

Figure 6.1   Types of marketing environment

MICROENVIRONMENT

Microenvironment begins with the company's environment itself wherein the marketing managers are necessarily required to handle:

1. Brand managers
2. Marketing researchers
3. Advertising and sales promotion specialists
4. Sales managers
5. Sales representatives

Microenvironment implies the factors and forces in the immediate environment which affect the company's ability to serve its market. These factors are otherwise called controllable factors. These factors are discussed in detail.

Suppliers

Suppliers are either individuals or business houses. They, combined together, provide resources that are needed by the company. Now the company should necessarily go for developing specifications, searching the potential suppliers, identifying and analysing the suppliers and thereafter choose those suppliers who offer the best mix of quality, delivery reliability, credit, warranties and obviously low cost. The developments in the supplier's environment have a substantial impact on the marketing operations of the company, since supply planning has become more important and scientific in recent years. Price trends need constant check and careful scrutiny. Supply shortages have to be fully monitored and plans have to be made to avoid the grip of supply shortages on marketing efforts. Regarding advertising, marketing, research, sales, training and marketing consultancy, the marketing managers are sole decisions makers.

Market Intermediaries

Market intermediaries are either business houses or individuals who come to the aid of the company in promoting, selling and distributing the goods to the ultimate consumers. They are middlemen (wholesalers, retailers, and agents), distributing agencies, market service agencies and financial institutions. Middlemen help to overcome the discrepancies in quantities, place, time, assortment and possession that would otherwise exist in a given condition. The marketing managers have to decide the most cost-effective modes of transportation and balancing the considerations of cost, delivery, speed and safety.

Customers

The company establishes faithful links with both suppliers and middlemen with two objectives in mind:

1. To supply appropriate products and services to its target market;
2. To see that consumer satisfaction is provided as per the dictates of the target market.

The target market of a company are of the following five types:

Consumer market   Individuals and householders

Industrial market   Organizations that buy goods for producing other products and services for the purpose of either earning profits or fulfilling other objectives or both.

Reseller market   Organizations that buy goods and services with a view to sell them to others for a profit. They may be selling intermediaries and retailers.

Government and other non-profit market   They buy goods and services in order to produce public services. They transfer them to those who need them for consumption, in most of the cases.

International market   Individuals and organizations of nations other than the homeland, who buy for either consumption or for industrial use or for both. They may be foreign consumers, producers, resellers and governments.

Though there are different target markets, the prime motto of marketing is consumer satisfaction.

Competitors

The competitive environment consists of certain basic things which every marketing manager has to take note of. Philip Kotler is of the opinion that "the best way for a company to grasp the full range of its competition is to take the viewpoint of a buyer. "What does a buyer think that eventually leads to purchasing something?" Kotler has illustrated by taking a person who has been working hard and needs a break. He may ask himself as to what ought for attaining this break after a sustained hard work. Among the possibilities that may pop up in his mind may be socializing, exercising, reading, going to cinema or hotels, watching television, etc. Kotler has also explained the types of competition (desire, generic, form and brand competition) and has summarized by pointing out that "a company must keep four basic dimensions in mind, which can be called the four C's of market positioning. They are Customers, Channels, Competitors and Company. Successful marketing is a matter of achieving an effective alignment of the company with customers, channels and competitors.

Public

General public do take interest in the business undertaking. The company has a duty to satisfy the people at large along with competitors and consumers. This is not a futile exercise. But it is an exercise which has a larger impact on the well being of the company for tomorrow's stay and growth. The actions of the company do affect the interests of other groups also. These other groups are those who form general public for the company, who must be satisfied along with the consumers of the company. A public is defined as "any group that has an actual or potential interest in or an impact on a company's ability to achieve its objectives". Public relations are certainly a broad marketing operation which must be fully taken care of. Companies would be wise to spend time monitoring the public understanding, their needs and opinions, and dealing with them constructively.

MACROENVIRONMENT

Environment provides resources and opportunities. It also puts limits and constraints on the organization, and influences its survival and growth.

Macroenvironment refers to those factors which are external forces in the company's activities and do not concern the immediate environment. Macroenvironment are uncontrollable factors which indirectly affect the concern's ability to operate in the market effectively. On the contrary, the microenvironment refers to internal factors that directly affect the market operating ability of the company and the factors are controllable. The company can manage these factors to its best advantage.

The uncontrollable external forces that have their own implications on the marketing strategy of a company are:

1. Demography
2. Economic environment
3. Social and cultural environment
4. Political and legal environment
5. Technological advancements
6. Ecology
7. Competition
8. Customer demand

To be successful in marketing, marketing managers must understand these uncontrollable forces, learn to accommodate them, and if possible take advantage of them in their marketing plans and policies. These uncontrollable forces are the parameters of the market. They act as constraints on the organization at all levels. Constraints are limitations on freedom of action. These limitations are described briefly below.

Demography

Market means people with money and with a will to spend their money to satisfy their demand. Hence, marketing management is directly interested in demography, that is, scientific study of human population and its distribution structure. Growing population indicates growing market, particularly for baby products. If a rise in birth rate is anticipated, the market potential is tremendous. But when we have reduction in the birth rate, and a lower rate of growth of population, many companies specializing in baby products will have to adjust their marketing strategy accordingly. Population forecasts for the next decade can be arrived at with considerable accuracy and on the basis of such forecasts, marketing management can adjust marketing plans and policies to establish favourable relationship with demographic changes. Demographic analysis deals with quantitative elements such as age, sex, education, occupation, income, geographic concentration and dispersion, urban and rural population, etc. Thus, demography (study of population) offers a consumer profile which is very essential in market segmentation and determination of target markets. The quantitative aspect of consumer demand is provided by demography, for example, census, whereas the qualitative aspect of consumer demand (for example, personality, attitudes, motivation, perception, etc.) is provided by behavioural analysis. Good demographic analysis combines several factors such as rate of growth of population, income or economic power, life cycle analysis of consumer, occupation, education and geographic segmentation. Both demographic and behavioural analysis enables marketing executives to understand the basis of market segmentation and to determine market reaction to a new product or consumer reaction to an advertising campaign.

Economic Environment

People constitute only one element of a market. The second essential element of a market is purchasing power and willingness to spend, called effective demand. Hence, economic conditions play a significant role in the marketing system. High economic growth assures higher level of employment and income, and this leads to marketing boom in many industries.

Marketing plans and programmes are also influenced by many other economic parameters such as interest rates, money supply, price level, consumer credit, etc. Higher interest rate adversely influences real estate market and markets of consumer durables sold on instalment basis. Exchange fluctuations, currency devaluation, changes in political and legal set-up influence international marketing. The level of take-home pay determines disposable personal income and it influences marketing programmes directly. Economic conditions leading to recession can influence product planning, price fixing and promotion policies of a business enterprise. Marketing mix must be formulated on the basis of important economic indices.

Since 1974, that is, after the energy (oil) crisis all over the world, there is an inflationary trend and a continuous price rise. A high rate of inflation affects the economic structure of a country. Inflation coupled with scarcity conditions can radically change consumer buying habits. Many purchases may be postponed or even eliminated. Higher petrol prices created a trend in favour of small cars and public transport. Inflationary conditions adversely affect the market of consumer durables. Economic forces can have positive or negative effects upon the promotion efforts of business units. Trade and business booms and slumps constitute the economic aspects of marketing environment.

Social and Cultural Environment

Social and cultural forces usually influence the welfare of a business concern in the long-run. In an ever-changing society, new demands are created and old ones are lost in due course. Marketing management is called upon to make necessary adjustments in marketing plans in order to fulfill new social demands.

There are three aspects of social environment:

1. Changes in our lifestyles and social values, for example, changing role of women, emphasis on quality instead of quantity of goods, greater reliance on governments, greater preference to recreational activities, etc.

2. Major social problems, for example, concern for pollution of our environment, socially responsible marketing policies, need for safety in occupations and products, etc.

3. Growing consumerism indicating consumer dissatisfaction since 1960. Consumerism is becoming increasingly important to marketing decision process. Social environment in many countries is responsible for emphasizing social responsibility of business and customer-oriented marketing approach.

Societal marketing concept demanding not only consumer welfare but also citizen welfare, is due to the prevalent social environment and social or cultural values in advanced countries. Marketers are now called upon not only to deliver higher material standard of living, but also assure good quality of life, for example, an environment free from pollution.

Political and Legal Environment

Political and legal forces are gaining considerable importance in marketing activities and operations of business enterprises. Marketing systems are affected by government monetary and fiscal policies, import–export policies, and customs duties. Legislation controlling physical environment, such as anti-pollution laws also influence marketing plans and policies. In many countries there are specific legislations to control marketing, such as forward markets of commodities and securities. Consumer legislation tries to protect consumer interests. There are also legislations to control and regulate monopoly and unfair trade practices in many countries. Marketing management cannot ignore the legislation regulating competition and protecting consumers. Marketing policy-making is influenced by government policies and controls throughout the world. In some countries the government, rather than the market, provides a dominating marketing mechanism. Business enterprises may not be allowed to resort to price discrimination, false and misleading advertising, exclusive distributorships and agreements, deceptive sales promotion methods, division of markets, exclusion of new competitors and such other unfair trade practices.

Technological Advancements

Unprecedented development of science and technology since 1940 has created a phenomenal impact on our lives. In one generation we have witnessed radical changes in our lifestyles, in our consumption pattern as well as in our economic welfare.

The phenomenal development of science and technology has completely transformed the life and living conditions in developed and developing countries. Ever-expanding markets create conditions that lead to technical progress. In most cases, the market was the mother of invention—the basic incentive for inventions is through research and development and for profit-seeking is through meeting market needs. Technology is the way by which things are done—the methods, materials and techniques used to achieve commercial and industrial objectives. Modern economics have been shaped by technology. New technologies are the main source of economic growth. Many business firms are earning handsome profits from products which did not exist some years back. Electronic industry is the best example of exploiting new marketing opportunities. Computers and airplanes are entirely new industries. Digital watches are killing the marketing prospects of traditional watches. Artificial fibre cloth has almost killed the pure cotton textile industries in many countries. Television has adversely affected radio and cinema industries. Nearly 70 per cent of food products, now available in highly industrialized countries, were simply non-existent thirty years ago.

Consumer purchase and the manner in which they are consumed reflect a society's lifestyle. Technological forces help to shape changes in the style of living of consumers. Marketing management with the help of technology can create and deliver standards and styles of life in many countries. It has the responsibility of relating changing lifestyle patterns, values and changing technology to market opportunities for profitable sales to particular market segments.

Competition

No marketing decision of major importance should be made without assessing competition in a free market economy. The marketing manager has little control over the actions of competitors. They can merely anticipate competitive actions and be prepared to deal with them. Competitors considerably influence the selection of target markets, suppliers, marketing channels as well as product mix, price mix and promotion mix. In fact, formulation of marketing strategy is in itself a plan to fight against competitors' move. An aggressive marketing manager knows that his marketing mix will encourage competition and he must anticipate the nature of this reaction while assessing his own situation. Similarly, he understands that activities of his rivals are bound to limit the marketing opportunities of his firm sooner or later. Marketing strategies recognize the force of competition in a free market economy and these strategic plans are always based on the anticipated moves of the opponent. You have to outmanoeuver your opponent and then only your survival is assured in a competitive environment. Competitive conditions within an industry are ever-changing and the marketing manager has to work hard to face the situation. After 1960, the marketing managers of cotton mills had to face competition from the synthetic fibre manufacturers.

Ecology

In the wider concept of marketing, ecological environment has assumed a unique importance in production and marketing in modern economics. Environmental experts are vigorously advocating the preservation and survival of our entire ecological system. It is said that pollution is an inevitable by-product of high-consumption economic systems prevalent in the advanced countries. The marketing system of an enterprise must satisfy not only the buyers of its products (consumers/users) but also societal wants which may be adversely affected by its activities and only then it is entitled to achieve its profit objective. The marketing executives must pay due attention to the quality of our life and our environment. They must take measures to conserve and allocate efficient use of our scarce resources that can restore the balance in our ecological environment. Economical use of energy and natural resources are the essential ingredients of marketing strategies.

Customer Demand

Customer demand is ever-changing, unpredictable and also immeasurable with accuracy. It is also complex and very intricate. Under the market-oriented, marketing philosophy, customer needs and desires act as the centre of the marketing universe. In fact, marketing system must respond to the customer needs and desires in all respects. Marketing policies, programmes and strategies are planned, organized and executed with the main objective of customer satisfaction and service. It is in marketing that we satisfy individual and social values, needs and wants—be it through producing goods, supplying services, fostering innovation, or through creating satisfaction. According to P. Drucker, There is only one valid definition of business purpose, "to create a customer". The business enterprise aims to earn profits through serving the customer demand. It now thinks more in terms of profitable sale rather than more sales volume. Today marketing in the firm begins and also ends with the customers. First we have to identify customers, that is, our market. Then we should develop a marketing programme in the form of the appropriate marketing mix to reach our customer, that is, our target market. We offer our output of goods and services primarily to secure continuous customer satisfaction. Repeat sales are possible only on customer satisfaction. The firm's profits, indeed its very survival is linked to the satisfaction of customer needs and wants. Despite this obvious logic, even today many firms are still production or sales-oriented and not market-oriented.

REVIEW QUESTIONS

I. Short-answers questions:

1. What is macroenvironment?
2. What is microenvironment?
3. What is economic environment?
4. What do you mean by marketing environment?
5. What are controllable factors?
6. What are uncontrollable factors?
7. What is technological environment?
8. What are external forces?

II. Essay-type questions:

1. What are the types of target market?
2. Explain briefly the various environmental factors affecting the marketing function.
3. What is marketing environment? Explain its main dimensions.
4. Explain the impact of environmental forces on marketing.
5. "Every change in Government regulatory environment creates adjustment problems for the marketer" – Explain.
6. Marketing has been described as a process of adjusting controllable factors to uncontrollable factors. List these uncontrollable factors.

7

MARKETING RESEARCH

INTRODUCTION

Marketers often need formal studies of specific situations in addition to information about competitors and environmental happenings.

For example, Toshiba might want to know how many and what kind of people or companies will buy its new superfast notebook computer. In such situations, the marketing intelligence will not provide the required information in detail. Managers will need marketing research.

A company with no research department has to buy the services of research firms.

MEANING AND DEFINITION

Marketing research is the systematic, objective and exhaustive search for and study of facts to any problem in the field of marketing.

Marketing research is a wider term and includes market research. Market research merely deals with the discovery of the capacity of the market to absorb a particular product; other areas covered by market research include location of the market, nature of market, product analysis, time, place and media of advertising, personal selling and channels of distribution.

Marketing research may be defined as the systematic collection, analysis and reporting of data relevant to a specific marketing situation faced by an organization. A company can conduct marketing research in its own research department or have some or all of it done outside, depending on its research skills and resources.

According to F.W Cundiff and R.L Still "Marketing research is the systematic gathering, recording and analysis of data about marketing problems to facilitate decision making".

According to Luck *et al.*, "Marketing research is the branch of marketing intelligence that conducts specific inquiries into problems in order to guide marketing decisions".

A.H.Delens observes that "marketing research is the systematic and continuing study and evaluation of all factors bearing on any business operation which involves the transfer of goods from producer to consumer".

OBJECTIVES AND FUNCTIONS OF MARKETING RESEARCH

The objectives of marketing research are:

1. To define the probable market for a particular product and to find out general market conditions and tendencies.
2. To assess competitive strength and policies.
3. To estimate potential buying power.
4. To indicate the distribution methods best suited to the product and market.
5. To assess the probable volume of future sales
6. To know customer acceptance.

7. To get information from recruits and competitor's employees.

8. To get information from people who do business with competitors.

9. To get information by observing the competitors.

10. To surf the Internet and online databases for information

KINDS OF MARKETING RESEARCH

1. *Market research* It covers the aspects regarding size and nature of market and dividing the consumers in terms of age, sex, and income (market segmentation). It may include market trends, market share and market potential.

2. *Sales research* It relates to studies about the problem of regional variations in sales, fixing sales territories, measurement of the effectiveness of a salesman, evaluation and impact of sales methods and incentives, etc.

3. *Product research* It relates to the analysis of the strengths or weaknesses of the existing products, product line decisions, etc.

4. *Packaging research* It is a part of product research. But recent developments in packaging and its contribution to advertising has given it an important position in marketing.

5. *Advertising research* It undertakes a study relating to the preparation of the advertisement copy (copy research), the media to be used (media research) and the measurement of advertising effectiveness.

6. *Business economic research* Problems relating to input–output analysis, forecasting, price and profit analysis and preparation of break-even charts are the main areas of this research.

7. *Export marketing research* This research is intended to study the export potentials of the products.

THE MARKETING RESEARCH PROCESS

The marketing research process has 4 stages (Figure 7.1), that are discussed in detail.

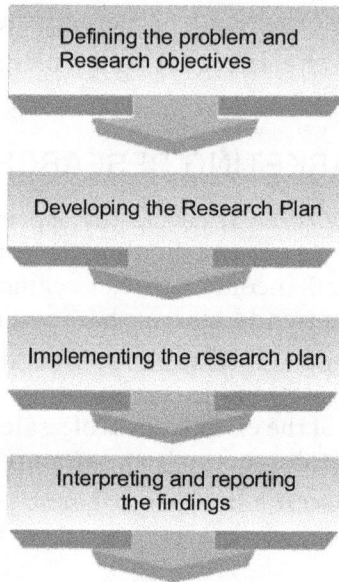

Defining the problem and Research objectives

Developing the Research Plan

Implementing the research plan

Interpreting and reporting the findings

Figure 7.1   Marketing research process

1. Defining the Problem and Research Objectives

Defining the problem and research objectives is often the hardest step in the research process. If the managers know only a little about marketing research, they may obtain the wrong information, accept wrong conclusions or ask for information that costs too much.

For example, managers of a large discount retail store chain hastily decided that falling sales were caused by poor advertising, and they ordered research to test the company's advertising. When this research showed that current advertising was reaching the right people with the right message, the managers were puzzled. It turned out that the real problem was that the chain was not delivering the prices, products and services promised in the advertising. Careful problem definition would have avoided the cost of advertising research.

After the problem has been defined carefully, the manager and researcher must set the research objectives. The objectives of exploratory research are to gather preliminary information that will help define the problem and suggest hypothesis. The objective of descriptive research is to describe things such as the market potential for a product or the demographies and attitudes of consumers who buy the product. The objective of causal research is to test hypotheses about cause-and-effect relationships. For example, would a 10% decrease in tuition fee at a private college result in increase in enrollment sufficient to compensate the reduced tuition fee ? Would a 10% decrease in price result in increase in sales to compensate the reduction in price?

Managers often start with exploratory research and follow with descriptive or casual research.

2. Developing the Research Plan

The second step of marketing research process calls for determining the information needed, and developing a plan for gathering it efficiently. The plan outlines the sources of existing data and spells out the scientific research approaches, contact methods, sampling plans and instruments that researchers will use to gather new data.

Determining specific information   Research objectives must be translated into specific information needs. For example, let us suppose Campbell decides to conduct research on how consumers would react to the company replacing its familiar red and white soup can with new bowl-shaped plastic containers. The containers would cost more, but would allow consumers to heat the soup in a microwave oven and consume it without using cooking utensils?

The research might call for the following specific information:

i.   The demographic, economic and lifestyle characteristics of people taking soups. (Busy working couples might find the convenience of the new packaging worth the price, families with children might want to pay less and use washable pan and bowls.)

ii.   Consumer-usage patterns for soups, how much soup they would eat, where and when. (The new packaging might be ideal for adults eating lunch on the go but less convenient for parents those feeding lunch to several children.)

iii. Retailer reaction to the new packaging.

iv.   Consumer attitudes towards the new packaging. (The red and white Campbell can has become an American institution. Will consumers accept the new packaging?)

v.   Forecasts of sales of both new and current packages (Will the new packaging increase Campbell's profits?)

Secondary data and primary data   Secondary data means data collected from the published sources. Primary data consist of information collected for the specific purpose at hand.

Companies can buy secondary data reports from external suppliers. Nielsen Marketing Research sells data on brand shares; Pharma Marketing Vendors specialize in providing quantitative and qualitative pharmaceutical market research services. Online databases, computerised collections of information available from online commercial sources or via the internet, are other sources of secondary data.

Advantages and disadvantages of secondary data   Secondary data can usually be obtained more quickly at a lower cost than primary data. A study to collect primary information might take weeks or months and cost thousands of rupees.

Secondary data can also present problems. Researchers can rarely obtain all the data they need from secondary sources.

Planning primary data collection While collecting primary data, it should be made sure if it is relevant, accurate, current and unbiased. Designing a plan for primary data collection calls for a number of decisions on research approaches, contact methods, sampling plan and research instruments.

Research approaches The different types of research approaches are:

Observational research It is the gathering of primary data by observing relevant people, actions and situations. For example, a maker of personal care product might pretest its advertisement by showing them to people and measuring eye movements, pulse rates and other physical reactions.

Observational research can be used to obtain information from people who are unwilling or unable to provide information. However, some things simply cannot be observed such as feelings, attitudes or private behaviour.

Survey research Survey research is the approach best suited for gathering descriptive information. The major advantage of survey research is its flexibility. It can be used to obtain many different kinds of information in many different situations.

However, survey research also has some problems. Some people are unwilling to respond to unknown interviewers or about things they consider private or they may try to help the interviewer by giving pleasing answers.

Experimental research Experimental research is best suited for gathering casual information. Experiments involve selecting matched groups of subjects, giving them different treatments and checking for differences in group responses. Thus experimental research tries to explain cause-and-effect relationships.

For example, before adding a new sandwich to the menu, researchers at McDonald's might use experiments to get answers for questions such as the following:

- How much will the new sandwich increase McDonald's sales?
- How will the new sandwich affect the sales of other menu items?
- How would different prices affect the sales of the product?
- At whom should the new item be targeted—adults, children or both?

To test the effects of two different prices, McDonald's could set up a simple experiment. It could introduce the new sandwich at one price in its restaurants in one city and at another price in restaurants in another city.

Contact methods   Information can be collected by mail, telephone, personal interview or computer.

Mail Questionnaires can be used to collect large amounts of information at a low cost per respondent. Respondents may give honest answers to personal questions on a mail questionnaire. Also, no interviewer will be involved in bias towards the respondents' answers.

The disadvantages are that mail surveys usually take longer to complete and the response rate is often very low, and the researcher often has little control over mail questionnaire sample. It is hard to control who at the mailing address fills out the questionnaire.

Telephone interviewing is the best method for gathering information quickly and it provides greater flexibility than mail questionnaire. Interviewers can explain difficult questions and thus can skip some questions. The main disadvantage is that the cost per respondent is higher than mail questionnaires. But the response rate tends to be higher than mail questionnaire.

Most research firms now do computer-assisted telephone interviewing. Professional interviewers call respondents around the country, often using phone numbers drawn at random.

When the respondent answers, the interviewers read a set of questions from a video screen, and type the respondent's answers directly into the computer.

Some firms employ, Completely automated telephone surveys (CATS) that is, voice technology to conduct interviews. The recorded voice or an interviewer asks the questions and respondents answer by pressing numbers on their push button phones.

Personal interviewing takes two forms: individual and group interviewing.

Individual interviewing involves talking with people in their homes or offices.

Group interviewing consists of inviting six to ten people to gather for a few hours with a trained moderator to talk about a product, service or organization. The participants are normally paid a small sum for attending.

Group interviewing is helpful for gaining insight into customer thoughts and dealings.

In Computer interviewing, respondents sit down at a computer, read questions from the screen and type their own answers into the computer.

Sampling plans A sample is a segment of the population selected to represent the population as a whole. Sample selected should help the researcher to make accurate estimates of the thoughts and behaviours of the large population.

Designing the sample requires three decisions. First, who is to be surveyed? (sampling unit).

For example, to study the decision-making process for a family automobile purchase, should the researcher interview the husband, wife, other family members, or all of these?

The researcher must determine what information is needed and who is most likely to have it.

Second, how many people should be surveyed (sample size). Large samples give more reliable results than small samples.

Third, how should the people choose the sample? (sampling procedure)

The Table 7. 1 shows the types of samples:

Table 7.1   Types of samples

Probability sample	
Sample random	Every member has equal chance of selection
Stratified random sample	The population is divided into mutually exclusive groups and random samples are drawn from each group.
Cluster (area) sample	The population is divided into mutually exclusive groups (such as blocks) and researcher draws a sample of the groups to interview.
Non-probability sample	
Convenient sample	The researcher selects the easiest population members to obtain information
Judgement sample	The researcher uses his judgement to select population members
Quota sample	The researcher interviews a prescribed number of people in each of the several categories

Research instruments   In collecting primary data, marketing researchers have a choice of two main research instruments: questionnaire and mechanical devices.

In preparing a questionnaire, the marketing researcher must first decide what questions to ask. Each question should be checked to see that it contributes to the research objectives.

The form of each question can influence the response. Marketing researchers distinguish between closed-end questions and open-end questions.

Closed-end questions include all the possible answers and respondents make a choice among them.

Open-end questions allow respondents to answer in their own words, for example, "What is your opinion about Indian airlines"? is an open-end question.

Researchers should also be careful in the wording and ordering of questions—they should use simple, direct, unbiased wording. Questions should be arranged in a logical order.

Mechanical instruments, for example, galvanometer measures the strength of interest or emotions aroused by a subject's exposure to different stimuli, such as to an advertisement or picture.

Eye cameras are used to study respondent's eye movements to determine at what points their eyes focus first and how long they linger on a given item.

3. Implementing the Research Plan

The researcher next puts the marketing research plan into action. Researchers must process and analyse the collected data to isolate important information and findings. They need to check data from questionnaires for accuracy and completeness and code it for computer analysis. The researchers then tabulate the results and compute averages and statistical measures.

4. Interpreting and Reporting the Findings

Managers and researchers must work together closely when interpreting research results and both must share responsibility for the research process and resulting decisions.

Information analysis Sometimes managers may need more help to apply the information to their marketing problems and decisions. Statistical analysis may be useful for the managers. Analytical model will help marketer to make better decisions.

Marketing scientists have developed numerous models that help marketing managers to make better marketing mix decisions, design sales territories, develop optimal advertising mixes and forecast new product sales.

Distributing information The information gathered through marketing intelligence and marketing research must be distributed to the marketing managers at the right time. Most companies have centralized marketing information systems that provide managers with regular performance reports and intelligence updates. Managers need these routine reports for making regular planning. But marketing managers may also need non-routine information for special situations and for the on-spot decisions.

For example, a sales manager having trouble with a large customer may want a summary of the account's sales and profitability over the past year.

With recent advances in computer software, most companies have decentralized their marketing information systems. Many companies have direct access to the information network through personal computers and other means. Managers analyse the information using statistical packages and models, prepare reports using word processing and presentation software.

ADVANTAGES OF MARKETING RESEARCH

1. It facilitates planned production. It enables a firm to forecast the demand for its product.
2. Marketing research is helpful in judging the acceptance of new products. It reveals changes required in the product to make it more acceptable to target customers.

3. Marketing research helps to study the effectiveness of pricing policies, channels of distribution, advertising, sales promotion and other marketing activities. With the help of such appraisal, defects in marketing programme can be located and eliminated.

4. Marketing research can be used to understand consumers' behaviour and to discover new products and new lines of production. It helps the firm to judge its overall standings in the industry.

5. Marketing research enables correct diagnosis of declining sales and helps in finding appropriate remedies. Sales resistance may arise due to several factors such as physical defects in products, inappropriate pricing policies, unsuitable distribution channels, ineffective advertising, changes in customer preference, etc.

LIMITATIONS OF MARKETING RESEARCH

1. Marketing research involves huge expenditure of money, time, and effort on the collection and analysis of data. Small business firms may not be able to afford marketing research.

2. The effectiveness of marketing research depends largely on the quality of research staff. It is not always possible to recruit and train the required staff. Moreover, results of a marketing research study may not be accurate due to bias or carelessness of the research staff. Sometimes, marketing research is used by executives to support their individual views and objectives and not those of the organization.

MARKETING INFORMATION SYSTEM VS MARKETING RESEARCH

Marketing information system (MIS) is wider in scope than marketing research. Marketing research is a vital component in the development of marketing information system. The major differences between the two are given below:

1. Marketing research is the systematic collection, recording and analysis of data about marketing problems. But MIS includes a set of procedures and methods for the continuous analysis and presentation of information for decision making.

2. Marketing research aims at solving problems whereas, But marketing information system is designed to solve as well as to prevent occurrence of problems.

3. MIS is a fairly wider concept. It suggests methods to prevent and solve the problems for the whole organization under different perspectives, for example, sales, advertisements, cost of distribution, whereas marketing research presents the problems pertaining to a particular field of activity.

4. Marketing research is conducted on a project-to-project basis. On the contrary MIS is a continuous process.

5. Marketing research is a part of MIS whereas MIS is an integral part of the organisation.

6. Scope of marketing research is only limited, whereas scope of MIS is wider.

REVIEW QUESTIONS

I. Short-answer questions:

1. What do you mean by marketing research?
2. Define marketing research.
3. What is questionnaire?
4. What is experimental method?
5. What are secondary data?
6. What is sampling?
7. What are the types of sampling?

8. What are primary data?

9. What is personal interview?

10. What is sales research?

11. What is advertising research?

12. What are the sources of secondary data?

13. What are research instruments?

II. Essay-type questions:

1. What are primary data? Briefly analyse methods of collecting primary data?

2. Explain the elements of marketing research.

3. What are the merits and demerits of marketing research?

4. Explain the marketing research process.

5. What are secondary data? Explain the sources of secondary data.

6. Differentiate between marketing research and marketing information system.

7. What are the methods used to collect information?

8

CONSUMER BEHAVIOUR

To understand marketing, one must understand buyer behaviour. Marketing success or failure depends on target consumers' individual and group reactions expressed in the form of buying patterns. The consumer market consists of all the households and individuals who buy goods and services for their personal use. Consumers vary tremendously in income, education level, taste, age and other factors. So the marketers classify the consumers into so many groups and develop products or services designed to suit their needs.

Consumer behaviour may be defined as "behaviour involved in planning, purchasing and using economic goods and services."

Consumer behaviour has two aspects:

1. The thought process which analyses and decides what to buy, when to buy, etc.
2. The resultant activity, that is, accepting or rejecting a product.

Definitions

According to Webster, "Consumer behaviour is all psychological, social and physical behaviour of potential customer as they become aware of, evaluate purchase, consume and tell other people about products and services".

Consumer behaviour is a process, which through inputs (buying power) and their use through process (perfection of wants, search, purchase decision, product use, and evaluation) and actions leads to satisfaction of needs and wants".

According to Boone and Kurtz, "Consumer behaviour is the outcome of both individual and environmental influences".

In the words of Glenn Wilters, "Human behaviour refers to the total process by which individuals interact with their environment".

Walters and Paul says that "Consumer behaviour is the process whereby individuals decide what, when, how and from whom to purchase goods and services".

IMPORTANCE OF CONSUMER BEHAVIOUR

1. A sound marketing programme should start with a careful quantitative and qualitative analysis of the market demand for the product or service. Market demand is the result of the consumer behaviour.

2. Changes in the market are brought about by the changing behaviour of consumers. So, to understand changes in markets or even to predict the changes, buyer behaviour must be studied.

3. Consumer needs should be converted into wants, thereby creating potential buyers. But needs are psychological and create uncertainty in their prediction. Grouping customers with identical behaviour (segmenting) can solve this problem.

4. Appealing to the right motive of the buyer is crucial for sales. This needs study of the behaviour of buyers.

An understanding of the buying behaviour of various segments helps sellers to select the most effective product design, price, advertising appeals, channels of distribution and many other aspects of their marketing programme.

Thus, studying buyer behaviour is essential to understand what consumers need and satisfying those needs most effectively by the producers.

CONSUMER DECISION BEHAVIOUR

It is a usual behaviour with most consumers to have the general objective of creating and maintaining a collection of goods and services that provides current and future satisfaction. For example, an average adult has to take several decisions daily regarding food, clothing, shelter, education, transportation, etc. but when they make decisions, buyers use different decision-making behaviours.

Types of Consumer Decision Making

There are three types of decision-making behaviour. They are as follows:

1. Routine response behaviour
2. Limited decision making
3. Extensive decision making.

Routine response behaviour It is usually found in the cases of frequently purchased and low-cost items. Lengthy search for products is not attempted and hence the decision effort needed is only minimum. Though consumers are brand conscious they are also aware of alternative brands. For instance, if you intended to buy a particular brand of tooth paste and if the brand is not available in the shop, majority consumers would switch over to a second preferred brand of their choice. Thus, products that are brought through routine response behaviour are purchased quickly with very little mental effort.

Limited decision making It is pertinent in the case of purchases made by the consumers less frequently. The investment needed is also comparably high. Hence, the consumers may acquire information about all possible brands and some amount of mental exercises would follow to arrive at a decision. For instance, buying of a washing machine makes the consumer to examine various models and brands, make causal enquires with the neighbours using washing machine, and discuss with family members before a final decision is made. In such cases the store loyalty (from where to buy) is also considered at length. Thus, limited decision making requires a moderate amount of time for information gathering and deliberation.

Extensive decision making This is required when a consumer wants to purchase unfamiliar products, which are totally new, having high unit value and bought preferably once

Type of consumer decission behaviour

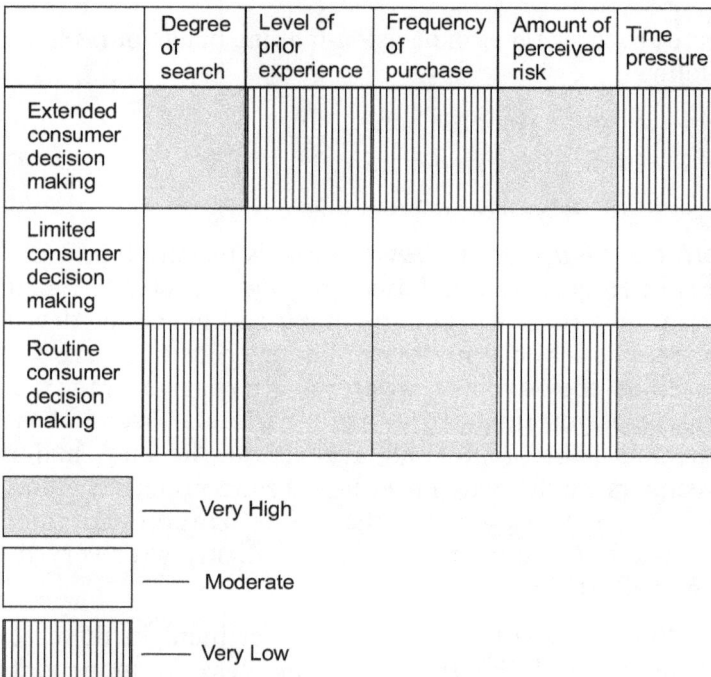

	Degree of search	Level of prior experience	Frequency of purchase	Amount of perceived risk	Time pressure
Extended consumer decision making					
Limited consumer decision making					
Routine consumer decision making					

———— Very High

———— Moderate

———— Very Low

Figure 8.1   Patterns of consumer decision-making behaviour

in his/her lifetime. Before such a product is bought, the consumer uses many criteria for evaluating alternative brands and substitute products and spends much time in seeking information and deciding on the purchase. Decisions on construction of a house, buying a car, etc., may be cited as examples. This process is the most complex type of consumer decision-making behaviour.

The types of consumer decision making is given in Figure 8.1.

FACTORS INFLUENCING BUYER BEHAVIOUR

Buyer behaviour is an orderly process whereby the buyer interacts with his or her environment for making a purchase decision on products.

A buyer's purchase decisions are highly influenced by the social, personal and psychological factors (Figure 8.2).

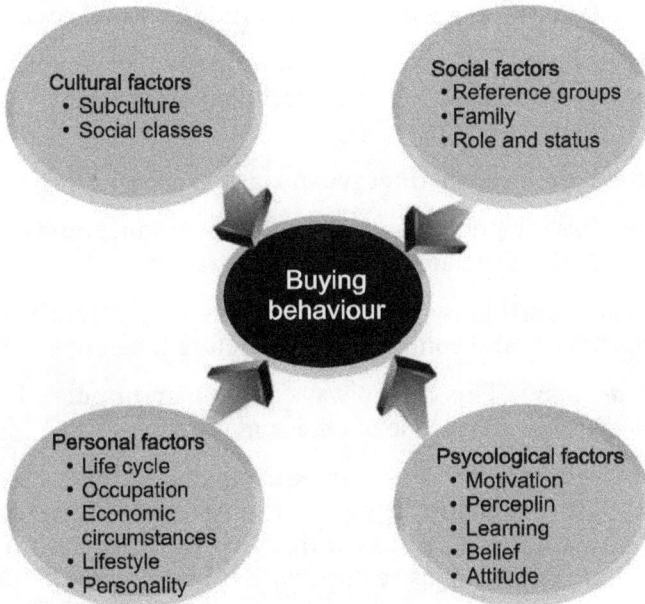

Figure 8.2   Factors Influencing Buying behaviour

1. Cultural Factors

Cultural factors have a deep influence on the buyer behaviour. Culture is the basic determinant of a person's wants. It refers to a set of learned beliefs, values, attitudes, morals, customs, habits and forms of behaviour that are shared by a society. These are transmitted from generation to generation. Culture is always alive, moving and ever-changing. Culture shapes the pattern of consumption and pattern of decision making.

Subculture Each culture consists of smaller subcultures that provide more specific identification and socialization for its members. There are four types of subcultures:

  i. *Nationality groups*—Chinese, Irish, Polish, etc.
  ii. *Religious groups*—Christians, Muslims, Hindus, etc.
  iii. *Racial groups*—Blacks, Whites, etc.
  iv. *Geographical groups*—North India, South India, etc.

Social classes These are divisions in the society which are hierarchically ordered and whose members share similar values, interests and behaviour.

There are three distinct social classes:

i. *Upper class* Upper class consumers buy products and brands that depict their social status. They are rational.

ii. *Middle class* This type of consumers shop carefully, read advertisements and compares prices before they buy.

iii. *Lower class* This class always buys on an impulse. Lower classes show limited sense of choice making.

Each class differ in their patronization, their reading habits, clothing habits, etc. For example, a family from a higher class would wish to eat in a five-star hotel. A middle class family might choose a hotel with best service and quality foods. A low class family may opt for a cost-effective restaurant.

2. Social Factors

Reference groups   These groups are the social, economic, or professional groups that have a direct or indirect influence on the person's attitudes or behaviours. Consumers accept information provided by their peer groups on the quality, performance, style, etc. These groups influence the person's attitudes, expose them to new behaviours and lifestyles and create pressures on the individual. A family, a circle of friends, a local club, an athletic team, and college living groups are examples of small reference groups. When a member is satisfied with a product, he becomes the salesman of the product. He influences the other members of the group.

Family   This constitutes the most influential group on one's attitudes. Personal values, attitudes and buying habits have been shaped by family influences. The members of the family play different roles such as influencer, decider, purchaser and user in the buying process. A person acquires an orientation towards religion, politics and economics and a sense of personal ambition. Though they do not interact with parents while purchasing, their family values and beliefs subconciously influence the buying behaviour. A person's behaviour is also influenced by his/her spouse and children. In Indian families, the wife is the purchasing agent. In case of expensive products, there is joint decision-making.

There are three patterns of decision making within the family and the product categories with which each is associated. These are:

i.	Husband dominant	:	Life Insurance, automobiles, television.
ii.	Wife dominant	:	Washing machines, Carpeting, Kitchen ware.
iii.	Equal	:	Housing, Vacation, outside environment.

Medias of communication play a major role in decision making. For example, Johnson baby products are advertised to mothers and not to small children (the actual consumers).

Role and status This factor also influences decision making. Roles are the activities of the person in a group. A woman plays the role of wife, mother and sister in a family. She plays the role of an employee in an organization. She may also play the role of a secretary of an association. Each role carries a status. People will choose products that will communicate their status to the society.

3. Personal Factors

A buyer's decisions are also influenced by personal characteristics, notably the buyer's age, that is the stage in his life cycle occupation, economic circumstances, lifestyle and personality and self concept.

Life cycle The life cycle of a person begins with child birth, shifts to dependant infancy, adolescence and teen, adults, middle-aged, old and then ends with death. Under each stage people's buying behaviour is different. Under the first three stages, decisions are not made by the consumer. They are totally dependent on their family. In the next stage, buyers not only make their decision but also influence other's buying decisions. In the later stage of life cycle, they are back to the early stages.

Occupation A person's behaviour depends upon his occupation. A company's Managing Director will prefer expensive suits, air travel, separate cottage, etc. A worker would prefer economic dresses, bus travel, etc. The occupation of a person decides his ability to buy. Hence, his need satisfaction depends on his occupation which provides him the means.

Economic circumstances Occupation gives rise to the economic circumstances. A person may have high desire to buy so many things. All his needs do not become wants. This is the result of his purchasing power. People's economic circumstances refer to their spendable income, savings, assets, borrowing power and attitude towards spending versus saving.

Lifestyle   Lifestyle may be defined as the pattern or way of living of a person, which are indicated through the person's activities, interests and opinions. A person may reside in a high income group (HIG) flat. He may have costly furniture. He shall buy his clothing's only from Raymonds. He may have his dinner only in Five Star Hotels. His hobby may be playing billiards. From above activities, we can understand the lifestyle of a person. Hence, his choice will be according to his lifestyle.

Personality and self concept   It is defined as the person's distinguishing psychological characteristics that lead to relatively consistent and enduring responses to his or her environment. Personality is described in terms of such traits as self-confidence, dominance, autonomy, deference, sociability, defensiveness and adaptability. A person, in order to maintain his personality, will decide his purchase accordingly.

4. Psychological Factors

Motivation   It is the driving force which makes the person to act. Motivation is the drive to act, to move, to obtain a goal or an objective. A human being is motivated by his needs. When these needs are backed by purchasing power, it becomes a want. Buyer behaviour, hence, is stimulated by motivation.

Perception   A motivated person is ready to act. How the motivated person actually acts is influenced by his or her perception of the situation. To perceive is to see, to hear, to touch, to taste, to smell and to sense something and to organize, interpret and find the meaning in the experience. Our senses perceive the colour, shape, sound, smell, taste, etc. of this stimulus. Our behaviour is governed by these physical perceptions. Perception is to select, organize and interpret sensory stimulation into a meaningful and coherent picture of the world.

Learning It describes changes in an individual's behaviour arising from experience. Learning refers to changes in behaviour brought about by practice or experience. Almost everything that one does or thinks is learning.

Belief A belief is a descriptive thought that a person holds about something. These beliefs may be based on knowledge, opinion or faith. They may or may not carry emotional change.

Attitude An attitude describes a person's enduring favourable or unfavourable cognitive evaluations, emotional feeling and action tendencies toward some object or ideas. In simple words, attitude is an emotionalized predisposition or inclination to respond positively or negatively to an object or class of objects. Attitudes lead people to behave in a fairly consistent way towards similar objects.

BUYING MOTIVES

Motives may refer to thought, strong feelings, urge, motion, drive, etc., which make a buyer to react in the form of decision. Any urge which makes a person to take purchase decision is called as buying motive. It is not a mere desire to buy. Prof.D.J.Duncan has defined buying motives as "those influences or considerations which provide the impulse to buy, induce action or determine choice in the purchase of goods or services". Some of the buying motives are instinctive, while others are acquired as a result of environment, education, culture, social status, age, sex, capacity, etc. Consumers buy goods for the satisfaction of their wants. They buy products for three reasons:

1. to satisfy their needs
2. to neuturalise the inner urge to purchase
3. reasoning

Maslow's Classification of Basic Needs

Marketing is to do with the satisfaction of human needs. Therefore attention has been focused on the nature of the "needs".

The term needs refers to a condition marked by the feeling of want of something or of requiring the performance of certain action. Hence, need is the first factor in a sequence leading to the purchase decision. It is the need which generates the motive for the consumer to take action with a view to relieve the tension arising from the felt need.

A.H.Maslow has classified the human needs into five stages in a pyramid form called "Hierarchy of needs" as given in Figure 8.3.

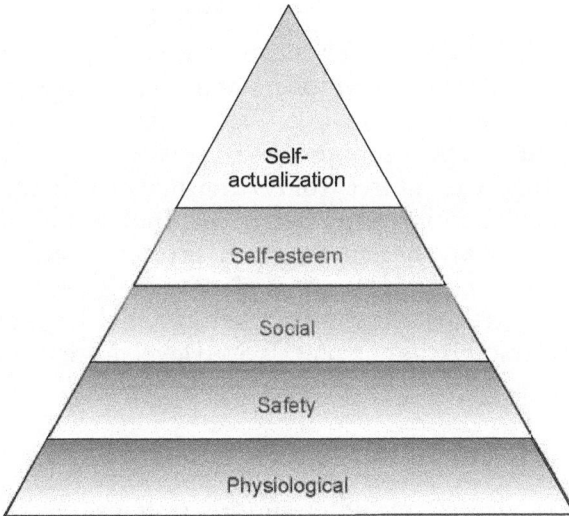

Figure 8.3 Maslow's Hierarchy of Needs

Physiological needs Physiological needs refer to the basic needs and therefore have the first priority. Until these needs are satisfied, other needs are of no significance. Need for food, cloth, shelter are the examples of physiological needs.

Safety needs This type of need arises to ensure economic and social security. For example, the need to protect oneself from physical harm, to obtain security and safety from unexpected dangers like accident.

Social needs   Social needs are also known as belongingness and love needs. This is the need for affectionate relationship with others in the society.

Self-esteem needs   This type of need arises to achieve self-respect and prestige in the society. Purchase of luxury items, for example, TV, fridge, etc, made to satisfy this need.

Self-actualization needs   Self-actualization needs are the result of a person's desire to achieve the maximum of his capabilities. Fulfillment of this type of need depends primarily upon the satisfaction of the basic needs.

With the help of Maslow's theory, it is simple and easy to perceive how particular products and services are related to particular needs. Various marketing and advertising activities can be undertaken, keeping these ideas in mind. However, Maslow's theory is not free from criticisms because this is only a broad categorization of human needs. Individuals, however, differ considerably in their need structure and need decisions. The actions of individuals are guided by their need structure levels. Therefore to succeed in marketing activities, a marketer should understand the customer's need level, foster these needs and fulfill them.

THEORIES OF CONSUMER BEHAVIOUR

The importance of consumer and his response to marketing programmes has been recognized for a long time. Different theories about consumer behaviour were formulated to understand the reactions, motives, etc. of the buyer.

1. Economic Theories

Marginal utility theory   This was originated by Marshall and is recognized as a classical economic theory.

The essence of the theory is that a consumer will continue to buy products which will deliver him maximum utility at relative prices.

The theory assumes that man is rational and his purchasing decisions are the result of economic calculations.

This theory fails to explain brand preferences or product preferences. Prejudices and beliefs affect rational behaviour of consumers.

Income and savings theory The core of this theory is that purchasing power is the real determinant of buying. Purchasing power depends on disposable income after tax and savings. So, consumers are expected to allocate their total income between savings and consumption.

This has led to two concepts—marginal propensity to consume and marginal propensity to save.

This theory concludes that spending for personal consumption tends to rise and fall at a slow rate than the disposable income.

2. Psychological Theories

These theories are called "learning theories". These theories are based on the fact that people learn from experience which will modify their actions in future dealings.

Brand loyalty and repeat purchases are explained by these theories.

Stimulus response theory Philip Kotler and others developed this theory on the basis of experiments with animals. They say learning occurs as a person responds to some stimulus and is rewarded with need satisfaction for a correct response.

The most recent and frequent stimuli are remembered and responded. Repeated advertisement is based on this approach.

This theory is based on four central processes—drive, cue, response and reinforcement.

Drives are strong needs or motives. Cue is a weak stimuli. Response is the reaction to stimuli.

Reinforcement is the process by which rewarding experiences in the past are strengthened. Free samples are like stimulus. Brand loyalty is the result of reinforcement.

Cognitive theory   Festinger has propounded this theory to explain post-buying behaviour.

The essence of this theory is that stimulation of "wants" is perception, beliefs and attitudes. Strong beliefs and attitudes are difficult to change. The resistance of customers can be overcome by strong appeals.

After purchase, consumer may feel discomfort or fear. Such customers need reassurance. This theory finds greater application in advertising and sales promotion.

Gestalt and field theory   This theory states that buying is not motivated by a single element, but is the sum total of many elements. Buyer behaviour is the result of "psychological field" existing at the time of buying.

Thus a buyer's decision is affected by product quality, price, advertising, retailers, etc., all combined in a particular pattern.

3. Psychoanalytic Theory

Sigmund Freud has postulated that human personality has three basic elements:

id   It refers to the free mental mechanism which leads to strong drives.

Ego   It refers to the mental act of weighing consequences of the drives and reconciling them with reality.

Super ego   It is a person's conscience. It tries to keep the drives and actions morally right.

Thus, id urges an enjoyable act. Super ego shows the moral issues involved and ego acts as the arbitrator to determine whether to proceed or not.

Freud's ideas have led to research on motivation. Buyer's behaviour from motivational angle is explained by this theory. Advertising and packaging have been benefitted by his approach.

4. Socio-Cultural Theory (Group Theories)

T. Veblen has formulated this theory and is called as "Veblenian model". According to this theory "man is primarily a social animal. His behaviour and wants are influenced to a large extent by the group in which he is a member. People try to fit in to their places in society".

Many goods of luxurious nature are bought because a friend or a neighbour of the same status has bought it.

As per this theory, culture, subculture, social classes, reference groups, and family are the different factor groups that influence buyer behaviour.

This theory explains different extraneous influences on a person's behaviour. It is useful for market segmentation.

Reference group This indicates the position of a particular group of persons in a society. Man is essentially a social being and interacts with other individuals in a variety of social groups.

In spite of personal differences, people may be forced to accept the decision of the society, e.g., the group insurance scheme where individual differences of opinion may not be given much consideration.

5. Comprehensive Theory of Buyer Behaviour

The different approaches or theories explaining buyer behaviour have been fragmented approaches. Recently some notable attempts have been made to formulate a comprehensive theory of buyer behaviour.

Howard–Sheth theory   Around 1970, J.A. Howard and Jagdish Sheth developed a model which assumes that

   i.   Buying is a rational exercise.

  ii.   Buying behaviour is systematic

 iii.   It is caused by inputs or stimuli and results in outputs or buying behaviour.

The theory then attempts to describe what occurs between inputs and outputs.

The theory concludes that:

- Most of the buying behaviour is usually repetitive.
- Decision mediators follow a set of rules, which helps the buyers to match their motives and the alternatives for satisfying their motives.
- Learning experience or outside information helps to rank the brands. From this ranking, predisposed attitudes and inhibitions are developed.

BUYING PROCESS

The buying process includes the following five steps:

1. Need recognition
2. Information search
3. Evaluating alternatives
4. Purchase decision
5. Post-purchase experience and behaviour

Need Recognition

Buying process begins when a person begins to feel that a certain need or desire has arisen. The need may be activated by internal or external factors. The intensity of the want will indicate the speed with which a person will move to fulfill the want. The buyer will postpone the less important motives. Marketing management should offer appropriate cues to promote the sales of the product.

Information Search

Aroused needs can be satisfied promptly when the desired product is not only known but also easily available. But when it is not clear what type or brand of the product can offer best satisfaction, the person will have to search for information. This may relate to the brand, location and the manner of obtaining the product. Consumers can use many sources, for example, family, friends, neighbours, opinion leaders and acquaintances. Marketers also provide relevant information through salesman, advertising, dealers, packaging, sales promotion, window displaying, and mass media like newspapers, radio and television. Marketers are expected to provide reliable, up-to-date and adequate information regarding their products and services. This is the pressing demand of consumerism.

Evaluating Alternatives

This is the critical stage in the process of buying. There are several important elements in the process of evaluation:

i. A product is viewed as a bundle of attributes. These attributes or features are used for evaluating alternative brands. For example, a product has certain common attributes such as taste, flavour, strength, aroma, colour, number of cups per packet and price etc.

ii. Information cues or hints about a set of characteristics of the product or brand, such as quality, price, distinctiveness, availability, etc. helps in the process of evaluation.

iii. Brand images and brand concepts can help in the evaluation of alternative.

iv. In order to reduce the number of alternatives, some consumers may consider more critical attributes and mention the level for those attributes.

v. Occasionally, consumers may use an evaluation process permitting trade-offs among different alternatives.

Marketers should grasp thoroughly the process and utility functions for designing and promoting the product.

Purchase Decision

While the consumer is evaluating the alternatives, she/he will develop some likes and dislikes about the alternative brands. This attitude towards the brand influences the intention to buy. Thus the prospective buyer heads towards final selection. In addition to all other factors, situational factors like dealers' terms, falling prices, for example, are also considered. Perceived risk may also influence the decision to purchase. High-priced products involve higher risk. Sophisticated products involve performance risk. Consumers may not have confidence in foreign products involving higher cost and they would prefer national brands to reduce risks and problems of service after sale.

Post-purchase Experience and Behaviour

The brand purchase and the product use provide feedback of information regarding attitudes. If the devised satisfaction is as per the expected satisfaction, it will create brand preference influencing future purchase. But if the purchased brand does not yield desired satisfaction, negative feelings will occur and this will create anxiety and doubts. This phenomenon is called cognitive dissonance. (Post-purchase anxiety). It is the lack of harmony between the buyer's beliefs and his/her purchase decision. Marketer may try to create dissonance by attracting users of other brands to his brands. Advertising and sales promotion can help marketer in this job of brand switching.

Different theories on buyer's behaviour throw light on different aspects of marketing mix. A deep study of these theories can provide valuable insights into consumer's behaviour which lead to successful marketing efforts.

BUYER BEHAVIOUR FOR NEW PRODUCTS

Marketers introduce new products to compete in the international market and attract the attention of the customers. Once a new product is introduced, majority of the consumers will not come forward immediately to buy the new product. They will wait for sometime and observe movement of new products in the market. Philip Kotler has defined new products as "a good service, or idea that is perceived by some potential customers as new".

Stages of Product Adoption

Consumers pass through five stages in the process of adopting a new product in order to become regular buyers.

The five stages are:

    i. Awareness

    ii. Interest

  iii. Evaluation

    iv. Trial

    v. Adoption (buy or use of product regularly)

The process of passing through the five stages is known as product adoption process. Everett M.Rogers in his book, *Diffusion of innovation*, has defined adoption process as, "the mental process through which an individual passes from first learning about an innovation to final adoption" and adoption is the "decision by an individual to become a regular user of the product".

i. *Awareness* Consumers come to know of the new product available in the market. But they do not know all the features of the product.

ii. *Interest* Once the consumers are aware of the new product, naturally, they become interested to know about the product. They try to get relevant information about the product from various sources (personal, commercial, public). It shows their interest towards the product.

iii. *Evaluation* After acquiring the required information about the new product, (personal, commercial, public) consumers will evaluate attributes of the product to assess whether buying the product is worthy to them or not. If they consider it worthy, they will go to next stage, trail.

iv. *Trial* After evaluating the attributes of the product, consumers go for trial purchase to experience performance of the product.

v. *Adoption* In the trial stage, if the perceived performance of the product is at par or above the expected performance, consumers will become regular buyers of the products and they will become loyal consumers in the future.

Some consumers may be interested to buy. But they do not know relevant information about product features. Some consumers after getting information about product features, may not go for trial purchase due to non-availability of money. After the trial purchase, some consumers may not become regular buyers, because they might seek some improvement in product features. Marketer should observe the problem faced by consumers in the various stages of product adoption and show helping hands to them to solve their problems.

Product Characteristics

Product characteristics decide the speed of product adoption. Some products will be adopted by consumers during a short span of time and some products after a long period of time. The following are product characteristics that decide the speed of product adoption:

i. *Relative advantage* Consumers try to realize the relative advantage of new product by comparing the existing one. They will buy the new product when the relative advantage of such product is more than the existing product. Increase in quality, competitive price and involvement of recent technology may be the relative advantages of the new product.

ii.*Compatibility* A new product introduced by the marketers should be compatible with the values, lifestyle and experiences of prospective buyers. If a new product is not compatible to the consumers, then the rate of adoption will also be very low.

iii. *Complexity* Any new product or the existing product should be easy to handle, use and repair and overhaul. If the new product is complex in nature, the rate of adoption will be very low. Consumers do not prefer products that are so difficult to use and complex in nature.

iv. *Divisibility* Divisibility is another characteristic of a new product that influences consumers to buy.

v. *Communicability* Communicability of a product will increase the rate of adoption. Consumers should feel comfortable in explaining or communicating innovativeness and characteristics of the new products to others. If the communication of the uses of the product to others becomes difficult the rate of adoption will be very low.

REVIEW QUESTIONS

I. Short-answer questions:

1. Define consumer behaviour.
2. What are cultural factors?
3. What do you mean by buying motive?
4. State the various buying motives.
5. State the major factor influencing consumer behaviour.
6. What is product adoption?
7. What is consumer behaviour?

II. Essay-type questions:

1. What are the major factors that influence the consumer decision making?

2. Define the concept of buyer behaviour. Why is it desirable to study it in marketing?

3. What do you mean by buying motives? Explain the importance of studying consumer behaviours in marketing.

4. Explain the various types of buying behaviours.

5. Explain the various stages in the buying decision process.

6. Write a note on product adoption.

7. Explain the stages in product adoption for new product.

8. Explain the Maslow's hierarchy of needs.

9. What are the types of consumer decision behaviour?

9

MARKET
SEGMENTATION

A market consists of large number of individual customers who differ in terms of their needs, preferences and buying capacity. Therefore, it becomes necessary to divide the total market into different segments or homogeneous customer groups. Such division is called market segmentation. The segments may have uniformity in employment patterns, educational qualifications, economic status, preferences, etc.

Market segmentation enables the entrepreneur to match his marketing efforts to the requirements of the target market. Instead of wasting its efforts in trying to sell to all types of customers, a small-scale unit can focus its efforts on the segment most appropriate to its market. Production-oriented firms treat their entire market as a single, undifferentiated unit. This is called as "market aggregation". Here only one product is produced and sold through one marketing programme.

"Market segmentation" is the exact opposite of "market aggregation". It is a consumer-oriented philosophy. It divides the market into "sub-markets" having homogeneous features.

DEFINITION

According to W.J. Wheldon, "Market segmentation is the process of taking the total heterogeneous market segments, each of which tends to be homogeneous in all significant aspects."

The needs of each sub-market are identified, products are designed, and a marketing programme is designed to reach the sub-market and satisfy the needs.

Market segmentation is compared to "rifle approach". It has "pinpointed targets" with separate programmes for each target.

Market aggregation is compared to a "shot-gun approach", where one programme is used for a broad target.

CRITERIA FOR SUCCESSFUL MARKET SEGMENTATION

Ideally, marketing management should segment its market in such a way that each segment will respond in a homogeneous fashion to a given marketing programme.

The following criteria, can result in effective segmentation of the total market into sub-markets:

1. *Substantiality*   Marketing efforts can be directed at viable segments only. When the segments are too small, it is not possible to develop a marketing mix for each of them. Small-sized segments may have to be ignored.

2. *Measurability*   Each market segment should be quantifiable. It should be amendable for accurate measurement.

Data for vague factors are neither readily available nor easily quantified.

For example, if India is divided on geographical basis, statistics can be easily obtained from published sources relating to population, colleges, output of products, etc. If India is divided on the basis of religious groups, exact statistics of population in different areas belonging to these religions may not be available.

Thus, subjective or vague basis should be avoided for segmentation because of the difficulties in collection and measurement of data.

3. *Accessibility*   The object of segmentation is effective direction of marketing effort to specific segments. So, the segments should be accessible through channels of distribution, advertising media, company sales force, etc.

If the access to the market segments is difficult, segmentation will become meaningless. Even those segments which are substantial and measurable should be within the reach.

For example, there are separate magazines for professionals. So, segmentation on the basis of profession is accessible.

4. *Representability*   Each segment should be large enough and profitable to be considered as a separate market. It must be representative in nature with individual characteristics.

For example, old people (based on age segmentation) can be a representative segment with special characteristics.

5. *Nature of demand*   If two or more segments consume identical quantity and variety of products, they can be treated as a single segment. The differentiation is of no practical use. In simple words, consumption rate or the product type must differ from segment to segment.

6. *Response rates*   The marketing mix must be able to obtain different responses from different segments. If two or more segments react in the same manner for increase or decrease in product prices, then separate pricing strategy is useless for the segments. Similarly, if promotional efforts like advertising elicit similar response from all segments, then segmentation is not effective.

NEED FOR SEGMENTATION

Segmenting the market into several sub-markets is necessary for the following reasons:

1. *Promotional methods* Potential customers may be a small part of the total market. Directing marketing effort to the entire market is a waste of resources and time.

2. *Consumers have diverse needs* A single product with given characteristics may not satisfy all customers. Segmentation helps the firm to come out with a product mix which can satisfy the diverse needs of the customers.

3. *Identification of potential sub-markets* Sub-markets offer maximum potential. A firm may concentrate on that portion of the market for maximum profitability.

METHODS OF CONSUMER MARKET SEGMENTATION

1. *Geographic or territorial segmentation* The market can be divided into several well-defined areas, each of which will be a sub-market, for example, states in India can be deemed as separate market segments. The benefits of geographic segmentation are:

   i.   It is possible to allot territories to salesmen.
   ii. Statistics and other data are easily available.
   iii. It is easier to promote the product. Advertising and publicity can be in local language.

2. *Demographic segmentation* Dividing the total market into different parts on the basis of population is demographic method. The categories based on which the market is segmented are:

i. *Age* Here, child, teenager and adult can be the basis of segmentation

ii. *Gender* Here, gender can be the basis of division or segmentation.

iii. *Literacy*   There are illiterate, semi-literate and literate groups, which form the basis of division. Promotional methods have to change according to the educational level of customers.

3. *Product segmentation*   The products may be divided on certain criteria which may suit particular segments of the people (Figure 9.1). For example, products may be divided into prestige products, anxiety products, functional products and maturity products.

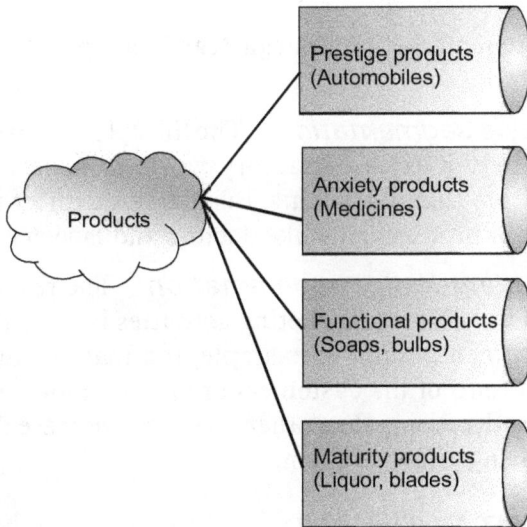

Figure 9.1   Product segmentation

4. *Socio-economic segmentation*   The segmentation here is done on the basis of social class like working class, middle income group, etc. Since marketing is potentially and intimately connected with the "ability to buy", this segmentation is meaningful in analysing buying patterns of a particular class. Socio-economic factors, especially when used together, can help locate a market precisely. This method is widely used because they not only help in locating segments but also in measuring the size of segments easily.

5. *Benefit segmentation* Consumers are interviewed to learn about the benefits they are expecting from a product. It may be classified into generic or primary utilities and secondary or evolved utilities.

But choosing the benefit to be emphasized is not an easy job, for the thrust of various utilities may shift from time to time.

6. *Volume segmentation* Buyers may be divided on the basis of quantity purchased—bulk users, moderate quantity buyers and single-unit buyers.

Different marketing strategies can be adopted to tackle each group.

7. *Lifestyle segmentation* The lifestyle of consumers may differ widely. Office or factory workers have a different lifestyle from that of students. Businessmen differ in lifestyle from that of professionals like doctors and lawyers.

8. *Marketing-factor segmentation* The responsiveness of buyers to different marketing activities is the basis for this type of segmentation. For example, if a manufacturer knows that one group of his customers are giving more response to change in advertising than others, he must increase the amount of advertising aimed at them.

SEGMENTATION AND MARKETING STRATEGIES

It is now certain that any market could be segmented to a considerable extent because buyer's characteristics are never similar. This, however, does not mean that manufacturers may always try to segment their market. In segmentation, Each segment is considered as "target market". Developing and implementing separate marketing strategies for each target market is called "target marketing". On the basis of the intensity of segmentation, marketing strategies to be adopted or the targeting techniques may be classified into the following.

1. Undifferentiated Marketing

This is called as "aggregation" technique or "total market concept". When segmentation is not possible or it is not useful the entire market is treated as a single entity or target.

In the case of fully standardized products and where substitutes are not available, differentiation need not be undertaken. Under such circumstances, firms may adopt mass advertising and other mass methods in marketing, for example, Coca Cola.

2. Differentiated Marketing

Here, appropriate products and marketing programmes are developed for each segment separately. This helps the firms to cater to the diverse needs of the customers. Thus intimacy develops between the producer and the consumer. Clothes of men and women, etc. demonstrate this marketing approach.

In recent years most firms have preferred to have a strategy of differentiated marketing, mainly because consumers' demand is diversified. For example, cigarettes are now manufactured in a variety of lengths and filter types. This provides the customer an opportunity to select his or her choice from among filtered, unfiltered, long or short cigarettes. Each kind offers the basis for segmentation also. Though the differentiated marketing is sales-oriented, it should also be borne in mind that it is a costly affair for the organization.

Differentiated marketing has the following demerits:

- mass production of products may not be possible because of the product differentiation.
- cost reduction becomes difficult.
- several marketing programmes and separate advertising campaigns become necessary.

3. Concentrated Marketing

Both the concepts explained above imply the approach of the total market either with segmentation or without it. Yet another option is to have concentrated efforts in a few markets capable of offering opportunities. Putting it in another way, instead of spreading itself within many parts of the market, it concentrates its forces to gain a good market position in a few areas. When new products are introduced and test marketing is conducted, this method is adopted. Recently for the consumer product "Boost", this method was adopted. The principle involved here is "specialization" in markets which are really potential. Another notable feature of this method is that here the advantage of one segment is never offset by the other. But in the case of the first two types, good and poor segments are averaged.

Undifferentiated and differentiated marketing methods target the entire market with or without segmentation. The concentrated marketing technique is selective. It concentrates on one or two segments of the market to get the maximum share in the segment. For example, MJP Publishers concentrates on textbooks at college level in the publishing industry. They rarely concentrate on school books. This method helps to concentrate on a particular segment and intensify marketing efforts to maximize profits. Selecting a particular technique or target depends on the product, resources of the firm and competition. The most profitable technique is usually adopted.

IMPLEMENTATION OF MARKET SEGMENTATION

Market segmentation is not an end by itself. It should be used as a basis for determining marketing strategies.

Different alternative strategies like differentiated marketing, undifferentiated marketing and concentrated marketing are there to choose from.

The following considerations affect the choice of the exact strategy:

1. *Firm's resources* Market segmentation and diverse strategies for each segmented market involves heavy expenditure. Different product promotion strategies for each sub-market, separate product mix, etc. involve huge investment.

2. *Stage of product in its lifecycle* Market segmentation is beneficial for products in their growth and maturity stages. For those products which are in declining stages, segmentation serves little purpose. It will result in loss of resources.

3. *Homogeneous nature of market* When the market is homogeneous, segmentation is unnecessary. Only when market is heterogeneous and consumer preferences vary from group to group, segmentation is practicable.

4. *Competitor's marketing strategies* Marketing strategies of competitors influence the choice of a firm's own strategies. When other firms are following differentiated marketing, undifferentiated marketing will not yield satisfactory results.

5. *Product characteristic* Most products are heterogeneous in character but certain products show homogeneity. In the former, market segmentation is necessary but in the latter, the necessity of segmentation is disputed. Salt, kerosene, etc. fall in the latter group and in their case undifferentiated marketing is enough.

Thus, selection of appropriate marketing strategy depends up on different considerations at a given time. But the strategies may have to be changed with time and market change.

BENEFITS OF SEGMENTATION

1. A firm can avoid wastage of marketing efforts over the entire market. This saves resources. Marketing efforts become more effective.

2. All customers are not treated alike. Product differentiation based on the segmented market offers more choice to each consumer.

3. Product alteration for changing tastes and even discontinuation of saturated products become easier with segmented markets.

4. Effectiveness of promotional tools can be easily assessed and evaluated for future efforts.

5. Concentrated marketing strategy becomes possible through segmentation. For example, Nippon Motor Co. concentrated on "Small Car market" in the USA in the 1960s.

REVIEW QUESTIONS

I. Short-answers questions:

1. What is market segmentation?
2. Define market segmentation.
3. Why do we need segmentation?
4. What is demographic segmentation?
5. What is undifferentiated marketing?
6. What is differentiated marketing?
7. What is concentrated marketing?

II. Essay-type questions:

1. Explain the criteria for segmenting the market.
2. Explain the benefits of market segmentation.
3. Explain the methods of market segmentation.
4. What are the factors to be considered while segmenting the market?
5. Explain the marketing strategies for segmentation.
6. Explain the importance of market segmentation.

10

PRODUCT

It involves development and commercialization of new product, the modification of existing lines and the discontinuance of marginal or unprofitable items.

The following are the usual functions undertaken by product planning:

1. Evaluation of the idea, market and product
2. Evaluation of company resources
3. Finding out customer specifications
4. Testing the product
5. Marketing the product

Product development includes the technical activities of product research, engineering and design. Product planning is usually described as "merchandizing" and it covers both the existing and potential products.

WHAT IS A PRODUCT?

A product consists of a bundle of utilities involving various product features and accompanying services.

These utilities are created by a set of tangible, physical and chemical attributes assembled in an easily identifiable form.

The product has a descriptive name and a brand name for easy identity.

Philip Kotler recognized three distinct concepts in a product. They are:

1. Tangible product (represents the physical entity of the product).
2. Extended product (represents the services a product could render to the users).
3. Generic product (represents the benefits a buyer can get by buying the product), for example, refrigerator.

A single product may have different meanings to different users, For example, to some smokers, a cigarette is a means of comfort. Some others view it as an outlet for nervous tension.

Product acts as a tool to achieve corporate objectives, and it satisfies customers need.

CLASSIFICATION OF GOODS

The two major categories of goods are consumer goods and industrial goods.

1. Consumer Goods

The American Marketing Association has defined the consumer goods as "Goods destined for use by the ultimate consumers or household and in such a form that they can be used without commercial processing." Meloin T. Gopeland divided consumer goods into three classes namely, convenience goods, shopping goods and speciality goods.

Convenience goods   The consumer goods, which a customer usually purchases frequently and requires immediately, with minimum efforts are called convenience goods.

They are low-priced, of low-value and are widely available at many outlets.

They may be further subdivided as:

Staple products Staple products include items like milk, bread, butter, etc., which the family consumes regularly. The purchase decision is programmed in the beginning only and it is usually carried on without change.

Impulse products Purchase of these is unplanned and impulsive. Usually when the consumer is buying other products, he buys these spontaneously, for example, magazines, toffees and chocolates. Usually these products are located where they can be easily noticed.

Emergency products Purchase of these products is done in an emergency as a result of urgent and compelling needs. Often a consumer pays more for these. For example, while travelling if someone has forgotten his toothbrush or shaving kit, he will buy it at the available price.

Shopping goods The customer buys these goods only after comparing quality, price, suitability and style. These are less frequently purchased and the customer carefully checks suitability, quality, price and style. He spends much more time and effort in gathering information and making comparisons, for example, furniture, clothing and used cars.

Speciality goods These are goods having unique characteristics and or brand identification which have a significant group of buyers; goods are comparatively of higher unit value and infrequently purchased. For example, electronic products.

Unsought products These are products that potential buyers are not aware of or not require, for example, life insurance, a lawyer's services in contesting a will.

The above product decisions are very important to ensure the sale of products. A product has both tangible and intangible components. While buying a product, the customer does not merely look for the physical product, but a bundle of satisfaction. Thus the impact that any product has upon a buyer goes well beyond its obvious characteristics. There is a psychological dimension to all customer purchases; what a customer thinks about a product is influenced by the product itself. For example, the buyers of an air conditioner are not only purchasing a cooling machine. They look for attractive colour and design, durability, low noise, quick cooling, etc. These influencing factors must be considered by small firms to meet the requirements of different kinds of customers.

2. Industrial Goods

The American Marketing Association has defined the industrial goods as "goods which are destined to be sold primarily for use in producing other goods or rendering services as contrasted with goods destined to be sold primarily to the ultimate consumers."

Industrial goods fall into four main categories:

i. *Raw materials*   Most of the agricultural products or semi-manufactured goods are raw materials, which require further processing.

ii. *Equipment*   Goods included in this category include installations, minor or accessory equipments, and plants and buildings.

iii. *Fabrication materials*   These industrial goods become a part of the finished goods. These products might have gone through complete manufacturing processes but reach the ultimate user only after they are assembled or combined with other products.

iv. *Operating supplies*   These products are essential to the business operations of industrial users, but they do not form a part of the finished products.

PRODUCT POLICY

The modern marketing concept is that it is not sufficient merely to produce better products, it is also necessary to bring it to the attention of the prospective customers. Hence, it is necessary to adopt suitable policy.

A policy sets the objectives to be achieved and also the limits within which the management has to operate. Policy is essential to make the product live up to the expectations of the consumers.

The important aspects analysed under product policy are:

1. The rate, nature and direction of change in demand for existing products.
2. Product elimination and new product development decisions
3. Product policy of the competitors.

It is to be understood that product policies do not provide readymade answers to the above problems. Product policy provides only guidelines for efficient planning and action. They are company's rules to guide those engaged in product planning and development, production or marketing. Product policies are applicable for both existing and new products.

Some people think that product policy simply relates to the quality of the product. High quality alone is not the ultimate reason for good sale. The sale depends on the extent to which a product is able to satisfy human wants. For example, when a car is bought, the motive is not conveyance alone, the car might have been bought for status, for economy or for some other purpose, say for carrying goods or for carrying passengers.

ELEMENTS OF PRODUCT POLICY

When a product policy is formulated, the following factors should be taken into consideration:

1. Product planning and development
2. Product mix, Product item and product line
3. Product standardization
4. Product identification or Branding

5. Product style
6. Product packaging and labelling

PRODUCT PLANNING AND DEVELOPMENT

It involves development and commercialization of new product, the modification of existing lines and the discontinuance of marginal or unprofitable items.

The following are the usual functions undertaken by product planning:

1. Evaluation of the idea, market and product
2. Evaluation of company resources
3. Finding out customer specifications
4. Testing the product
5. Marketing the product

Product development includes the technical activities of product research, engineering and design. Product planning is usually described as "merchandizing" and it covers both the existing and potential products.

PRODUCT ITEM, PRODUCT LINE AND PRODUCT MIX

1. Product Item

Product item means a specific version of a product that has a separate designation in the sellers list. It refers to a particular product.

2. Product line

Product line refers to a group of products that are closely related because they satisfy a class of needs, are used together, are sold to the same customer groups, are marketed through the same type of outlets within given price changes.

3. Product Mix

The product policy decisions are made at three different levels product mix, product item and product line. These "three-in-one" elements make the product planning effective.

Product mix is the list of all products offered for sale by a company. The product mix is three-dimensional. It has breadth, depth and consistency.

Breadth is measured by the variety of products manufactured by a single manufacturer. For example, Bajaj Electricals produces a variety of electrical appliances such as fans, lamp, etc. Depth refers to the assortment of sizes, colours and models offered within each product line.

Consistency refers to the close relationship of various product lines—either to their end use or to production requirements or to distribution channels. Bajaj Electricals, for example, produces those goods which fall under the category "electrical appliances" so, there is consistency in their products. In contrast to this, Godrej shows inconsistency in its product line, manufacturing process and even in its channels of distribution.

Factors influencing product mix The fundamental reasons for changing product mix (adding or eliminating products) is the change in the market demand. Change in demand occurs due to the following factors:

- Population increase
- Changes in the level of the income of the buyers
- Changes in consumer behaviour
- Marketing influences
- Production influences and
- Financial influences

All the activities arise out of the internal economics of a firm. As long as the profit motive is the criterion for the existence of the firm, changes in product mix are inevitable.

Any change in the product line or product item naturally changes the product mix and vice versa. The following are instances where the product mix is altered:

Product modification   Product modification may be defined as a deliberate alteration in the physical attributes of a product or its packaging. Modification is necessary to suit the changing demand on account of fashion changes.

Such a decision is required at a time when the product is in the maturity stage of product life cycle.

Product elimination   Some products cannot be improved or modified to suit the market. Here, the profitable alternative would be to withdraw the product.

Product line modification   Product line is altered or modified through the following methods:

i. *Product line contraction*   It is a method by which a fat and long product line is thinned out. It is also termed as "simplification". It may be due to marketing problems or very poor returns yielded by the product.

Sick products, in course of time, eat away the profits earned by the other products. The decision to give away a product often results from changes in the market. Market saturation makes a product unprofitable. Products may also be abandoned, even though still profitable, if the management feels that the same resources could yield a higher profit from other products.

ii. *Product line expansion*   It is just the opposite of contraction of product mix. To utilize the marketing opportunities, a firm may expand, product or production or both and depth of products. The expansion of the product line is undertaken by increasing the lines or items of products.

New lines may be related or unrelated to the present products. For example, manufacturers of radio sets may start producing television sets and tape recorders.

iii. *Diversification*   It means that something new is added. It may be new products, new technologies or even a new company. Generally, it means adding a new product to the existing product line or mix.

For example, if a wholesaler dealing in engineering goods starts selling confectionery items, simultaneously it is a case of diversification.

Diversification is necessary under the following circumstances:

- There is a technological development in the process of production.
- New markets are to be created.
- There is a constant threat for the existing product due to abrupt changes in fashion.
- The spare capacity of the factory is to be fully utilized.

Diversification prevents recessionary trends entering the industry. The usual way in which diversification is brought about is by means of mergers like one company acquiring another.

Hindustan Machine Tools offer a good example in this regard. Started as a company manufacturing various machine tools, it moved into the field of watch making.

iv. *Changing models or styles of the existing products*   Continuous changes in fashion create a problem for the producer to assess in advance. Such changes, furthermore, the desires and needs of the consumers are also subjected to continuous change.

A car or a bike Company introduces different models of bikes? "because different individuals have different tastes.

v. *Quality variations*   Under certain circumstances, a producer, is forced to produce differing qualities of a particular product. Even if the quality of the product is good, a single quality may not be enough to retain the market.

For example, manufacturers of pens invariably market pens of different varieties with varying quality at different prices.

The process of changing the quality falls under two heads— trading up and trading down.

i. *Trading up* The process of introducing higher quality products by a manufacturer, whose low-quality products are famous is called trading up. High quality invariably demands a high price too. This is practicable only when the manufacturer has already earned a reputation for his quality products.

ii. *Trading down* It is the opposite of trading up. It happens when a manufacturer of high-quality producing starts selling a low-quality product. High quality followed by high prices may fit only certain markets. For a manufacturer who purposely wishes to widen the market for his products, this policy is an apt one. The policy will be most effective where the manufacturer has already established a name for high-quality products.

PRODUCT STANDARDIZATION

Standards are fixed taking into consideration the process involved, the nature of the product, consumer demand, etc.

While fixing the standard, the following physical properties of the product are considered:

1. Weight and measures
2. Size and shape
3. Chemical or technical properties
4. Product performance
5. Other characteristics apparent to human senses

Standardization includes various elements such as grading, packaging, labelling and branding.

The different kinds of standards are:

1. *Product standards* They establish ingredients, physical characteristics, quality and performance of a particular product. Product standards generally help the consumer by assuring him of uniformity in quality and performance.

2. *Engineering standards* These standards are concerned directly with the parts that make up the product.

3. *Materials standards* The materials that are used in production (raw material) are standardized in quality and other physical aspects.

4. *Quality standards* The economical quality to be produced is decided earlier and this assumes the standard for production.

5. *Process standards* The operation method in a factory or industry is standardized to get the maximum benefit of ease and economy in production.

Standardization vs Simplification

These two terms are often used interchangeably. Simplification is commercial in nature, while standardization is technical.

For example, when a manufacturer of electric fans reduces his line of electric fans from six models to two, he has simplified his product line.

When the same manufacturer establishes a modified new regulator or any additional special features for each model, he is said to have established standards for the product.

Maintaining the Standard

If standards are registered, the manufacturer is obliged to maintain them. The ISI inspectors, throughout the country, draw samples from various places and these are tested in laboratories to find out their conformity with the standards. Besides the legal obligation, a manufacturer is bound to maintain the standards or else he will fail in the competitive market. Most of the manufacturers have their own quality control departments. Modern management uses techniques like statistical quality control (SQC) to ensure standards.

PRODUCT IDENTIFICATION

Once a manufacturer has decided to introduce a new product he decides to give his product an identity—a brand name. Brand names help the buyers to identify the products in the market place. But the brand image is not a permanent one and cannot retain a perpetual market. Brand is only a name and the acceptance of a product finally rests on the real worth of a product.

Brand

Branding is the management process by which a product is branded. It is a general term covering various activities such as giving a brand name to a product, designing a brand mark, establishing and popularizing it. A brand is a name, term, symbol or design or a combination of them which is intended to identify the goods or services of one seller or a group of sellers and to differentiate from those of competitors. For example, Lux Soap is a brand. They assist the producer in many ways. They add prestige to the product, aid in creating, stimulating and maintaining the demand and facilitate effective sales promotion techniques.

Functions of branding

- It helps in product identification.
- Indirectly it denotes the quality or standard of a product.
- It ensures legal right on the product.
- It helps in advertising and packaging.
- It helps to create and sustain brand loyalty to particular products.
- It helps in price differentiation of products.

Kinds of brands

Thomas F. Schutte in *The Semantics of Branding* classifies brands into two broad categories:

1. *Manufacturers' brands*

- National brands—The same brand used on a national level
- Regional brands—Brands for particular regions
- Advertising brands—Brands stressing symbols
- Blanket brands or single brands or family brands—One brand name for all the products of a manufacturer, for example, Godrej Products.
- Multiple brands or individual brands—Brand name given for each variety of product, for example, various brand soaps of Tata.

2. *Distributors' brands*

- Private brand
- Store brand
- Dealer brand
- House brand

Distributor's brand stresses the identity of the retailer.

There is a great controversy and difference of opinion about the purpose, use and effectiveness of each of these brands.

The first controversy is between manufacturers' and distributors' brands. Some authorities argue that the manufacturers' brand is strong and more purposeful. Some others are of the view that distributors' brand is more popular because it is they who ultimately deal with the customers. They feel that it is not the manufacturer's brand alone which decides a sale. In the USA this controversy is termed as "brand battles".

In India, however, this does not have much relevance. In India, the retailers are not very strong to carve out their own name in the distribution field, except a very few like Spencers.

The next conflict is between the use of family brand and individual brand. Each has its own advantages and disadvantages. Where a manufacturer has established a name, he may prefer to introduce the new products under the same brand name used for his previous product. The new product will also enjoy the reputation created by earlier brands without any additional expenditure.

At the same time, it may turn out to be disadvantageous in case the new product fails. The failure will affect the market of the earlier products also. Using one brand name also reduces the advertisement expenditure.

In contrast to this, the use of individual brand name calls for high advertisement cost for its establishment. The greatest disadvantage is that the products of the same manufacturer will compete with each other. It is, however, advantageous for clear identification where different quality and variety of products are manufactured. Bata Shoe Company manufactures a variety of shoes and individual names are essential to identify a particular variety.

The decision of a manufacturer to choose a family brand or individual brand depends on the following factors:

- Name of the product
- Varieties manufactured
- Promotional aspects
- Nature of the market for which the product is intended
- Consumer's attitudes and sentiments.

Kinds of brand names Brand name is a part of a brand consisting of a word, letter, group of words which helps to identify the goods or services of a seller. Brand names are divided into:

Coined name A purposely created name puts more stress on producer's identity. For example, the word a "Parker" alone is meaningless unless it is attached to a Pen.

Arbitrary name   A name neither relating to product nor the producer.

Suggestive name   A name which suggests something about the product or its functions. For example, Band-aid sticking plaster, Kesavardhini hair oil.

Descriptive name   A name that describes the product fully, for example, glucose biscuit, cocoa sweets.

Characteristics of a good brand name are:

- The name should readily come to the minds of the customers.
- It should be easy to pronounce.
- The name should be easy to read and understand.
- The name should be appropriate for the product.

The brand name, packaging are only ancillary things and customer is really influenced by the quality and performance of the product.

Advantages of brand names

The advantages of using brand names that could be easily recognized for each group of participants in the marketing, viz., manufacturers, consumer and distributors are as follows:

To the manufacturers:

- It identifies the product and distinguishes it from other competing products. Thus, it protects the interests of the manufacturer.
- It saves advertising cost, if the brand name is popular.

To the consumers:

- It affords an easy way for purchase by easily identifying a product.
- It assures fixed prices. Even the distributors cannot unjustifiably vary prices.

To the distributors:

- Widely popular brands ease the selling process and lead to large sales.

- The distributor can easily find out the quick moving products.

- Special selling efforts need not be undertaken. This reduces the cost of distribution and hence the final low price.

Brand mark   A mark is the part of the brand which appears in the form of a symbol, design or distinctive colouring or lettering.

It could be recognized only by sight but may not be pronounceable, for example, the symbol of "Maharaja" of Air India, the picture of "Gopuram" of the Tamil Nadu Tourist Development Corporation.

Brand image and product image

Every brand image is partially derived from the product image. The product image relates to the fundamental aims and satisfactions which the consumers find in a particular product.

In the present day markets, branding is inevitable and it plays an important role in demand creation. A large number of products live in the market even today mainly due to the effective use of brand names. For example, Usha Fans. This brand name is so common that one does not even recognize the manufacturer, viz. "Jay Engineering". Similar instance is found in the case of "Dettol". It is simply an antiseptic lotion. But the manufacturers were successful in creating an impression in the minds of most of the people that Dettol means antiseptic lotion and vice versa.

The importance of branding arose mainly because of overemphasis on advertisement. In fact, the brand name is the child of advertisement and the trademark is the legal guardian of a brand name.

Arguments against branding The severe criticism levelled against branding is that it leads to some kind of monopoly known as "brand monopoly". The brand monopoly is created by gradually creating a brand loyalty to the products in the minds of the consumers.

This criticism is baseless since such a situation is not possible in the case of consumer goods unless they are really necessary items. When a monopolistic tendency is found, consumers will change the brand.

It is difficult to establish a brand and the expense of advertising in the initial stages is very high, which raises the cost.

Manufacturers sometimes place inferior goods in the market under a glamorous brand name.

Branding decisions Brand managers have to develop a logical order of action in developing brand awareness and ultimately leading to brand loyalty. These phases may be as follows:

i. *Brand preference* Making the consumers buy a particular brand.

ii. *Brand insistence* It is the stage in which consumers will not accept any substitute product.

iii. *Brand loyalty* Last stage in the branding process when consumers make repeat purchases of the same brand.

Trademark When a brand name or a brand mark is registered, it becomes a trademark. Thus registered brands are trade marks. In that sense "all trademarks are brands but not all brands are trademarks." Trademark protects the manufacturer's right to use the brand name or brand mark.

Trade name A trade name is the name of business, preferably the name of the organization itself. A trade name may also be a brand name, but in such a case, it serves two separate purposes. It brings out the identity of the manufacturer and the product. Tatas is solely a trade name of the maker of various brands of cosmetics (for example, jasmine soap, hair oils, powders, etc).

Godrej is both a trade name and a brand name for most of their products (for example, Godrej locks, Godrej soaps).

Patents   Patents are public documents conferring certain rights, privileges, titles or offices. A patent confers the right to the use of a technical invention. It is applicable in the case of new inventions such as a new process, a new product or a new machine.

A patent prevents unauthorized persons from making commercial use of a new and a useful technological invention.

Copyright   This is applicable in the case of books and issued in the same meaning as that of patents. It is a sole right to reproduce literary, dramatic, musical or artistic work. Copyright is available for the entire life of the author and fifty years after his death.

PRODUCT STYLE

Most of the products are bought by consumers to meet the psychological needs. For example, powder, perfume, shaving lotion, etc. have only very little functional value. Physiologically these products are not necessities. Therefore their need is only subjective and not objective.

Yet, this completely subjective force is recognized and is called "style". This element is so dangerously dynamic that a product becomes obsolete in no time.

A firm may stress the need for the product with a changed emphasis. For example, "toothpaste" was introduced in the market as an anti-decay medicine.

PRODUCT PACKAGING

Packaging

Until recently packing was being considered as a minor element in the marketing mix of a product. But now it has become an integral part of the product itself. Packages act as the major means of creating product preference. It is a vehicle by which the brand of a product is carried through the consumer. It is a powerful selling tool. Hence, it has become a highly important area of managerial decisions.

Packing and packaging   Packing is the process of covering, wrapping or crating goods into a package. This is done for the purpose of delivering the product.

Packaging involves designing and producing the container or wrapper for a product. The potentialities of packaging, essentially in the field of demand creation, have been widely accepted now. It is often remarked as a silent salesman. Packaging decision may affect production, distribution, research and development, sales, accounting, and finance.

Packaging is an effective selling tool. For example, Gillette Company introduced a package for keeping blades. This packaging has come to be known as "razor blade dispenser". This dispensing packaging not only includes space for new blades, which could easily be ejected, but contained space at the bottom of the dispenser in which old and useless blades could be kept.

Functions of package

Packaging has a two-dimensional function. First, it must protect the product. Then it has an important promotional role.

Thus, the functions can be categorized into the following headings:

i. *Protection and preservation*   The basic function of packaging is to protect and preserve the contents during transit from the manufacturer to the ultimate consumer.

- Most of the damage occurs in the handling process. The more frequently the products are handled in the distribution process, the greater is the need for protection. Damaged goods have to be replaced as they may cause loss and inconvenience to the seller as well as to the purchaser.

- Certain products, if exposed, may be lost. Powder, oil and petroleum products are examples.
- Pilferage
- Contamination by dirt or dust, for example, clothing.
- Moisture gain and loss, for example, cement.
- Chemical change, for example, metal corrosion.
- Insect attack, for example, moths in clothing.

ii. *Containment* Most products must be contained before they can be moved from one place to another. To function successfully, the package must contain the product. This containment function of packaging makes a huge contribution to protect the environment. A better packaging helps to maintain the quality of the product and reachability of the product in the consumer's hand without spillages. It gives better image to the organization.

iii. *Communication* A major function of packaging is the communication of the product. A package must communicate what it sells. When international trade is involved and different languages are spoken, the use of unambiguous and readily understood symbols on the distribution package is essential. It helps in appropriate communication to the consumer about the product, how to use it and other utility information. Packaging protects the interests of consumers. Information includes quantity, price, inventory levels, lot number, distribution routes, size, elapsed time since packaging, colour, merchandizing and premium data.

iv. *Convenience*

- Properly packed goods require less space.
- Easy methods could be suggested to take goods out from a pack and keep the rest intact.

v. *Economy* Package provides various economies, both to the producers and the consumers.

- Loss in quantity is prevented thereby avoiding the monetary loss also.

- Creates an opportunity to communicate with the customers.

vi. *Promotion function*

- *Self-service* The package must be and capable of performing many of the sales tasks. It must attract attention, describe the products' features, give consumer confidence and make a favourable overall impression.

- *Consumer affluence* The prestige of a product is maintained with the help of proper packaging. Good packaging is capable of projecting various qualities of the product as well as that of the manufacturers.

- *Integrated marketing concept* Brand names now occupy a dominant role in marketing. The brand names are popularized through advertisement but the reminding of brand names and making the brands acceptable to consumers are achieved through packaging.

- *Innovational opportunity* Packaging is capable of bringing large-scale gains.

Packages also perform a large and increasing variety of other individual functions.

Some of these functions are:

- To assemble and arrange the contents in the desired form.

- To identify the contents, the brand and the maker. (Product differentiation is perfected through this function).

- To provide a suitable product mix including size, weights, prices, grades and packages.

- To facilitate retailer's functions.

- To facilitate transporting, storing and warehouse handling.

- To enable the display of contents.

- To encourage repurchase.
- To help in complying with legal requirements.
- To provide opportunity and space for advertising.

Kinds of packaging Kinds or methods of packaging will depend largely on the nature of the contents in terms of their value, physical composition and durability.

The length of the distribution channel, the amount of handling which the container receives, and variations in climatic conditions encountered between the points of manufacture and sales are also to be taken into account .

For example, products in liquid form require containers made of glass or similar materials. For fragile articles, wooden containers are used.

On the basis of nature, packaging is classified into the following:

i. *Family packaging* A package of a particular manufacturer, packed in an identical manner is known as family packaging. The shape and colour, the materials used for packaging will be similar for all the products in such cases.

ii. *Reuse packaging* Packages that could be used for some other purposes after the goods have been consumed is known as reuse packaging.

iii. *Multiple packaging* It is the practice of placing several units in one container. This helps to introduce new products and increase sales.

iv. *Transport packaging* The product entering into the trade needs to be packed well enough to protect against loss or damage during handling, transport and storage, for example, fibreboard, wooden crate, etc.

v. *Consumer packaging* This packaging holds the required volume of the product for ultimate consumption and is more relevant in marketing, for example, beverages, tobacco, etc.

Test to check packaging

There are various mechanical tests to check the method of packaging. They are:

i. *Drop test* This test helps to measure the ability of the container to provide protection to its contents and to withstand rough handling.

ii. *Vibration test* This test is used to determine the ability of the container to withstand vibration and the protection offered by materials used for interior packing.

iii. *Compression test* This test is carried out, generally, on empty containers, to measure the ability of the container to resist external compressive loads applied to faces or applied to diagonally opposite edges or corners.

iv. *Inclined impact test* This test helps to study the extent of damage in a way of crushing, breaking, cracking, distortion and shifting during handling, storage and transport which occurs to the container and its contents.

v. *Rolling test* This test helps to evaluate the overall strength of the container and the cushioning material provided inside.

vi. *Drum test* This test helps to evaluate loaded shipping containers with respect to general overall durability and the protection afforded to the contents against certain hazards of handling and shipment.

Various climatic tests are available to check the effect of various climatic factors on packaging:

i. *Rain test* This test is conducted in a simulated rain condition to assess its impact on the test area for two hours.

ii. *Sand and dust test* This test evaluates the resistance of a package to the penetration of sand and dust.

iii. *Salt spray test* This test evaluates the resistance of a package to corrosion by salt spray and if serves as a general standard for corrosion.

The following points need to be taken into consideration while packaging:

- Cost of packaging
- Appearance
- Kinds of designs
- Convenience
- Reuse

AIDA formula AIDA formula is applicable in packaging decisions too.

This formula represents the following four basic requirements.

A—Attention, that is, getting the attention of the public.

I—Interest, that is, creating an interest over the product.

D—Desire, that is, creating desire to purchase the product.

A—Action, that is, compelling the consumers to take action (that is, purchase)

Engineering tests are necessary to know whether the package will withstand handling. Visual tests are done to prove its attractiveness. Dealer tests and consumer tests are also conducted to assure favourable response from these two groups.

In spite of its various advantages, packaging has been subjected to criticisms. One among them is that it adds to cost. It is true that packaging expenses definitely increase the cost. But the benefits derived are sufficient to compensate the increase in the cost.

For example, the medicine which we buy is not consumed at once. Its preservation is very important. Only a good package can render this service.

Kinds of materials used for packaging

Earthenware It is an old method of preserving products of liquid nature.

China jars They are used where protection is required against light and corrosive action.

Wooden boxes They prevent breakage due to rough handling.

Cardboard containers These are mostly used in specialist goods which are not bulky.

Straw baskets These are meant for keeping vegetables.

Gunny bags Gunny bags are popular for packing goods like rice, grains, sugar, cement, white and colour washing meterials, etc. Gunny bags cannot give protection to the goods.

Glass Glass is used to pack liquid products. It affords protection against the action of most of the chemicals.

Tin containers Tin containers are used to pack liquid and solid products. They are light and strong.

Plastic containers Plastic containers are gaining extreme popularity. Plastic containers are used to pack liquid and solid products. It involves low cost, good appearance, convenience and ability for reuse.

Paper bags Paper bags are used to pack products which are in solid form. They are commendable. But their limitations are that the freshness of the product cannot be preserved.

Cellophane paper Cellophane is a good substitute for paper as packing material. It protects the contents from moisture, but it cannot protect the products against harmful effects of light.

Cushion materials Cushioning is that part of packaging, which protects the article from damage due to shock and vibration. The main functions of cushioning materials are:

- Shock protection against vibration
- Protection against abrasion
- Protection of grease-proof and water-proof barriers at the point of contact with solid blocks

- Protection of moisture vapour barriers at points of contact with sharp edges of the article itself
- Protection of small projections
- Filling of void space in the container

Packaging cost

The most important aspect of packaging is the packaging cost. Packaging cost includes the following:

Material cost   It means the cost of the pack and quality control cost.

Storage and handling cost of empty packages   This includes the handling cost of bulky packages, heavy materials of construction, drums, etc.

Packaging operation cost   This includes the cost involved in operations like cleaning the package, product filling, closing, labelling, unitizing, stencilling, handling cylindrical drums, etc.

Storage of filled packages   This includes the cost incurred to shift the goods from one form of packaging to another.

Transportation cost of filled packages   This involves the transportation cost by sea, air, etc.

Loss and damage cost   It is related to the loss and damage during operation, transportation, delivery, etc.

Insurance cost   It varies depending on the vulnerability of package.

Effect of packages on sales   The package that influences the sales.

Obsolescence cost   This cost is incurred when changes in the packaging materials, packages and labels happen.

Package developmental cost   This includes the evaluation cost, pilot test cost, field testing cost, consumer research cost, feedback cost, final trial cost, etc.

Labelling

Labelling is another product feature that requires managerial attention. Packaging, branding and labelling go together and are integral part of product planning. The purpose of labelling is to give the consumer, information about the product he is buying and what it will and will not do for him.

What is label? Label is a part of the product. It gives verbal information about the product of the seller. The information to be conveyed may be either printed on the container itself or affixed on or printed on a separate slip of paper and delivered to the consumer along with the product. This is called labelling.

Functions of labelling

  i. It encourages production of only standardized and quality products.
 ii. By mentioning prices, undue price variations caused by the intermediaries are avoided.
iii. Identification of a product is easy.
 iv. It specifies the special features of the product.

Kinds of labels Labels can be classified as follows:

i. *Brand labels* These are meant for popularizing the brand name of the product. Cosmetics manufacturers prefer to use this kind, for example, sweets, cigarettes.

ii. *Grade labels* These labels give emphasis to standards of grades, for example, Cloth, leaf tea.

iii. *Descriptive labels* (Illustrative in nature) In addition to the product feature, they explain the various uses of the product. Most of the milk-food products and other similar household products invariably have descriptive labels.

iv. *Informative labels* These labels contain details in addition to product features, methods of using it properly, etc, for example, medicines—specify the side effects in using them.

Advantages of labelling

- It is a social service to customers, who often do not know anything about product features.
- It avoids price variations by publishing the price on the label.

Demerits of Labelling

- Labelling is effective only when standardization is compulsory.
- It enables the customer to weigh and compare the advantages of products before they are used. This ultimately ends in discarding a product in favour of the other.

PRODUCT POSITIONING

Product positioning means "relating a product to the market." In simple words, group of customers with common characteristics are first identified. It also involves analysis of product strengths and weaknesses and competitor's ability to meet customer needs. It is necessary to differentiate products from their competing ones.

Designing of new products always raises a number of problems. One of them is their failure in a very short span. The reasons for product failures are as follows:

1. *Inadequate market analysis* Biased information or improper analysis will yield only wrong data. Acting on such data leads to product failure.

2. *Product defects* This arises out of technical flaws in the process of production.

3. *Higher costs* Higher final costs than anticipated at the time of product planning is another reason for product failure.

4. *Poor timing* It is necessary to find out the exact time at which the product is to be introduced in to the market. A close analysis of the market condition and consumer behaviour is necessary to avoid product failures.

5. *Competition* There are various methods to overcome competition, including price cuts and various kinds of discounts, etc.

6. *Insufficient marketing efforts* Proper selection of the channels of distribution helps in proper and efficient marketing of products. Promotional activities should be backed by adequate sales force.

Product failures can be prevented by adopting the following methods:

- By making a product that is acceptable to the society.
- By using continuous and efficient demand creation methods.
- Analysis of customer—as to who wants what and where.
- Analysis of product features including the price.
- Design-efficient organizational structure for the distribution of products.
- Undertaking consumer tests on the basis of results obtained and the rescheduling of the entire process if necessary.

PRODUCT LIFE CYCLE (PLC)

Every product passes through four stages in its life namely, introduction, growth, maturity and decline. The concept of product life cycle (PLC) highlights that sooner or later, all products will die and that if entrepreneurs wish to sustain its revenues, they must replace the products in the declining stage with the new ones. With the product passing through different stages the small-scale entrepreneur faces varying challenges, opportunities and problems. Smaller businesses have a good reputation for innovation. Their greatest advantage is the speed at which they can respond to the demands of the market.

Every firm makes sales forecasts during introduction, growth and maturity stages of the PLC. To achieve the sales target, it formulates promotional, pricing and distribution policies.

Thus the concept of PLC facilitates integrated marketing policies relating to product, price, promotion and distribution.

The life cycle of a product has many points of similarity with the human life. From its birth, a product passes through various stages, until it is discontinued from the market.

The advantages of forecasting the life cycle of a product to a firm are as follows:

1. When the PLC is predictable, the entrepreneur can take in advance before the decline stage, by adopting product modification, pricing strategies, distinctive style, quality change, etc.

2. The firm can prepare an effective product plan by knowing the PLC of a product.

3. The entrepreneur can find new uses of the product for the expansion of market during growth stage and for extending the maturity stage.

4. The entrepreneur can adopt latest technological changes to improve the product quality, features and design.

STAGES IN PRODUCT LIFE CYCLE

As the product moves through the different stages of its life cycle, sales volume and profitability change from stage to stage as shown in Figure 10.1.

Product Life Cycle

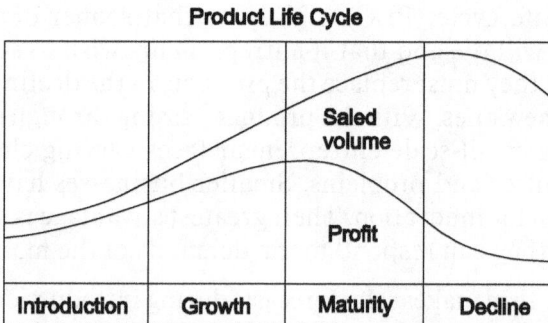

| Introduction | Growth | Maturity | Decline |

Figure 10.1   Product life cycle

The entrepreneur's emphasis on the marketing mix elements also undergoes substantial changes from stage to stage. A brief discussion of the marketing strategies in different stages of the PLC is discussed in the following sections:

Introduction Stage

The first stage of a product life cycle is the introduction or pioneering stage. In this stage, the fixed costs of marketing and production will be high, competition is almost non-existent, markets are limited, and the product is not known much. Prices are relatively high because of small-scale production, technological problems and heavy promotional expenditure. Profits are usually non-existent as heavy expenses are incurred for introducing the product in the market. Heavy expenditure on advertisement is made to inform the customers about its qualities and characteristics and it is made popular among its users, through promotional efforts. As the consumers are unaware of the products, characteristics, the sales do not pick up much. Consequently the quantum of profits is low or rather negligible in this stage but the risk factor is much higher.

To introduce the product successfully, the following strategies may be adopted:

- When advertising the product, "Money back" guarantee may be given to stimulate the people to try the product.
- Attractive gift to customers as an "introductory offer" can be offered.
- Attractive discount to dealers can be given.
- Higher price of product to earn more profit during the initial stages.

Growth Stage

After the product is introduced in the market, the product enters the second stage, viz. growth stage. The sales as well as the profits increase rapidly as the product is accepted in the market. The promotional expenses remain high although its ratio to sales volume tend to fall. Quite often, smaller firms move into the market during the growth phase. With their flexibility, they can move very quickly and capture a valuable part of the market without huge investment risks of the development phase. In this stage, the competition increases and distribution is greatly widened. The marketing management focuses its attention on improving the market share by deeper penetration into the existing markets and entry into new markets. Sometimes major improvements also take place in the product during this stage.

The product gains popularity and recognition from the customers. The demand and sales go up tremendously due to promotional efforts. Consequently profits of the firm start rising because of two primary reasons: (i) production and sales go up, hence firm gets economies of large-scale production and sales, and (ii) although advertising and distribution costs go up, per unit cost is reduced. High profits attract the competitors, so they enter the field.

The following strategies are followed during the growth stage:

- The product is advertised heavily to stimulate sale.
- New versions of the product are introduced to cater to the requirements of different types of customers.
- The channels of distribution are strengthened so that the product is easily available wherever required.
- Brand image of the product is created through promotional activities.
- Price of the product is fixed in such a way that it is competitive.
- Greater emphasis on customer service is adopted.

Maturity Stage

The product enters into the maturity stage as competition intensifies further and market gets stabilized. There is saturation in the market as there is no possibility of sales growth. The product has been accepted by most of the potential buyers.

Profits come down because of stiff competition and marketing expenditures rise. The prices are decreased because of competition and innovations in technology. This stage may last for a longer period as in the case of many products with long-run demand characteristics. But sooner or later, the demand of the product starts declining as new products are introduced in the market. Product differentiation, identification of new segments, and product improvement are emphasized during this stage. The advertisement and distribution costs increase in order to make the product survive. The profit rate begins to decline. The producers search for new markets. Market and marketing research expenditure goes up. The prices come down due to stiff competition.

In order to lengthen the period of maturity stage, the following strategies may be adopted:

- Products may be differentiated from the competitive products and brand image may be emphasized more.
- The warranty period may be extended.
- Reusable packaging may be introduced.
- New markets may be developed.
- New uses of the product may be developed.

Saturation Stage

The next stage is comes the saturation stage point. The sale volume comes to standstill despite best efforts but it is at all time high . The competition is also at its peak in this period. Competition brings the cost of distribution and promotional efforts to new heights. Thus prices begin to fall and therefore profits come down. Fresh efforts are made in this stage to improve the product. New makes are tried.

Decline Stage

This stage is characterized by either the product's gradual displacement by some new products or change in consumer's buying behaviour. The sales fall down sharply and the expenditure on promotion has to be cut down drastically. The decline may be rapid with the product soon passing out of market, or it may be slow if new uses of the product are found. Profits are much smaller and companies need to assess their investment policies, looking towards investing in newer and more profitable product lines. This stage brings gradual displacement of the products with some new innovation or changes in consumer behaviour. New products are introduced in the market by competitors. Cost control becomes necessary to reduce the price in order to compete. As far as possible, attempts should be made to avoid the decline stage.

But if it has started, the following strategies may be useful:

- The promotion of the product should be selective. Wasteful advertising should be avoided.
- The product model may be abandoned and all the good features may be retained in the new model of the product.
- Economical packaging should be introduced to revive the product.
- The manufacturer may seek merger with a strong firm.

Obsolescence Stage

As new products are developed and introduced by the competitors, the company's product dies out. Its demand and sales are likely to taper off. Profits are reduced to the negligible point. At this stage, it is advisable to stop the production of the product and switch on to other products.

Utility of Product Life Cycle Concept

The concept of product life cycle is very important, from the marketing point of view for a producer or a marketer. The main utilities of the concept are:

Life of a product is limited   According to the concept, the life of a product is always limited. The product will die out over a period of time irrespective of the fact that the product had made tremendous progress during the past.

Estimation of profits   The quantum and rate of profits increase or decrease with the quantum of turnover. At the introductory stage, profits are negligible, then they go up and after some time, they begin to fall and gradually they move to nil.

Marketing programmes   Different policies, procedures and strategies are followed in the different stages of the life cycle of a product. So, management can prepare the marketing programmes accordingly and may get success.

PRODUCT DIVERSIFICATION

To utilize the marketing opportunities, a firm may extend in both breadth and depth. Depth refers to the number of product items offered by the organization within a particular product line. Width refers to the extent of different product lines in the product mix offered by an organization. Consistency describes the goodness of the various product lines.

For product diversification, increasing depth of the product helps the organization to attract customers with deficient needs and preferences. This helps the concern to capitalize on its established reputation and marketing skills. Increasing consistency of the product mix helps the concern to capitalize on the existing facilities of the production and distribution and establishes a high self-reputation.

Diversification by definition means addition of something new to the product line. It is opposite of simplification. It may be new products, new markets, new technologies, even a new company. Generally it means adding a new product, and not various qualities of the same product, to the existing product line or mix. For example, if a fan manufacturing company starts producing sewing machines, it is a case of diversification. It does not mean that the new product should be complementary or an allied product to the existing one. It may be a product which may be entirely distinct and different from existing products.

The term "diversification" is applicable not only to production but also to selling. For instance, if a wholesaler dealing in engineering goods starts selling woollen textiles simultaneously, it is also a case of diversification. Some of the reasons why such a change is necessitated are:

- There is a technological development in the process of production.
- New markets are to be created.
- Existing products reputation need to be spread to other products.
- There is constant threat for the existing product due to abrupt changes in fashion.

Diversification is profitable only in the case of large companies which have multi-market and multi-products. Such companies should be financially viable, supported by a well-organized management. Diversification of products to a very large extent is capable of preventing recessionary trends entering the industry. The usual way in which diversification is brought into effects is by means of mergers like one company acquiring another.

Objectives of Product Diversification

i. *Suitability in earnings and organization*

- To eliminate seasonal slumps.
- To eliminate cyclical slumps.
- To reduce the danger of declining demand.
- To acquire social approval.

ii. *Efficiency in utilization of company resources*

- To make use of the discoveries, accidental or purposeful in the company laboratories.
- To use excess productive capacity arising from abrupt decline in demand and from imbalance of the vertical integration.
- To capitalize an unique production process.
- To capitalize the foreseen demands for a product developed for company's own use.
- To utilize profitably the by-products.
- To meet the government requests arising out of the knowledge of the company's resources.
- To make full use of a developing management and staff.

iii. *Efficient marketing*

- To increase the sale of the basic products.
- To meet the demands and convenience of the diversification retailer.
- To exploit the value of an established trademark.
- To meet the requests of specific customers.
- To reduce the ratio of sales costs vs total sales.

iv. *Profitable use of opportunities*

- To use cash and undistributed earnings during high-profit periods.
- To take advantage of the large company's access to debt financing at relatively low rates.
- To manipulate capital gains versus income and inheritance taxes for the material benefit of the buyers and sellers in perspective mergers.
- To capture merger bargains.
- To avoid the cost of constructing facilities under existing economic conditions.
- To make the best of diversification, willingly or unwillingly acquired, with a purchased company.

Various Forms of Diversification

There are three popular forms of product diversification:

1. Diversification into related product line
2. Diversification into unrelated product line
3. Product replacement

Diversification into related product line When diversification is planned in products which are related to the existing product lines, then the suggested products may be grouped with the existing products. For example, Hindustan Unilever Limited produces several food articles and detergents. The purposes of such types of diversification are to reduce the average selling cost, to reorganize its sales organization, to combat competition and to increase the profits.

Diversification into unrelated product line The company may diversify in such product lines which are quite unrelated to each other. They cannot be grouped together. For example, Hindustan Machine Tools manufactures machine tools, watches, tractors, etc. These products are not related to each other. The decision to diversify in this form is taken to get the following advantages: (a) to capture the market (b) to take advantage of its goodwill in the market (c) to have stability in the trade, etc. This type of policy requires extensive market analysis before taking a decision to diversify.

Product replacement In this form of diversification, a new product is added to the product line to replace the other product of the same product line. If the company thinks that a product is in its final stage adds another product of similar nature to the market so that the company can maintain its sale-volume and profits. It is a defensive policy against the risk of dying out of one of the products of the company.

Factors Motivating Product Diversification

Following are the various factors that motivate product diversification:

   i. Utilization of unused capacity
   ii. Scientific and technical development
  iii. Efficient management
  iv. Industrial and economic policies of the government
   v. Social changes
  vi. Desire of the producer
 vii. Consumer satisfaction

PRODUCT PLANNING FOR EXISTING PRODUCTS

New products are the results of planned discovery. Huge investment and innovation are necessary for developing new products. At the same time, management should also review the profitability of current items (existing products) in the product mix.

Product planning deals with changes in:

- the quality levels acceptable to various classes of consumers.
- the degree of distinctiveness.

The following are the basic changes that may be required in product planning:

- Improving the existing products.
- Weeding out unprofitable items in the product line (simplification).
- Expansion of the current product line (diversification).
- New product development for the present customers.
- New product for new customers.

Deletion of a product requires careful planning. A definite procedure for the deletion of the product must be worked out beforehand. It is necessary to gather information about the product proposed to be deleted. Proper analysis of the information might show that the existing product could be modified to suit the needs of the customers. Before taking a decision to discontinue a product, careful analysis is required.

Time limit should be set on making the item profitable or finding a convenient way to drop the product.

Sometimes, it is necessary to eliminate a product when it does not find a proper place in a firm's product line. Many drug manufacturing concerns are forced to delete a product simply because the product does not fit exactly into their product line.

The appearance of substitute products is another instance where a product has to be eliminated.

The decision to delete a product normally creates certain problems. They are:

- The capital invested on a "to be deleted" product becomes a waste.
- Such deletion can be implemented only after the entire stock is sold-out.
- Customers might suffer on account of the deletion of a product. For example, when a particular variety of product (say a car) is dropped from the product line, it becomes the duty of the producer to supply spares until the product life cycle is completed.

It is also necessary that the product elimination should not cause inconvenience to customers. They should be informed about the elimination far in advance so that they can make replacements, if necessary.

Similarly, the process of deletion should be properly timed so that it exactly coincides with the end of the selling reason. This will also help in clearing out the products by recovering at least the cost of production.

In the case of most of the consumer durables, the investment cost is high. So it may not be advisable to decide the outright deletion. Product modification would be equally profitable.

For example, in the case of refrigerators, washing machines, radios etc. the product features are modified to attract customers.

Every management must review its products on a continuous basis. The needs of consumers undergo a change and the appearance of rival products creates the need to modify the existing products.

Introduction of new product is a lengthy process. In the case of consumer goods it is an easier task since they have regular pattern. Product replacement in the industrial field is often a case of changing technology.

PRODUCT PLANNING FOR NEW PRODUCTS

Customer's needs must be identified, competing and substitute products should be evaluated, and above all, the strength of the company should be examined before deciding to produce a new product.

Product failure defeats not only the objectives of a firm, but also ends in waste of money, material and time.

The following steps are recommended in the planning of products:

Exploration

One must begin with an idea. Ideas may be generated from the following sources:

i. Own research and development department

ii. Distributors

iii. Competitors

iv. Professional inventors

All the ideas may not have immediate market potential. At the same time, a firm must always keep a collection of ideas ready in stock. The specific activities performed in this stage are:

- Determining the product fields of interest to the company.
- Establishing a programme for planned idea generation.
- Collecting ideas through an organized work.

Screening

At this stage, the ideas collected are scrutinized to eliminate those inconsistent with the product policies and objectives of the firm. Some ideas may already have been protected by patents and some others may not be red because of non-availability of raw materials for production. Thus most of the ideas are dropped at this stage.

The procedure followed includes:

i. Expanding each idea into full product concept.
ii. Collecting facts and opinions to decide whether the product idea could be converted into business proposition.
iii. Assessing each idea for its potential value to the company.

Business Analysis

At this stage product features are analysed and a rough programme for its development is fixed.

Development

During this stage, "the idea on the paper" is turned into a product on hand. This stage is also termed as "technical development."

Once the management decides to go forward with the product idea, the following activities are undertaken:

i. Establishing development projects for each product.
ii. Building the product with the changed specifications if necessary.

iii. Completing laboratory evaluation and releasing the product for testing.

TESTING

It is at the stage of testing that one could verify the accuracy of information. The object of this stage is to assess whether the product meets the technical and commercial objectives envisaged in the original proposal.

There are three types of tests that are usually conducted, namely: 1. Concept testing, 2. Product testing, and 3. Test marketing

Concept Testing

This is concerned with measuring customer reaction to the idea or concept of a product. The idea of a product with as many details as possible, is made known to the customer either verbally or through the use of suitable blueprints. The response of the customers is checked and only if it is found encouraging, the development of the product prototype is taken up. For instance, while the rest of the world had largely gone in for a synthetic detergent in the powder form, it was decided by the Hindustan Lever Limited to test a detergent bar as a concept, because in India most people do not use washing machines and are accustomed to using a bar to rub on the fabric.

The major advantage of concept testing is that the management could form early judgements on the likelihood of the market success of the new ideas.

The other objectives of concept testing are:

i. To determine the size of the potential market.

ii. To evaluate the relative merits of several new product proposals.

iii. To guide the management to adopt suitable marketing policies in advance.

Concept testing has a few drawbacks. They are:

i. It entails some risk of disclosing the company's plans to competitors.

ii. There is a time-lag for obtaining and assessing the results.

iii. Respondents may overstate their interest and encourage unsound development.

Product Testing

Once the concept test of the product is successful, the next step is to put the real product into a few selected markets. This test will prove whether the product performs as expected or whether it lives up to the promise of the concept. Such a test enables the management to find out the likes and dislikes of the consumers towards the product.

Product testing helps:

i. to assess product performance.

ii. to minimize the risks attached to the full-scale launching of a new product.

iii. to identify the most productive market segments.

However, this test is not a fool-proof system for predicting the future. It cannot help to forecast the market size, sales volume, repetitive buying, etc. Correct pricing can also not be assessed.

Test Marketing

Even the most favourable results from the two tests mentioned above are not a conclusive evidence for the success of a product. It is therefore logical to examine the total marketing mix using test marketing methods.

The objectives of test marketing are :

i. To evaluate a complete marketing plan including advertising, distribution, sales, pricing, etc.

ii. To determine media mix, sales channel, etc.

Test marketing has the following limitations

i.   It is a costly affair.

ii. It is a time-consuming method. Many firms avoid test marketing, since they want to be the first in the market.

In spite of the limitations most firms do resort to test marketing. For example, Liril soap, introduced by the Hindustan Lever Ltd., was originally tested in two towns. (Hyderabad and Lucknow). These towns were selected because of their different characteristics which make them representative of a large spectrum of towns in India.

The results of the test enabled the company to make several improvements which were successfully incorporated before the product was nationally extended.

To make test marketing more fruitful, a post-launching survey should be conducted. This survey will reveal whether the earlier satisfaction continues to be derived, whether the advertising is appealing, etc. On the basis of the findings, changes will have to be incorporated before the product is finally launched in the market.

COMMERCIALIZATION

In this stage, the product is submitted to the market and thus commences its life cycle. It is necessary to check whether advertising and personal selling have been done effectively and whether proper outlets have been arranged for distribution. Unforeseen events can impair commercialization seriously.

The following activities are undertaken during this stage:

i.   Completing final plans for production and advertising.

ii. Initiating coordinated production and selling programmes.

iii. Checking results at regular intervals.

It should be remembered that new products should be launched in the market only stage by stage.

MARKETING PLAN

While determining the marketing strategy, factors such as market penetration, market share, profit margins, budgets, financial analysis, capital investment, government actions, demographic changes, emerging technology and cultural trends should be addressed.

There are two major components to a marketing strategy:

1. How to address the competitive marketplace
2. How to implement and support to day-to-day operations.

In today's competitive market place a strategy that will outsell the competition is critical. Several factors must be considered in the process of creating a marketing strategy. The most critical ones are discussed below:

1. The creation of the strategy begins with deciding the overall objective of the enterprise. In general this falls into one of four categories:

    i. If the market is very attractive and the enterprise is one of the strongest in the industry it will invest its best resources in support of its offering.

    ii. If the market is very attractive but the enterprise is one of the weaker ones in the industry it will concentrate on strengthening the enterprise, using the offering as a stepping stone towards this objective.

    iii. If the market is not especially attractive, but the enterprise is one of the strongest in the industry, then an effective marketing and sales effort for the offering will be good for generating near-term profits.

iv. If the market is not especially attractive and the enterprise is also one of the weaker ones in the industry, it will promote this offering only if it supports a more profitable part of the business (for instance, if this segment completes a product-line range) or if it absorbs some of the overhead costs of a more profitable segment. Otherwise, it will determine the most cost-effective way to divest itself of this offering.

2. Having selected the direction most beneficial for the overall interests of the enterprise, the next step is to choose a strategy for the offering that will be most effective in the market. The various strategies are discussed below:

   i. *A cost leadership strategy* It is based on the concept that one can produce and market a good quality product or service at a lower cost than the competitors. These low costs should translate in to profit margins that are higher than the industry average. Some of the conditions that supports a cost leadership strategy include an on-going availability of operating capital, good process engineering skills, close management of labour, products designed for ease of manufacturing and low-cost distribution.

   ii. *A differentiation strategy* It involves creating a product or service that is perceived as being unique throughout the industry. The emphasis can be on brand image, proprietary technology, special features, superior service, a strong distributor network or other aspects that might be specific to the industry. This uniqueness should also translate in to profit margins that are higher than the industry average. In addition, some of the conditions that exist to support a differentiation strategy include strong marketing abilities, effective product engineering, creative personnel, the ability to perform basic research and a good reputation.

iii. *A focus strategy*   It is the most sophisticated of the generic strategies, in that it is a more intense form of either the cost leadership or differentiation strategy. It is designed to address a focused segment of the marketplace, product form or cost management process and is usually employed when it is not appropriate to attempt an "across the board" application of cost leadership or differentiation strategy. It is based on the concept of serving a particular target in such an exceptional manner that others cannot compete. Usually this means addressing a substantially smaller market segment than others in the industry. Due to minimal competition, profit margins can be very high.

REVIEW QUESTIONS

I. Short-answer questions:

1. What is a product?
2. What are the features of a product?
3. What is product mix?
4. What is product policy?
5. What are the elements of product policy?
6. What is product item?
7. What is product line?
8. What is product modification?
9. What is trading down?
10. What is trading up?
11. What are the ways to prevent product failures?

12. What is testing?
13. What are the stages in product life cycle?
14. What is concept testing?
15. What is PLC?
16. What are the factors influencing product mix?
17. What is marketing plan?
18. What is branding?
19. What is a brand?
20. What is trademark?
21. What are the functions of branding?
22. What is a patent?
23. What is copyright?
24. What is packaging?
25. What is AIDA formula?
26. What is a label?
27. What is labelling?
28. What are the functions of labelling?
29. What is product diversification?
30. What are the factors motivating diversification?

II. Essay-type questions:

1. Explain the types of products.
2. Explain the elements of product policy.
3. Write short notes on product standardization.
4. Explain about product planning and development.
5. What is PLC? Explain the stages in product life cycle.
6. What are the steps to be taken to introduce a product?
7. What are the types of testing and explain each of their.
8. What are the strategies followed for preparing marketing plan?

9. Explain the product planning strategies for existing products.

10. What are the types of brand?

11. Explain the advantages of branding.

12. What are the kinds of brand name?

13. Explain the functions of packaging.

14. What are the types of packaging?

15. Discuss the different kinds of materials used for packaging?

16. Explain the significance of packaging.

17. What are the kinds of labels?

18. Explain the merits and demerits of labelling.

19. Explain in detail about the product diversification.

20. What are various forms of product diversification?

11

PRICING

Marketing objectives are realized through proper pricing policies. It is through effective pricing techniques the external forces are brought under control. Inflation, recession, government regulation and increasing consumerism are other factors that have forced marketing managers to become more price conscious.

The price of the product should be related to the achievement of marketing and corporate goals. Price not only affects the profit margin but also affects the quantity sold.

IMPORTANCE OF PRICE

Price can spell success or disaster to a firm. Furthermore, prices are important economic regulators.

In perfect markets, price is determined by supply and demand. Buyers are fully informed about the supply available and are free to come into the market or go out of the market at will. Actually it is doubtful whether such state exists.

Theoretically it is possible to explain the relationship between marginal revenue and marginal cost and their relationship to price and quantities. But for practical application, data are not available for all these and a businessman has to depend on some other practical methods. Pricing is a point where theory and practice do not reconcile.

The concept of the elasticity of demand describes the relationship between changes in prices and the accompanying changes in demand. But the theory fails to give any indication in exact terms.

FACTORS AFFECTING PRICING DECISIONS

In short, businessmen when setting the price of goods consider various factors like consumer demand, competition, political consequences, legal aspects and even ethical aspects of pricing. In addition, they must consider their own costs, the cost of channels they use to reach the market and the various activities they have to perform in connection with the sale (such as advertisement and sales promotion, freight, handling costs, discount, etc.).

For convenience, the factors that influence price decisions may be divided into two:

1. Internal factors
2. External factors

Internal Factors

Internal factors are generally within the control of the organization. They are sometimes referred to as built-in factors that affect the price. These factors include costs and objectives.

i. *Costs*   The most decisive factor is the cost of production. The main defect in this approach is that it disregards the external factors, particularly demand and the value placed on goods by the ultimate consumer. Furthermore, finding the cost of production is not so simple today on account of various lines of production and distributing the overhead (indirect) costs among the various products is also difficult.

ii. *Objectives*   Many companies have established marketing goals or objectives and pricing contributes its share in achieving such goals. These goals may together be termed as pricing policies. Such pricing policies may be classified into:

- Target rate of return (rate of return on investment or on net sales).
- Stability in prices.
- Maintenance or increase of market share.
- Meeting or preventing competition.
- Maximizing profits.

External Factors

External factors are generally beyond the perfect control of an organization. They include demand, competition, influence of distribution channel, political consequences, legal aspects, etc.

i. *Demand* In consumer-oriented marketing, the consumers influence the price. If the customers does not consider the value of the product worth the price, they will refuse to buy. In pricing not only the total demand be determined but also the rate at which this demand must be met has to be included. It is here that marketing research is used as an effective aid, in providing answers to these questions.

ii. *Competition* No manufacturer is free to fix his price without considering competition unless, he has the monopoly. It is necessary to consider the availability of substitutes.

Sometimes a higher price may in itself differentiate the product. This is known as "prestige" pricing. But this is possible only when the product is backed by perfect quality.

Sometimes, management may decide to price below cost, mostly in the initial stages. This is referred to as "markdown" prices.

iii. *Distribution channels* It is necessary to compensate middlemen working in the channel of distribution. The compensation is included in the ultimate price the consumer pays.

Legal constraints, government interference such as control of prices, and levying of taxes are other considerations which also affect the pricing of products.

PRICING OBJECTIVES AND POLICIES

Any good pricing policy must be aimed at offering a reasonable price to the consumer, ensuring a fair return on investment to the manufacturer and providing a reasonable price stability.

In addition, good pricing policy meets competition and complies with legal requirements.

Pricing Objectives

The pricing objectives are discussed below:

i. *Return on investment (ROI)*   From the point of view of investors, the principal pricing goal is to achieve the expected profit. The profit must compensate the investment made.

ii. *Market share*   Increase in market share is the best method of evaluation as far as efficiency of pricing is concerned. Market share and ROI are closely related. For example, a larger market share might increase profitability because of greater economies of scale and market power.

iii. *Meeting competition*   Price cutting may have to be adopted without incurring huge losses. The pricing method adopted in this regard is referred to as extinction pricing. It is used as a way of eliminating competition. It involves pricing the product below variable cost. This will eliminate marginal competitors and then prices will be raised to normal levels.

Correct pricing involves finding the best possible exchange value for the products. Modern manufacturers must understand what constitutes value to the customer. They must also know what competition offers, what substitutes are available, etc.

Consumer situation   Utility to the buyer, return to the buyer, comparable and substitute products, prestige position of the product and brand, presence of buying habits, motives, etc. has to be considered while fixing the price.

Other factors include the following:

- Stages in the product life cycle—Usually high price in the introduction stage, stable price in growth stage, and price decline in maturity stage
- Distribution strategy.
- Promotion strategy.

Basic Pricing Policies

The following are the basic policies recognized for pricing:

i. *Cost-oriented pricing policy*   It is also referred to as "cost-plus pricing". This pricing method assures that no product is sold at a loss, since the price covers the full-cost incurred.

Cost-plus policies are often used by retail traders and manufacturing industries where the production is non-standardized. Thus the retail price of a particular item might be the manufacturer's cost plus his gross margin plus the wholesaler's gross margin plus the retailer's gross margin. This method is known as sum of margins method.

Another common method used under cost-oriented pricing is known as "target pricing". This is invariably adopted by manufacturers who fix a target return on its total cost. Manufacturers these days use break-even analysis for deciding cost-plus pricing. However, this method ignores the demand factor. The break-even analysis helps a firm to determine at what level of output the revenues will equal the costs assuming a certain selling price.

ii. *Demand-oriented pricing policy*   As the name suggests, under this method of pricing, the demand is the deciding factor. Price is fixed by simply adjusting it to the market conditions. A higher price is charged when or where the demand is intense, and a low-price is charged when the demand is low.

iii. *Competition-oriented policy*   Most companies set prices after a careful consideration of the competitive price structure. Deliberate policies may be formulated to sell above, below or at same price with competing products. One important feature of this method is that there cannot be any rigid relation between the price of a product and the firms own cost or demand.

KINDS OF PRICING

Firms may choose various kinds of pricing for their products by adopting the basic principles explained above. These are discussed below:

1. *Odd pricing*   The term "odd prices" is used in two ways. It may be a price ending in an odd number or a price little less than a round number. Such a pricing is adopted generally by sellers of speciality or convenience goods. For example, a shoe manufacturer may fix the price of his product at say Rs. 49.92.

2. *Psychological pricing*   The price under this method is fixed as a round number. The price-setters feel that such a price has an apparent psychological significance from the buyer's point of view. The experiments conducted proved that the change of price over a certain range has little effect until some critical point is reached.

3. *Customary pricing*   Such prices are fixed by custom, or in other words, it is the pricing where a product traditionally sells for a certain price, for example, sweet manufacturers price their products in such a way that a particular variety of sweets is sold at approximately the same price. Soft drinks are also priced in the same manner.

4. *Pricing at the prevailing prices*   This kind of pricing is undertaken to meet the competition. Hence, such a pricing is also termed as "pricing at the market".

In simple words, a price above those of the competitors would sharply bring down sales, while a lower price would not significantly increase them.

Obviously such a policy is aimed at avoiding price competition and price wars.

5. *Prestige pricing* Many customers judge the quality of a product by its price. Generally prestige pricing is applied to luxury goods, where the seller is successful in creating a prestige for his product.

6. *Price lining* Under this policy, the pricing decisions are made only initially and such prices remain constant over long periods of time. Any change in the market conditions are met by adjustments in the quality of merchandise.

7. *Geographic pricing* This policy is sometimes used where a manufacturer serves a number of distinct regional markets. The manufacturer can adopt different prices in each area without creating any ill-will among customers. For example, petrol is priced in this way, depending on the distance from the storage area to the retail outlet.

The different methods relating to the absorption of distribution cost in the price are:

i. *Free on board (FOB) pricing* It is of two types: FOB origin and FOB destination. In the first case, the buyers will have to incur the cost of transit and in the latter, the price quoted is inclusive of transit charges.

ii. *Zone pricing* This denotes some amount of equality of prices for the same product. For instance, if India is divided into south zone, north zone, etc, a product will be sold in the south zone at the same price irrespective of the difference in distance between two places in that zone.

iii. *Basic point pricing* This system charges the buyer the transportation cost from the basic points to the buyer's location.

8. *Dual pricing* When a manufacturer sells the same product at two or more different prices, it is dual pricing. The dual pricing is adopted in railways. For the same distance of travel, in the very same vehicle, the services are sold to passengers at different prices under different classes. This is also referred to as "discriminatory pricing."

9. *Administered pricing*   This applies to the practice of pricing the products for the market on the basis of the policy decisions of the sellers. The administered prices remain unchanged for sometime.

10. *Monopoly pricing*   Since competition is absent, the seller has a free hand in fixing the price.

11. *Skimming pricing*   This is also termed as "skim-the cream pricing". It involves setting a very high-price for a new product initially and then reducing the price gradually as competitors enter the market.

The initial high-price serves to skim the cream off the market, that is relatively insensitive to price. In the case of pricing of textbooks, this method is followed by setting a high price for the first edition and lesser price for subsequent editions.

12. *Penetration pricing*   This method is the opposite of skimming method. In this method of pricing, low price is adopted in the initial period or till such time that the product is finally accepted by customers. Low-starting price sacrifices short-run profits for long-run profits and therefore, discourages potential competitors.

This method is desirable under the following conditions:

i.   When sales volume of the product is very sensitive to price.

ii.   When the product faces a threat from competitors.

13. *Expected pricing*   In this method, the price that will be accepted by the customers is found out. Naturally a fixed price cannot be decided beforehand and hence price range is offered. The response of consumers to the price is analysed and later a price is fixed.

14. *Sealed bid pricing*   This method is followed in the case of specific job works. Government contracts are usually awarded through a system known as tenders. The expenditure anticipated is worked out in detail and the competitors offer a price (known as contract price). The minimum price quoted is accepted and the work is awarded to the party.

15. *Negotiated pricing* This method is invariably adopted by industrial suppliers. Manufacturers who require goods of highly specialized and individually designed nature often negotiate and only then fix the price. For example, in the case of automobiles, various components required for the manufacture are not actually produced by the companies marketing the automobiles. They find out the suppliers and entrust them with the work of manufacturing and supplying various components. Under such circumstances, the prices are negotiated and fixed.

16. *Markup pricing* This method is adopted by wholesalers and retailers in establishing a sale price. When the goods are received, the retailer adds a certain percentage to the manufacturer's price to arrive at the retail price. For example, an item that costs Rs. 20 is sold for Rs. 25, the markup is Rs.5 or 25%. The initial markup is also referred to as "markon".

PRICE DETERMINATION

The following steps may be followed to determine the price:

1. Market segmentation
2. Determining or estimating the demand for the product
3. Anticipating and analysing the competitive reaction
4. Establishing the expected share of the market
5. Select pricing strategy to reach market target
6. Considering company's marketing policies
7. Setting the price

Market Segmentation

The very first procedure for price determination is market segmentation. Marketers will first decide the type of products to be produced or sold and also decide the types of consumers or market segments they want to tackle.

Determining the Demand for the Product

The second stage in pricing a product is to estimate the total demand for it. There are two practical steps in demand estimation. They are:

    i. To determine whether there is a price which the market expects

    ii. To estimate the sales volume at different prices.

Determining the expected price   Expected price for a product is the price what the customers think the product is worth. Determination of expected price can be assessed in three ways. They are:

    i.   The producer may submit the product to an experienced retailer or wholesaler for appraisal

    ii.   Comparison of the prices of the comparable rival products

    iii. Survey the potential consumers. They may be shown the product and asked what they would pay for it. This can be done in a few limited test areas.

Estimating the sales at different prices   Another method of estimating the demand for the product is to estimate the sales at different price levels. For this estimate, demand elasticity of the product should be considered. If the demand for the product is elastic the price must be fixed low.

Anticipating and analysing the Competitive Reaction

Present and potential competition is an important influence on price determination. Competition may arise from

    o similar products

- close substitutes
- unrelated products seeking the same consumer's disposable income

When the marketing field is easy to enter, then the number of competitors is greater, and there is a room for more revenue. To anticipate the reactions of the competitors, it is necessary to collect information about their product, cost structure, market share etc.

Establishing the Expected Share of Market

The next step in price determination is to determine what share of the market the company expects. Low-priced products can capture larger share of the market and a high-priced product may capture a small share of the market. Larger share of the market can also be captured by advertisements and non-priced competition. Share of the market is also influenced by factors like present production capacity, cost of plant expansion and ease of competitive entry. If the management feels that there will be easy competitive entry, the initial price can be fixed high.

Selecting Pricing Strategy to Reach Market Target

A good and proper pricing policy may be employed to achieve the predetermined share of the market. There are two methods:

  i. Skimming pricing
  ii. Penetration pricing.

Considering Company's Marketing Policies

Another major stage in pricing procedure is to consider the company's marketing policies with respect to the product itself, the distribution system and promotional programme.

i. *Product itself* The price of product is influenced by the nature of product's durability, perishability or non-perishability. Perishable products have to be disposed of within a limited time, for example, fruits, milk, vegetables etc. The prices of durable products, for example, car, radio, cloth, scooter, etc. need not be reduced. But when the fashion changes, the marketer may compel the stockist to sell out the stocks before they become obsolescent.

ii. *Channels of distribution* Channels of distribution select the types of middlemen, and the gross marginal requirements of these middlemen will influence the manufacturer's price. Wholesalers as well as retailers may purchase from a producer, who often sets a different factory price for each of them.

iii. *Promotional methods* Larger the promotional methods used, larger will be the expenses and this will reflect in the manufacturer's price, as the set price has to cover the expenses.

Setting the Price

It is the process of price determination for the products by the producer. There is no specific method for setting the price. Procedures used for setting a specific price vary under different competitive conditions. Complexity of the pricing policy has led to the development of numerous approaches to price setting. The following are the basic policies generally recognized for pricing:

    i. Cost-oriented or cost-based pricing policy
    ii. Demand-oriented or demand-based pricing policy
    iii. Cost–demand-oriented pricing policy
    iv. Competition-oriented or competition-based pricing policy

PRICING OF NEW PRODUCTS

Pricing a new product is an art. New products when introduced, appeal to many as novel items. But this distinctiveness created by novelty is only temporary. The price factors which may be ignored would become important when the product becomes an ordinary one because of its constant use. Furthermore, competitors may also appear in the market. Therefore, the new products are hard to be priced, especially with a right price. For setting a price on a new product, three guidelines are to be adopted:

1. Making the products acceptable.
2. Maintaining the market
3. Retaining the profits.

There are two options available for pricing a new product: skimming and penetration pricing.

1. *Skimming* If a product is entirely new in all respects, skimming method could be used. A strategy of high prices coupled with large promotional expenditure in the initial stages has proved successful in a number of cases. Skimming pricing is recommended because it helps to take the cream off the market through high prices. However, it should be noted that high-initial prices may also prevent quick sales.

2. *Penetration pricing* The second option is to adopt penetration pricing. A comparative analysis of these two pricing system reveals that both these methods are not free from errors. The difference between these two methods could be illustrated through the following example.

When an electric clock was first introduced, consumers were reluctant to buy it because it was relatively low-priced when compared to a quality spring-wound clock. Consumers apparently felt that a quality clock could not be sold so cheap. The clocks were withdrawn from the market and reintroduced subsequently at a higher price; after that they sold more clocks successfully.

In the case of new products, pricing has to be made with a little knowledge of demand, cost and competition.

The new product has to bear the cost of primitive or creating a market. The initial cost therefore will be definitely greater. The cost incurred in constructing a proper channel of distribution may also be accounted for, in pricing.

SPECIAL PROBLEMS IN PRICING

After fixing a price, a manufacturer is often beset with the problems of price reduction. It is needless to say that this should be considered even before fixing a price. Hence, there must always be "built-in flexibility" in the price structure to accommodate such requests. These are known as discounts, allowances and guarantees.

Discounts

Discounts are deductions allowed by the seller from the base price of a product. These discounts could be of the following types.

Trade discount   They are usually found in bulk purchasing. These discounts are given as a consideration for performing marketing functions.

Quantity discount   Quantity discounts may attract large buyers or induce small buyers to large quantities.

Cash discounts   It is a deduction granted by the seller to the buyer for paying his dues in time. Some suppliers offer a special discount for payment within a stipulated period from the date of invoice.

Seasonal discount   This refers to discounts offered during a particular season. It is usually done during the off-peak periods, for example, fans sold during winter season.

Allowances

These are also the same as discounts but are usually given as a consideration for performing specific services. Allowances are of two types. They are:

Promotional allowances   Samples given at concessional rates or supplying advertising materials are included in promotional allowances.

Brokerage allowances This is another form of trade discount.

Besides the above deductions, the manufacturers have to sometimes bear the cost of marketing also. For example, when FOB price is quoted, the manufacturer will have to bear a part of freight. This definitely reduces his profit margin.

LEGAL RESTRICTIONS ON PRICING

There are various legislations that exist in India mainly to protect consumers' interests. The major laws affecting pricing decisions are:

1. *Monopolies and Restrictive Trade Practices Act 1969* This Act prohibits the increasing of prices unreasonably.
2. *Essential Commodities Act 1955* This imposes price controls on most of the products.
3. *Drugs (Price Control) Act* This controls the prices of drugs.

RESALE PRICE MAINTENANCE

Resale price maintenance is a policy adopted by a manufacturer whereby he fixes a price for his products to be sold to customers by retailers.

In case the dealer does not maintain the specified prices, the supplier will even withhold further supplies. Normally, strict enforcement of the suggested price is possible only when a manufacturer uses a selective or exclusive distribution system. Another condition is that the particular brand should have achieved a high-degree of customer acceptance and popularity.

It should be noted that when manufacturers use their own retail (Chain shop) outlets, it is a case of direct price maintenance. This is different from resale price maintenance.

In India, resale price maintenance is controlled through MRTP Act. Resale price is fixed in any one of the following ways:

1. A minimum price below which the products cannot be sold (Restrictive Trade Practice).
2. A maximum price above which the product cannot be sold.
3. A stipulated price from which no changes are allowed (Restrictive Trade Practices).

The second one allows flexibility for the retailer to fix the final price. Hence, it is not treated as a restrictive trade practice. But any agreement relating to resale price maintenance must be registered with the Registrar of restrictive trade agreements.

The original idea behind the Resale Price Maintenance (RPM) was to avoid unhealthy competition among retailers. But later this has become as a source of additional profit for the manufacturers through exclusive or selective distribution system.

APPLICABILITY OF MRTP ACT IN TRADE PRACTICES

1. The terms and conditions relating to minimum price maintenance in any contract are void.
2. The manufacturers and wholesalers are prevented from fixing a minimum price to the retailer.
3. No retailer should be compelled to sell the goods at the retail price fixed by the suppliers.
4. Even the patented articles are included under the provisions of this Act.

These regulations are basically meant to protect the interests of the customers.

REVIEW QUESTIONS

I. Short-answer questions:

1. What is pricing?
2. What are the factors that affect pricing decisions?
3. What are the internal factors that affect pricing?
4. What are the external factors that affect pricing?
5. What is cost-oriented pricing policy?
6. What is demand-oriented pricing policy?
7. What is competition-oriented pricing policy?
8. What is odd pricing?
9. What is skimming pricing?
10. What is penetration pricing?
11. What is trade discount?
12. What is cash discount?
13. What is resale price maintenance?

II. Essay-type questions:

1. What is the importance of pricing?
2. Explain the pricing objectives.
3. What are the factors affecting pricing and explain them.
4. Explain the types of pricing.
5. Explain the procedure for price determination.
6. What are the special problems faced in pricing?
7. Explain the various pricing policies.
8. Explain the pricing for new products.

12

CHANNELS OF DISTRIBUTION

Goods produced by the manufacturers must come to the knowledge of the ultimate consumers and the products must reach their hands for use. Channels of distribution are paths through which the products move from the points of production to the points of consumption. Distribution channels (Figure 12.1) are also called trade channels.

- A manufacturer may use different channels at different times for different products in different markets.
- A channel represents three types of flows: (i) Goods flow downwards from producer to consumer, (ii) Cash flow upwards from consumers to producer representing payment for goods, (iii) Information flows both downstream and upstream, representing two-way traffic of communication. Upward flow of information indicates feedback of information, that is, consumer feelings, desires and reactions.

The most common routes used for bringing the products to the market from producer to consumer are as follows:

1. *Manufacturer–consumer (direct sale)* There are three alternatives in direct sale to consumers. They are: (i) Sale through advertising and direct methods (mail order selling),

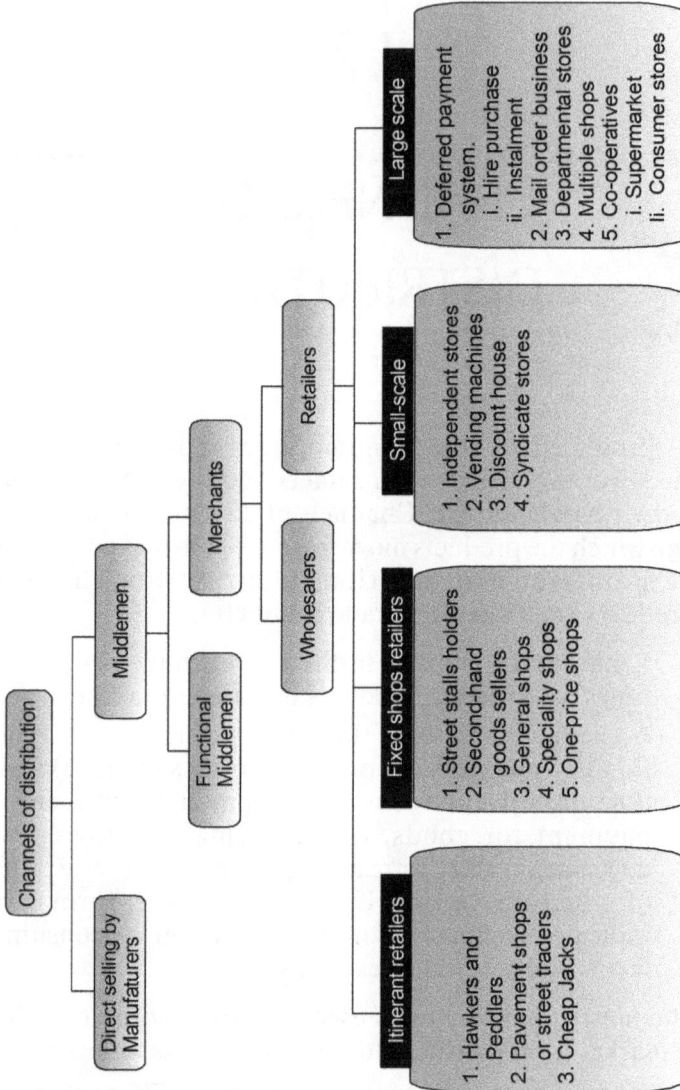

Figure 12.1 Channels of distribution

(ii) Sale through travelling sales force (house to house canvassing), (iii) Sale through retail shops of manufacture, for example, shops selling mill cloth. Bata Shoe Company outlets, etc.

2. *Manufacturer–retailer–consumer* This channel option is preferable when buyers are large retailers, for example, a departmental store, discount house, chain stores, super market, big mail-order houses or cooperative stores. The wholesaler can be by-passed in this trade route. It is also suitable when products are perishable and where speed in distribution is essential. However, the manufacturer has to perform the functions of a wholesaler such as storage, insurance, financing of inventories and transport.

3. *Manufacturer–wholesaler–retailer– consumer* This is a normal, regular and popular channel option used in groceries, drugs goods, etc. It is suitable for producers under the given conditions: (i) They have a narrow product line (ii) They have limited finance (iii) Wholesalers are specialized and can provide strong promotional support, (iv) Products are durable and not subject to physical deterioration or fashion changes.

4. *Manufacturer–agent–wholesaler–retailer–consumer* In this channel the producer uses the service of agent middlemen such as a sales agent, for the initial dispersion of goods. The agent in turn may distribute to wholesalers, who in turn sell to retailers. There may be a sole selling agent for many manufacturers, for example, Voltas. Many textile mills have sales agents for distribution. Agent middlemen generally operate at the wholesale level. They are common in agricultural marketing.

Agent middlemen sell directly to wholesaler or to a large retailer on commission basis. They are used by manufacturers for marketing of this goods.

5. *Manufacturer–wholesalers–consumer* Wholesaler may by-pass retailer when there are large and institutional buyers, e.g. industrial buyers, for example, government, consumer cooperatives, hospitals, educational institutions, business houses, etc.

DETERMINANTS OF CHANNEL CHOICE

The problem of selecting the most suitable channel of distribution for a product is complex. The following are the factors that determine the channel decision:

Product

   i. If a commodity is perishable or fragile, a producer prefers a few and controlled levels of distribution. For perishable goods, speedy movement needs shorter channel or route of distribution.

  ii. For durable and standardized goods, longer and diversified channels may be necessary.

 iii. For custom-made products, direct distribution to consumer or industrial user may be desirable.

  iv. System's approach needs a package deal and a shorter channel serves the purpose.

   v. For technical products requiring specialized selling and serving talents, shortest channel is desirable.

  vi. Products of high-unit value are sold directly by travelling sales force and not through middlemen.

 vii. For food products, both wholesaler and retailer are required. Here, size and average frequency of customer orders influence channel decision.

Market

   i. If the market size is large, it may require many channels, whereas in a small market direct selling may be profitable.

  ii. For highly concentrated markets, direct selling is enough but for widely scattered and diffused markets, many channels are necessary.

Middlemen

i. Middlemen who can provide the required marketing services will be given first preference.

ii. The selected middlemen must offer maximum cooperation, particularly in promotional services. They must accept marketing policies and the programmers or the manufacturers actively help them in their implementations.

iii. The channel generating the largest sales volume at lower unit cost will be given top priority. This will minimize distribution cost.

Company

i. The company's size determines the size of the market, the size of its accounts and its ability to get middlemen's cooperation. A big firm may have a shorter channel.

ii. The companies with substantial financial resources need not rely too much on the middlemen and can afford to reduce the levels of distribution. A weaker company has to depend on middlemen to secure financial and warehousing relief.

iii. New companies rely heavily on middlemen due to lack of experience and ability of management.

iv. A company desiring to exercise greater control over the channel will prefer a shorter channel as it will facilitate better coordination, communication and control.

Marketing Environment

Marketing environment can also influence the channel decision. During recession or depression, shorter and cheaper channels are always preferable. In times of prosperity, there is a wider choice of channel alternatives. Technological innovations also have an impact on distribution. The distribution of perishable goods, even in distant markets, has become a reality due to cold storage facilities in transport and warehousing.

Competitors

Marketers closely watch the channels used by rivals. Many a time, they prefer similar channels to bring about distribution of their products also. For instance, they may by-pass retail store channel and adopt door-to-door sales.

CHANNEL DECISION—MARKET COVERAGE

Once the company decides the general channels to be used, it has to decide on the number of middlemen in each channel, that is, intensity of distribution. There are three alternatives.

1. *Extensive distribution* Extensive or broadcast distribution is essential when the price is low, buying is frequent and brand switching is a common phenomenon. Extensive distribution secures rising sales volume, gives wider consumer recognition and creates considerable impulse purchasing. But it creates problems of motivation and control and it may generate unprofitable sales due to high-marketing costs. There are maximum number of retail outlets for mass distribution of convenience goods as consumers demand.

2. *Selective or limited distribution* When special services are needed, for example, TV sets, or a prestige image is to be created, we have selective distribution. The number of outlets at each level of distribution is limited to a given geographical area. When we have limited number of middlemen, they can spend more on sales promotion and offer maximum cooperation. By this mode the consumer brand preference can be established and selective distribution will be more profitable.

3. *Exclusive distribution* When final buyers do not need any product service, mass or extensive distribution is adopted. But if the amount of product service expected by final buyers is considerable, exclusive distribution is preferred.

There are four major aspects of exclusive distribution:

i. *Exclusive dealing contracts* They prohibit the dealer from selling products of rivals.

ii. *Closed sales territory* It limits each dealer to sell only to buyers located within the assigned area.

iii. *Tying contracts* They compel the dealers purchase to full product line of a manufacturer.

iv. *Franchise selling* Franchise means a privilege or an exceptional right granted to a person. Franchise selling is a term to describe in effect the selective or exclusive distribution policies.

MIDDLEMEN IN DISTRIBUTION

In all commodity markets, whether primary or central, there are a host of middlemen acting as essential functionaries:

1. *Brokers* Brokers are agents who do not have direct physical possession of goods they deal with but they represent either the buyer or the seller in negotiating purchase or sales for his principals. They may be organized as individuals, partnership or even companies.

2. *Commission agents* In each primary and central market, individuals, firms or even companies are organized to buy or sell commodities, acting as buying or selling agents of producers, dealers or manufacturers who convert the commodities into consumer goods. They may buy or sell on their own account and at their own risk of loss. In that case, they are called commission merchants or factors.

3. *Dealers* In all primary and central commodity markets, we invariably have merchant dealers. They are great risk-bearers in the physical or spot markets. They are the backbone of our markets. These dealers act as principals, buying and selling commodities on their own account and at their own risk merely for a chance of profit.

WHOLESALERS

Wholesale trade is concerned solely with the distribution of large quantities of goods received directly from the manufacturers or dealers and sold in small quantities to retailers. The wholesalers are the first important link in the field of distribution of goods. They connect both the manufacturer and the retailer. That is why they are called as middlemen.

Characteristics of Wholesalers

i.   The wholesaler is mainly concerned with the assembling and dispensing function in marketing. The products assembled from different manufacturers are kept in stock by the wholesalers and are distributed to retailers who may be widely scattered.

ii. They deal in large quantities of goods.

iii. They deal in a particular commodity.

iv. They also arrange, grade, transport, finance, etc.

Wholesalers' Services to the Manufacturer

i.   The wholesaler places large orders for goods to the manufacturer. Thus large-scale production is possible and the manufacturer is benefitted.

ii. The producers also get financial help in the form of advances from the wholesaler.

iii. As the wholesaler stocks the goods for future sales, the manufacturer need not stock the goods. This gives great relief to the manufacturer.

iv. They study the trends in the market—changes in tastes, fashion and demand—and keeps the manufacturer informed of the preferences of consumers as revealed to him by the retailers.

Wholesalers' Services to the Retailer

i.   A retailer with small capital deals with a large variety of goods. Since the goods are kept by the wholesaler in large quantities, a retailer can get all his requirements conveniently from the wholesaler.

ii. The retailer usually makes only small orders. Most of the large producers do not entertain small orders. But the wholesalers take this trouble of selling the goods in small quantities to retailers.

iii. The wholesalers also provide financial facilities to retailers. They are given credit facilities by wholesalers. This enables the retailers to manage their business with a small amount of capital.

iv. The retailers easily come to know of any new product from the wholesalers.

v. The wholesalers are specialized businessmen. Therefore they take advantage of the favourable price movements. A part of these benefits is passed on to the retailer by the wholesaler.

vi. The retailer can personally inspect the goods at the wholesaler's warehouse. Thus selection of goods is made possible to retailers.

vii. As the wholesaler alone keeps large stock of goods, the risk of falling prices and spoilage involved in goods will not affect the retailer.

viii. The wholesalers are experts and specialists. They create a market for the goods by undertaking sales promotion measures. They provide the retailers a ready market.

Types of Wholesalers

i. *Limited function wholesalers* They are basically merchant wholesalers but do not provide full services, and often provide only the minimum services among the limited functions.

ii. *General merchandise wholesalers* Such a wholesaler never restricts the varieties of products to be handled. He may even handle unrelated product lines. For example, a wholesaler may stock food items together with hardware.

iii. *General line wholesalers* Contrary to the above two types, these wholesalers deal in closely related items, for example, various types of cosmetics.

iv. *Specialty wholesalers*   As the name suggests, this kind of wholesalers have introduced specialization in the wholesale trade. Such a wholesaler deals only in one merchandise.

v. *Functional wholesalers*   This kind of wholesalers actually fall under the category of agent middlemen. They do not take title to merchandise nor do they see the goods they sell. Their main function is to facilitate selling, although there are some buying functional middlemen.

RETAILERS

A retailer or a retail store is a business enterprise which sells primarily to ultimate consumers. The retailer is also known as a dealer. The word "distributor" is sometimes used wrongly to denote a retailer. The distributor is a wholesaling middleman and not a retailer.

Functions of Retailing

i. The physical movement and storage of goods.

ii. The transfer of title of goods.

iii. The provision of information concerning the nature and use of goods.

iv. The standardization, grading and final processing of goods.

v. The provision of ready availability of goods.

vi. The assumption of risk covering the precise nature and extent of demand.

vii. The financing of inventory and the precise nature and extent of credit to consumer.

Services Rendered by the Retailers

i. The retailer keeps stock of different varieties of goods.

ii. Most of the demand creation methods are undertaken by retailers for the manufacturers and the wholesalers.

iii. The retailer is an expert in the distribution of consumer goods. Out of their experience, training and intimate knowledge of the goods, the retailers are in a position to help the customers in the proper selection of goods.

iv. The retailers often extend credit facilities to the consumers. They also provide many personal services to the customer such as home delivery, after-sales services, etc.

Kinds of Retailers

1. *Itinerant retailers* These traders are mainly dealers in agricultural products. They have no fixed business places and move from place to place as the season changes. Their prices are considered to be the cheapest.

i. *Hawkers and peddlers* Sale by hawkers and peddlers is of very old origin. They generally handle cheap goods with low-unit value like pens, handkerchiefs, towels, toys, etc. There cannot be any guarantee about the quality of goods, as they are of inferior quality.

ii. *Market traders* Market traders are those retailers who open their shops at different places on fixed days known as market days. The days may be fixed on weekly or monthly basis.

iii. *Cheap jacks* The retailer known as a cheap jack has an independent shop in a business locality. The shop may not be permanent and he may shift his shop to some other locality the moment he finds that another locality is more profitable.

iv. *Street traders* The very name indicates that this type of retailers carry on their business in the busy streets or on footpaths of busy town roads. They are very often found near railway stations, bus stands and similar places where there is a huge floating population.

2. *Fixed shop retailers*

i. *The street stall holders* The street stall holders have their stalls in streets where they may find heavy traffic. They exercise much care in selecting the location and such a location may be permanent. They sell articles like pens, banians, etc.

ii. *Second-hand goods dealers* These dealers deal in second-hand goods like books, furniture, clothes, etc. They purchase and sell such goods particularly to those customers who cannot buy new goods at higher prices. These dealers mainly get their supplies from public auctions.

iii. *Specialty shops* In such shops, goods of a particular variety are sold. The dealers specialize and deal only in one line of goods. Shops exclusively meant for books, leather products, drugs and readymade garments are examples.

iv. *General shops* These shops sell the entire line of products required for everyday use. These shops, depending upon the amount of capital invested, may assume a large size also.

v. *One-price shops* These shops sell all variety of goods at one fixed price. Some times they may be seasonal shops also.

3. *Small-sized retail shops*

i. *Independent stores* These are small, non-integrated retail establishments having a lesser degree of specialization in their management.

ii. *Vending machines (Automatic selling)* Vending machines have become big business in recent years. A variety of products are sold through coin-operated machines.

iii. *Discount houses* The discount houses grew as a result of the practice of manufacturers giving large discounts to retailers on certain types of goods. Jewellery, household appliances and articles and similar merchandise often carry high percentage of margin for the retailers.

iv. *Syndicate stores* A syndicate store is in fact an extension of the chain and mail order house but relatively on a small-scale. One of the chief characteristics of syndicate stores is that while they offer a wide variety of merchandise to customers, they seldom sell known brands.

Large-scale retailing institutions

i. *Departmental stores*   A departmental store is defined as a large-scale retailing business which handles a wide variety of shopping and speciality goods and is organized into separate departments for the purpose of promotion, service and control.

ii. *Chain stores or multiple shops*   The name multiple shop indicates that under this organization similar shops are established in multiples by the same management. A chain store system consists of four or more stores which carry the same kind of merchandise and are centrally owned and managed and usually are supplied from one or more central warehouses.

iii. *Mail order retailing*   This is also referred to as non-store impersonal retailing or shopping by post or selling by post. A mail order house is that type of retail institution which solicits patronage by means of catalogues sent through mail and containing detailed descriptions or merchandise for sale.

iv. *Deferred payment system*

Hire-purchase   Hire-purchase trading is a method by which the seller agrees to sell the article on the condition that the buyer shall pay the purchase price by a fixed number of instalments. Under this method the article is not legally sold out but is only hired by the buyer.

Instalment selling   It is basically the same as hire-purchase but with certain legal differences. Unlike the hire purchaser, the instalment buyer gets legal as well as physical possession rights over the product. This system is also referred to as deferred payment system.

v. *Cooperative retailing*   Severe criticism against wholesalers and various kinds of middlemen gave way to this type of retailing, where the principles of cooperation were extended to the retailing store. There are two types: retailers' cooperatives and consumers' cooperatives:

vi. *Supermarkets* Supermarkets are also self-service stores. They concentrate on food and grocery items. They are located in places where consumers are given facilities like parking. No credit facilities are offered.

REVIEW QUESTIONS

I. Short-answer questions:

1. What is a channel of distribution?
2. Who is a middleman?
3. Who is a broker?
4. Who is a retailer?
5. Who is a wholesaler?
6. What are characteristics of a wholesaler?
7. What are the functions of retailing?
8. Who is an itinerant retailer?
9. Who are called as fixed shop retailers?
10. Who are cheap jacks?

II. Essay-type questions:

1. Explain the types of channels of distribution.
2. What are the determinants channel of distribution?
3. Explain the factors to be considered for channel decision
4. Explain the role of middlemen in distribution.
5. Explain the services of wholesalers.
6. What are the types of wholesalers?
7. Explain the services rendered by retailers.
8. What are the types of retailers?

13

PROMOTION

INTRODUCTION

Promotion is the process of marketing communication involving information, persuasion and influence. It communicates marketing information to consumers, users and resellers. It is not enough to communicate ideas. Promotion persuades and convinces the buyer. The promotional activities always attempt to affect knowledge, attitudes, preferences and behaviour of recipients, that is, buyers. The element of persuasion to accept ideas, products, services etc., is the heart of promotion.

Promotion includes a variety of activities designed to increase sales volume and make selling of goods easy. It comprises sales promotional activities such as personal selling and advertising.

The American Marketing Association defines promotion as "The personal or impersonal process of assisting or persuading a prospective customer to buy a product or service or to act favourably upon an idea that has commercial significance to the seller."

Objectives of Promotion

i. To provide information to prospective customers about the availability, features and uses of products.

ii. To stimulate demand by creating awareness and interest among customers.

iii. To differentiate a product from competitive products by creating brand loyalty.

iv. To stabilize sales by highlighting the utility of the product.

KINDS OF PROMOTION

The different kinds of promotion are:

1. *Informative promotion* This type of promotion concentrates on informing the target market segment about the products and services offered by a firm. The emphasis is on information, not on sales.

2. *Persuasive promotion* The purpose of this method is to persuade people to buy. This method is more appropriate in the growth stage of products.

3. *Reminder promotion* When a product reaches maturity and saturation stages, this method is applicable. The central aim of this method is to emphasize brand names and product features in competitive terms.

4. *Buyer behaviour modification* Repeated advertisements and constant personal selling methods are designed to modify buyer behaviour. Brand preference and loyalty are the objectives in this type of work.

Generally promotion makes use of the "AIDA" approach where customer's Attention is obtained, Interest is created, Desire is stimulated and Action is prompted.

PROMOTIONAL MIX

It is a well-known fact that in the absence of promotional activities, even good products fail. Promotional mix is a strategic combination of these elements such as advertising, personal selling and sales promotion. Promotional mix or promotional blend should be balanced between the different elements.

Advertising represents mass impersonal selling methods. Personal selling refers to face-to-face selling through salesmen. Sales promotion refers to other promotional measures like point-of-purchase displays, exhibitions, dealers' contests, premiums to customers, etc.

1. *Advertising* It is defined as any paid form of non-personal presentation and promotion of ideas, goods and services by an identified sponsor. It is impersonal salesmanship for mass selling.

2. *Publicity* It is non-personal stimulation of demand of a product, service or a business unit. It is done by placing commercially significant news in a publication or obtaining favourable presentation of it on radio, television, or stage that is not paid for by the sponsor.

3. *Personal selling* It is the best means of oral and face-to-face communication and presentation with the prospect, for the purpose of making sales. They may be one prospect or a number of prospects in the personal conversation.

4. *Sales promotion* It covers those marketing activities other than advertising, publicity and personal selling that stimulate consumer purchasing and dealer effectiveness. Such activities are displays, shows, exhibitions, demonstrations and many other non-routine selling efforts at the point of purchase. Sales promotion tends to complement the other means of promotions.

Pull Blend

This is a promotional approach in which mass impersonal sales efforts are given the greatest emphasis. Advertising dominates this type of promotional mix. Personal selling is of no importance in this approach. Sales promotion measures may be used to support advertising. This method is expected to "pull down" the product from the manufacturer.

Push Blend

In this type of promotional mix, the emphasis is on personal selling. The product is pushed through the channel of distribution.

Advertising is minimal and sales promotion measures may be used wherever necessary.

When promotional mix is considered, the following are the aspects closely examined:

i. The most effective method of informing the consumer of the products such as the nature of the product, its durability, the targeted customer, etc. decide this aspect.

ii. The methods of marketing to be used such as sales objectives, required turnover, competitor's products and methods influence promotional mix.

iii. The direction of promotional effort, that is, whether it should be customer-oriented or dealer-oriented, personal or impersonal, should be decided.

After the above three aspects are carefully considered, the marketing budget is allocated to advertising, personal selling and promotional measures, as per the strategy developed.

Promotional mix is not static. It differs from product to product. It may differ even for the same product at different stages in its life cycle.

SALES PROMOTION

The main objective of sales promotion is to attract the prospective buyer towards the product and induce him to buy the product at the point of purchase. At retailer's level, its purpose is to sell a particular manufacturer's product. At consumer's level, it aims at persuading the consumer to buy more quantity, more frequently. Thus it is also called as Catch-all method.

Merits

i. Sales promotion policies supplement the efforts of personal and impersonal measures like personal selling and advertising.

ii. Good sales promotion makes salesmen more effective.

iii. The advertising creates favourable impression about a product in consumers which is enhanced by sales promotion.

iv. Sales promotion results in accelerated sales in the short-run which paves the way for mass production and lower production cost.

Demerits

i. Some consumers believe that the prices are fixed at a higher level and then concessions are given. This may be true of some middlemen, but most of the manufacturers genuinely implement promotional measures.

ii. When concessions are withdrawn, consumers may draw away. But the purpose of these measures is to draw customer's attention. If the product has intrinsic merit, customers will stick to it.

Sales Promotion Measures

Sales promotion is done at different levels and these are discussed below.

Sales promotion measures at dealer level Dealers are responsible for success or failure of most of the consumer durables when competition is intense. For example, colour TV, refrigerators, motorbikes and scooters, fans, etc. are some of the consumer durables which are facing severe competition from different brands because of a large number of manufacturers. Many producers find it imperative to offer inducements to the dealers to show special interest and enthusiasm in pushing their products, attracting customers and creating demand.

Dealer's contests The contests may be in the form of window display, interesting store display, sales volume, etc. There may be prizes at regional level or national level or both. The winners of the contests may get cash rewards or fully paid foreign holiday trips, etc.

Consumer durables of fairly high value like scooter, cars, etc. are the most suitable for such contests. The method should not be a one-time affair. It must be repeated periodically to sustain dealer's interest.

Advertising materials   Producers can supply carefully planned and prepared advertising materials to the dealer. These materials may include banners, shelf-signs, boards, store-signs, etc.

Special displays and shows   The products of a company may be displayed prominently with attractive lighting arrangements, neon signs, etc. Usually such methods are used for important occasions like Diwali, Christmas, trade fairs, exhibitions, etc.

Store demonstration   Some products like washing machines, cookers, etc. may need demonstration of their working to the prospective customer. The dealer's premises may be used for such demonstrations.

Dealer premiums   Dealer may be offered gifts for lifting stocks above a particular limit in a given period. The gift may be in cash or kind, or cash discount on the purchase value.

Dealer's meetings   A manufacturer may conduct dealer's meetings in an attractive city or summer resort. Usually star hotels may be used. Such meetings may be used to launch new products on a large-scale.

Advertising allowances   Dealers may be entrusted with local publicity work and an allowance may be given for such purpose. This method is more suitable for exclusive distribution agents who do not deal with any other products.

Sales promotion schemes at consumer's level   There are numerous promotional schemes at consumer's level, followed by different firms. The basic objective of all of them is to attract consumers to a particular retailer or to a particular producer's products. Most of the schemes aim at persuading the consumer to make repeat purchases.

The following are the most popular schemes adopted at consumer's level:

Coupons   Coupons of a stated value are given to the consumer either by the retailer or the coupons are kept inside the package. The coupons entitle the consumer to receive a price reduction of the stated value at the time of purchase. The retailer collects the coupons, extends the price reduction and gets reimbursement from the manufacturer.

This method does not directly affect the selling price of the brand. The original price can be continued after the time limit stipulated for the coupons offer.

Bargain offers   This is also called as "price-off" offer. This method is used to stimulate sales in off-season or slack season. For example, price-off is usually announced for fans in winter season.

When the offer is withdrawn, sales may be adversely affected. Consumers may switch to products on which bargain offer is made. Such offers may affect development of brand loyalty.

Samples   A small quantity of a product may be handed over to a prospective customer. This may be done by mail or through retailers or personally handed over by salesmen. This is a fast method of demand creation. The customer is given a chance to verify product quality. This method is the most effective to promote products of genuinely high quality. It leads to brand loyalty when customer is satisfied. The results of the method are immediate.

However, this is a costly method. Samples may have to be prepared separately and pains must be taken to distribute them. If actual product does not confine to the quality of the sample, it may create wrong impression and sales may be adversely affected.

Money refund offers   Some producers offer to refund full purchase price within a specified time if the product is returned by unsatisfied customer. For example, Amway Company offers to return purchase price of their products if the customer is not satisfied. Usually such offers are printed on the package.

Trading stamps   The customers of a producer's goods may be offered a premium in the form of trading stamps. The value of stamps given at the time of selling is linked to the value of the goods purchased. Separate trading stamp redemption centres may be specified where the stamps are exchanged for goods from a premium catalogue. This method aims at sustaining customer's interest for some time through the process of accumulation of sufficient stamps.

Buy-back allowance (or) "trade-in" method   When an article is sold, assurance is given that it can be exchanged for a new one or improved model after a specified period. Credit is given for the used article at an agreed rate. This method creates automatic demand for future models or new articles. It also induces customers to go faster for fresh purchases. This method is quite common for cars in the US. In India also some dealers follow this method for consumer durables.

Premiums   There are different types of premiums offered that give customers "two-in-one" benefit. Here the customer gets an additional article apart from what is purchased.

Factory in-pack premiums   The manufacturer packs the premium article inside the box of the product or it may be attached to the box, for example, spoons, cups, measuring glasses, etc. Plastic, animal-shaped toys were packed along with Binaca toothpaste tubes, small toys were packed along with kinderjoy chocolate. These premiums are inexpensive and mostly given along with tinned food items.

Self-liquidation premiums   Here purchasing an article may entitle a buyer to get some other article at low-concessional price, for example, buying a one kg washing powder may entitle the buyer to get a plastic bucket at half the normal price. In this method the customer feels the advantage. The articles bought in bulk may not involve additional cost to manufacturer because the price collected may be their cost.

Sales promotion schemes at salesman level
In the channel of distribution, the role of salesman is very important.

The idea of sales force promotion is to make the salesman's efforts more effective.

The tools for sales force promotion are:

Bonus to sales force   The manufacturer sets a target of sales for a year. If the sales force sell products above the targeted sales, bonus is offered to them. This is an encouragement incentive given to the salespeople to sell more products to cross the quota or targeted sales.

Sales force contests   To increase the interest and efforts of sales force over a specified time, these contests are announced. The prizes are given to the salesman who sources the maximum sales in sales contests. Thus it stimulates the salesman to sell more products.

Salesmen meetings and conferences   The idea behind these is to educate, inspire and reward salesmen. Encouragement is given to them during the discussion. New selling techniques are described to them and discussed in the conference.

PERSONAL SELLING

Personal selling is a method where consumers are personally persuaded to buy goods and services offered by a manufacturer. Personal selling forms a part of promotional mix of a firm. In fact advertising and sales promotion measures are impersonal in nature whereas personal selling establishes direct contacts with prospective buyers. Thus, "personal selling" is the "actual contact point" between a producer and consumer.

Functions of Personal Selling

i.   It enables the customers to decide what to buy.
ii. It creates demand to precede supply.
iii. It creates new wants among the consumers.
iv. It collects and transfers market information to the manufacturers.

Benefits of Personal Selling

i.   It helps to establish a binding relationship between consumer and the supplier. This relationship leads to long-term benefits to the selling firm.

ii. It arouses wants of the consumers. Consumers may be in need of so many goods. But, making a consumer "want" things is the greatest benefit of the personal selling or salesmanship.

iii. The consumers obtain useful information and technical assistance from personal selling.

iv. It not only sells products, but also "ideas", which have long-term implications.

v.   It fulfills the basic objective of marketing, that is, satisfying consumer's needs.

vi. It contributes to the growth of business by increasing sales and profits.

SALESMANSHIP

Salesmanship is concerned with persuasion. It is directed at prospective consumers.

Personal selling and salesmanship are often synonymously used. Salesmanship is broader in scope and is like an art or discipline. Personal selling is a way of practising salesmanship.

Salesmanship embraces all those activities which are to be undertaken to convert a trying "subject" into a "prospect" and then the "prospect" into a "customer". Salesmanship aims at a satisfied customer.

The modern salesman has a large number of scientific aids. He can use scientific inventions like computers and other modern communication devices.

In reality, salesmanship is neither completely based on scientific knowledge nor is it a pure art. It combines scientific principles and the creative abilities of an artist. It can be concluded as a scientific art.

Kinds of Salesmanship

Salesmanship can be classified into two types—creative and competitive.

Salesmanship based on creative thinking, imagination and resourcefulness is called as creative salesmanship. Creating markets for branding new products, creating new market for old products, etc., come under this category. It needs persuasive and informative efforts to tackle customers.

Creative selling involves selling intangibles, like insurances, high-technology products like computers, and fashion products.

When substitutes from competitors appear in the market, competitive salesmanship is needed to persuade consumers to buy particular brands.

Competitive salesmanship needs thorough knowledge of competing products, minor differences in quality, price terms, etc. Creative salesmanship is essential at the stages of introduction and maturity of a product. Competitive salesmanship is needed during growth and maturity stages of a product.

Qualities of a Good Salesman

The qualities required for a good salesman can be broadly divided into three groups—physical qualities, personality traits and information in his possession.

1.*Physical qualities*

Appearance   Salesmen must be well-dressed, neat and impressive in their appearance.

Health and fitness   They must be healthy and capable of hard work. Irregular working hours and travelling necessitate a good constitution.

Countenance   A smiling face and assured physical movements can create confidence in others.

2. Personality traits

Ability to communicate   They must be able to express their ideas clearly and persuasively. This needs good language and delivery and a pleasing voice.

Gregarious nature   They must not be shy or hesitating. They should be able to meet people and mix with them easily. They must be mentally alert, self-confident, imaginative and resourceful. These mental qualities help them in dealing with different kinds of people.

Character   They must be honest, reliable, stable and ambitious. These qualities can instill confidence in their superiors and pave way for their progress.

3. Information possession

Product data   They must know everything about their products. The uses, the varieties, prices, contents, etc. of the product, the brand variations and packaging must be known.

Company data   They should have knowledge of their company's history, achievements, sales outlets, distribution policies, different products and services, etc.

Customer data   They should know the different types of customers, their needs, likes and dislikes, motives, brand preferences, etc. They should also know possible complaints or arguments customers may have against their products or company. They should also develop reasonable and diplomatic answers for them.

Knowledge of sales technique   Salesmen should have expert knowledge of different methods, skills and techniques in selling.

Knowledge of self   Every salesman should be aware of his personal strengths and weaknesses.

Different Kinds of Salesmen

Salesmen can be divided into different kinds on the basis of the nature of their work. They are:

i. *Creative salesmen*   Salesmen who create demand for new products and new market for existing products can be called as creative salesmen. They are also called as "pioneer salesmen".

ii. *Service salesmen*   Those who sell services alone are called as service salesmen. They sell intangibles.

Services are generally credited with some special characteristics:

- They are not standardized. Service to one customer can rarely be the same as to another.
- Intangibility is the nature of all services. There is no product to show and demonstrate.
- Services usually cannot be postponed. If they are not booked in time, somebody else may take away the opportunity.

iii. *Detail salesmen*   They are also called as "indirect salesmen". They do not approach actual users of the product, but those who decide the usage. Salesmen of drug companies approach doctors and inform them about their products and give samples. Patients buy medicines on doctor's prescriptions.

iv. *Manufacturer's salesmen*   They are appointed by manufacturers to sell their goods. They may sell to ultimate consumers or middlemen like wholesalers and distributors.

v. *Wholesaler's salesmen*   They are appointed and controlled by wholesalers. They book orders from retailers. Mostly, they deliver goods and collect payments.

vi. *Retailer's salesmen*   There are two kinds of retailer's salesmen: Indoor salesmen and outdoor salesman: indoor salesman work inside a retail store. They execute customer's orders and sometimes collect cash. They may have to show the product and convince the customer, for example, cloth stores. Indoor salesmen need courtesy, good manners and prompt attention to customer's needs.

Outdoor salesmen travel and book orders. They themselves may deliver goods and collect money.

vii. *Special salesmen*   Salesmen who sell or book orders for high-priced durable goods like cars, refrigerators, bikes, etc, are called as special salesmen. Consumers may have fixed ideas about their brand preferences. Thus these salesmen need special tactics to convince unfavourably disposed prospects.

viii. *Staple salesmen*   Salesmen who sell necessary articles like stationary, food, soaps, etc. are called as staple salesmen. Most of these goods are convenience goods and brand preferences play a lesser role. Persuasion is hardly required but supplying goods in the right place and at the right time is required.

ix. *Exporter's salesmen*   Generally they are not employees of exporters. They are middlemen who act on commission basis. "Indent houses" are traditionally exporter's agents-cum-salesmen. The indent houses are professionals with regular contacts with buyers.

Salesmen have to identify prospective customers, approach and persuade them, and finally conclude a sale by booking an order and delivering goods.

Selling Process

The selling process consists of the following steps

i. *Prospecting*   Identifying prospective customers and arranging to meet them is called prospecting. Prospecting may be based on lists prepared in advance. The lists may be those of old customers or lists of likely persons noted through different types of contacts. Prospecting may be helped by the firm's plans or marketing research. A salesman himself may find prospects or may be directed by his superiors.

ii. *Approach*   Advance planning on the part of salesman regarding the contact is essential. The points to be stressed, the mode of conducting the interview, the possible points of resistance, ways of overcoming them, etc. must be pre-planned. It saves time and proves effective.

iii. *Overcoming objections*   Objections must be predicted in advance and forceful ways of dealing with them must be kept in reserve.

iv. *Closing the sale*   Closing a sale happens when products or services are delivered to the customers, their satisfaction is met and payment is received.

Sales Management

The sales management or marketing management is the term applied to the process of distributing the goods from the producer to the ultimate user or consumer. It covers selling, advertising and sales promotion, transporting, handling, financing and risk-taking.

The sales management represents one of the most important functional areas of management and all the principles of general management such as planning, organization direction, motivation and control are applied to sales management for securing better business performance, viz., reasonable profits through service.

Functions of sales management   Sales management is usually responsible for the following:

i.   Selection of the right type of salesmen
ii. Training of the sales personnel
iii. Controlling the salesmen
iv. Remunerating salesmen, and
v.   Evaluating and motivating the sales force.

The term salesman applies to all persons who are engaged at all levels of selling, ranging from a retail sales clerk to a broker or an agent who negotiates for contracts. From the modern point of view, the salesman is a vital member of the customer-oriented marketing. In this process, the salesman has to plan, forecast, establish procedures and programmes, final schedules, and finally coordinate all these activities to achieve customer satisfaction.

The following points are to be considered to make the selling efforts fruitful:

- The salesman must understand what basic needs are satisfied by the product or service.
- The salesman must be able to identify the prospects who have those needs.
- The prospects must recognize their own needs.
- The prospects must be convinced that the product will yield full or partial satisfaction of their needs.
- The salesman must give the prospect an opportunity to accept the product.

The above facts point out that a salesman's job is totally different from any other job in the following four ways:

- Salesmen are persuasive rather than analytical.
- Salesmen are intuitive rather than analytical
- Salesmen have higher average energy levels.
- Salesmen are more strongly motivated by the desire for prestige, power and material gain than by service ideals.

These aspects underline the need for sales management to perform the following activities.

1. Selection and Recruitment

A salesman is an important cornerstone upon which a sales organization is built. Sales management is confronted with the task of planning a sound selection programme for salesmen. Training, motivation etc, are other prime factors in developing an effective sales organization.

A firm intending to recruit salesmen can use various sources. On the basis of exact requirements of the firm, a particular source may be selected. The followings are the steps involved in the selection of salesmen:

i. *Deciding the quantity and quality of sales force* This depends up on the amount of work involved. The variables influencing the size of sales force are:

- Number of existing customers
- Number of potential customers
- Ideal frequency of calls
- Average length of each call
- Selling time.

These variables make the decision of the size of sales force a numerical one. Once these variables are properly estimated, the number of salesmen needed can be easily computed.

A different way of estimating the size of sales force is called as "marginal analysis". Here new salesmen are continuously appointed till the profits on the last man's sales are equal to the cost of manufacturing that salesman.

Job description   The different responsibilities and work to be performed by persons to be recruited should be clearly noted. A job description is the list of functions, duties, responsibilities, skills, etc. needed for the position which is vacant.

Employee specification   Based on job description, the qualifications, experience and qualities required in the person to be appointed should also be listed. Some qualifications may be essential and some other may be desirable.

ii. *Sources for recruitment of salesmen*   The different sources for recruitment of salesmen are:

Internal staff   Employees in other departments of a firm can be considered for salesmen's job. This method ensures loyalty and cooperation. The training requirement may be lesser and remuneration may not be too high. The only drawback is to reorient the employees to the sales job from their earlier work.

Competing firms   Highly efficient and suitable persons from competing firms may be "lured away", offering better prospects. This method may not be ethical, but highly useful and effective. Competitor's methods and ideas can be known. Very little training may be involved.

Employment agencies There are a large number of government-sponsored and private employment agencies. Generally untrained and inexperienced people can be recruited from this source.

Educational institutions Campus interviews may be conducted in educational institutions to recruit bright prospective scholars. IITs, IIMs, engineering and polytechnic institutes, etc. are the appropriate places for recruiting technical salesmen.

Press advertisements Advertisements may be given in popular newspapers with job description. From the applicants, suitable candidates can be selected.

Casual applicants Employment seekers may voluntarily submit applications or register their names with the firm. From such applicants selection may be made.

Recommended candidates Existing salesmen or executives or other employees may recommend suitable candidates. This method has the advantage of "reference" for the candidates selected.

iii. *Selecting proper plan*

Application form Applications in detail may be received from prospective candidates. Comparison with job description and employee specifications can help to "weed out" unsuitable applicants.

Psychological tests and group discussions The short-listed applicants may be asked to take psychological tests, mostly written, and also participate in group discussions. Based on these some candidates may be selected or they may be called for personal interview.

Personal interview Candidates may be interviewed to test their communication ability, personality and physical appearance. At this stage tentative selection may be made.

References Candidates may be asked to provide references. If references are satisfactory, final list of selected candidates may be prepared.

iv. *Finalizing the employment*   The selected candidates may be asked to report for duty on a given date. They may be allowed to report directly or after a medical test, to make sure that they don't suffer from hidden defects or diseases.

2. Training of Sales Personnel

Salesmanship being an art, most people even today believe that a perfect salesman is born and cannot be made. This is absolutely incorrect, Similarly, there is some truth in the statement that a good salesman can sell anything. But the increasingly sophisticated needs of modern industry and trade require better salesman. It is definite that the better trained salesman could make more positive effect on customers. Further the qualities required of salesmen are so varied that they cannot achieve them without proper training.

The characteristics of a successful salesperson are given below:

i.	Physical	Health, appearance, voice, dress and neatness
ii.	Mental	Alertness, initiative, self-confidence, resourcefulness, imagination, memory and foresight
iii.	Social	Courtesy, refinement, good manners, open-mindedness, patience, ability to move with the public
iv.	Human	Maturity, tactfulness, straightforwardness, loyalty
v.	Honesty	Reliability, stability, ambition

Advantages or Benefits of Training Salesmen

- Training increases overall sales volume of the firm because of higher efficiency of the salesmen.
- Higher sales can result in lower cost of production which helps to reduce selling prices or increase the profits.

- Trained salesmen can spend lesser time in tackling the customers. This can help in increasing the volume of sales of each salesman. Number of salesmen required can be reduced.

- Trained salesmen can look after the customers' needs in a better way. So there will be fewer complaints from the customers.

- Trained salesmen can keep the customers fully informed about the products, their uses, etc. So the customers can make better use of the products.

- Trained salesmen can give more effective product demonstrations wherever necessary.

Different Methods of Training Salesmen

It is necessary to train the salesmen to make them effective in their work. Untrained salesmen may spoil a firm's image. Sales may be adversely affected.

Before adopting a particular method of training, training scheme should be prepared to make the chosen method effective. The scheme should prepare the salesman for his job. He should be told what is expected of him and how it must be done. The salesman must be allowed to do his work under supervision initially and his performance must be analysed.

Training schemes are effective when prepared on "ACMEE" principles. These include **aim** of training, **content** of training, **method** of training, **execution** of training, and **evaluation** of training. Salesmen should be oriented towards customers' problems and needs.

Once training scheme is prepared there are five different methods which can be used to train salesman:

i. *Individual methods* Here the salesman is expected to see, observe and learn the work by himself.

Initial break-in-training The salesman may be asked to work in different departments and study the work.

Special assignments   Easier independent works may be given to a salesman and his performance may be observed. Any deficiencies may be pointed out to him.

Field coaching   Newly recruited salesman may be asked to work along with experienced salesman in the actual field. This method is effective and fast, giving confidence to the new recruit.

Sales manuals   Highly experienced persons may prepare sales manuals which contain guidelines, problems expected and possible ways of tackling. A new salesman has to study the manual, learn the salient points and then take up his actual work.

ii. *Group methods*   Large-sized modern firms with groups of salesmen employ group methods of training. The following are the variations in practice:

Lecture method   For batches of new recruits, lectures may be arranged by experienced persons in the field. Clarifications, discussion, etc. can provide valuable information to the trainees.

Audio–visual methods   This method is mostly used as a supplement to lecture method. Slides, charts, posters, film strips, etc. are the visual aids used.

Conference methods   This method is more useful for sharing experiences and discussing common problems. Sales conferences of salesman in an area may be highly useful. But as a method of training new recruits, this may not be effective.

Discussion and case method   Salesman can be divided into several groups and may be asked to discuss particular problems. The opinions expressed may be analysed together. This makes every salesman knowledgeable about different aspects of every problem.

Panel method   A panel is a permanent group for particular problems. The same members discuss similar problems at different times. For new recruits, this may not be useful.

Role playing   Here each salesman may be asked to play a role, just like in drama rehearsals. Then the roles played are analysed for any defects. This is an interesting method of teaching dramatically.

iii. *On-the-job methods*   Under these methods the new recruits actually work on the jobs which they are going to perform in the future. These methods are practice-oriented.

Farm system   The new salesman may be sent to different branches or even wholesaler's places to get first-hand experience of the work. In this way, a salesman is "farmed" to perform higher level jobs. This method is suitable for big organizations with large number of branches.

Job rotation   A new salesman may be trained in all departments and every section of each department. This gives a thorough knowledge of inter-relationship of different sections, departments and their work.

iv. *Off-the-job method*   Associations of salesmen publish professional journals and bulletins to help members to perform their duties efficiently. Trainees may be asked to study and learn from these publications. This is in addition to the above three methods.

v. *Follow-up training*   This is a method of further training. Salesmen trained once and working in jobs may be given further training. This is also called as refresher training. Large firms have regular training centres to provide follow-up training. This helps existing salesmen to learn latest methods and ideas.

3. Methods of Controlling Salesmen

Once the training is over and the salesman is put to field work, a sales manager is confronted with the problem of extracting work from him. If salesmen are within reach, it is easy to control them. But if the salesmen are working at different places direct contact is out of the question.

Employees in an office can be controlled through physical supervision of their movements and work. But salesmen are mostly in the field and only remote control methods can be used to control them.

i. *Performance standards* Standards may be set in quantitative terms or monetary terms for the work of salesmen. Usually this takes the form of sales quotas. Each salesman may be required to accomplish a minimum volume of sales during a given period. The quotas may also be set for number of orders, new customers, etc. The different kinds of quotas are:

Volume quota This may be in value or units.

Profit quota In business where commission is earned from clients, the gross profit to be earned by the salesmen may be fixed as quota.

Expense quota Each salesman may be allotted a ceiling for expenditure on daily or weekly basis while attaining performance targets.

Activity quota This refers to contacts to be made or work to be turned out on daily or weekly basis. When quota is fixed they must be:

- Scientifically determined
- Attainable by average salesmen
- Incentive linked
- Flexible for changing circumstances

Merits

- A salesman knows exactly what is expected from him.
- The management can assess performance.
- Production and sales can be properly coordinated.

Demerits

Highly efficient salesmen may limit their work to the quotas.

ii. *Sales territories* A sales territory may be a geographical area or a group of potential customers or any other determinable market segment. Different salesman may be allotted different sales territories. Producer should ensure the following:

- The entire market is fully covered.
- Each salesman's work is comparable to others.
- Opportunities are equalized for all the salesmen.
- Overall selling cost is in control.
- Overlapping of territories is scrupulously avoided.
- The coverage of territory should be possible for an average salesman.

This method is more organized, systematic and efficient. However, the territories may have various prospects. Favouritism in allotment can be easily suspected.

iii. *Control through reports and records* The salesmen are instructed to give regular reports about their work and maintain records of stocks, sales and other work done.

Merits

- This method helps sales executives ascertain what is going on in the field regularly.
- Reports from different areas can indicate trends in total sales and area-wise sales. This helps in production planning. It also helps in revising marketing strategies.
- The reports and records can draw attention to problem areas for special attention and effort.

The reports and records, if systematically collected and followed up, can provide a clear idea about the overall progress of selling programme. Maximum precautions should be taken against false report.

iv. *Personal control* When sales force is small in number and concentrated in a limited area, personal supervision method may be effective.

v. *Sales bulletin* This is like a circular, showing the progress of work in different areas, new products and policies introduced, etc. These bulletins are periodical with up-to-date data.

This method cannot be the sole method of controlling salesmen. It can be an accessory to other methods.

4. Remunerating Salesmen

The sales force plays a significant role in the success or failure of many companies. The sales operation is regarded as an integral segment of the "total corporate effort". Therefore, the compensation of sales personnel is important.

The compensation plan must be such that it must be capable of achieving the following objectives:

   i.   The compensating plan should motivate the sales force towards the attainment of established quotas.

   ii. If the compensating plan is devised in such a way that it increases along with sales, every salesman would strive hard to get the maximum.

   iii. Maximum coverage of markets.

   iv. The compensating plan must be capable of controlling sales expense.

   v.   It must be simple and flexible.

   vi. It must motivate salesmen to perform their duties diligently.

   vii. It must be equitable compared to the same type of job.

Remuneration plan Basically the remuneration that is given to salesmen is justified on two factors viz., (1) the amount of sales made and (2) the amount of time spent on the job of selling.

Objectives of remuneration plan

Simplicity and flexibility   The plan must be simple to understand by the salesman. It should be flexible to accommodate any future changes.

Increase in sales   The remuneration should have connection with the sales volume.

Coverage of market   The remuneration plan should provide incentive for enlisting new customers and getting fresh business apart from existing customers and business.

It should be able to keep sales expenditure within reasonable limits.

Methods of compensating salesmen

Regular salary method   Salesman may be paid monthly salary and fixed jobs may be allocated to them.

This method is simple, easy to follow and sales expenditure is in control. However, it does not provide any incentive for efficiency. All salesmen may be treated alike irrespective of their work. It may be suitable for new recruits.

Sales commission method   Salesmen may be paid a fixed commission or progressive commission based on their sales performance. This method provides ample incentive to work harder and earn more. However, the salesmen may be depressed when product demand decreases and sales come down.

Salary and incentive method   Here salesmen are paid a reasonable regular salary. Incentive is offered if sales of each person cross particular levels, determined in advance.

Additional incentives

Bonus   Salesmen may be paid bonus periodically or at the end of every year. The bonus may be related to sales volume, seasonal work, firm's profits, etc. The bonus is linked to specific events and does not form a part of salary or commission.

Fringe benefits Housing, medical facilities, vehicles, provident fund, etc. are the additional benefits that may be provided.

Sales contests Occasional or periodical contests may be conducted to arouse enthusiasm and initiative among salesmen.

5. Motivating Sales Force

Motivation is a psychological process involving complex problems.

The more provision of a good remuneration alone is not sufficient to motivate a salesman. He should be appreciated for his efforts and talent and given respect. He should have an opportunity to improve by training and must be given responsibility and authority.

The following are the methods that sales management may use to motivate salesmen:

i. Providing assistance through personal calls.

ii. Arranging sales meetings and conferences.

iii. Arranging sales contests.

iv. Devising fair performance evaluation schemes, assisting men to develop their own capabilities.

v. Reducing unnecessary administrative procedures

vi. Providing equipment and information to assist in the selling operation, for example, sales manuals, samples, demonstration models etc.

ADVERTISING

Advertising is one of the promotional elements in a firm's promotional mix.

Objectives

i. Primary function is demand creation to enable sales function to be performed smoothly and effectively.

   ii.   Secondary function is maintaining and enhancing the firm's image and goodwill.

  iii.   Psychological function is persuading and convincing people, thus removing mental reservations.

  iv.   Economic function is benefiting consumers and the firm economically.

   v.   Social function is to inform about product availability, to build brand recognition or brand insistence, to increase market share, to modify existing product appeals and buying motives, to reach new areas or new segments of population within existing areas and to develop overseas market.

Features

   i.   Advertising is a paid form of publicity. Publicity can be free or paid for. So advertising is a commercial transaction.

  ii.   Advertising is non-personal. Its appeal is general. It is directed against large groups of people. It may be visual or vocal or written. It is never addressed to particular individuals.

 iii.   It presents and promotes either goods and services or ideas. Goods and services are advertised for immediate benefit. Ideas are promoted for long-term benefit.

Advertising is either by identifiable firms or individuals.

Benefits

To producers

   i. Advertising helps producers to increase their sales, achieve economies of mass production, and reduce cost and prices.

  ii. Advertising helps producers to introduce new products. Prospective consumers can be made aware of the product uses and qualities before it is made available to them.

 iii. Advertising establishes direct, one-way channel between producer and consumer. Producers can convey what all they think necessary, to the prospective buyers.

To wholesalers and retailers

i. Advertising makes goods familiar to the customers. This makes selling easier to the middlemen.

ii. The selling activities of middlemen are supplemented by the impact of advertising.

To salesmen

i. Advertising acts like a "spade work" for a salesman job. His time and efforts are saved due to advance impact created by advertising.

ii. Salesman's legitimacy is accepted by the consumers. Suspicion or disbelief is lesser for advertised products when salesman approaches.

To consumers

i. It informs them where and when different products are available. This helps them to avoid wastage of time in searching.

ii. Advertising educates consumers about different uses of an existing product and new products available for different purposes. This educational value of advertising is considered by many as its greatest benefit.

To society

i. Advertising makes newspapers, magazines available at low prices. Without advertising revenue, newspapers have to be sold at high prices.

ii. Advertising provides employment opportunities for artists, copywriters and several other people connected with it.

Kinds of Advertising

The following are different kinds of advertising depending on the nature and characteristics of advertisements:

i. *Product advertising* Here the emphasis is on using a product than a particular brand of a manufacturer. It creates a primary demand for the product.

ii. *Institutional advertising* Here the advertisements focus on a company to project its image and services. The aim may be to build-up a company's goodwill among shareholders, creditors and also consumers.

iii. *Primary demand advertising* When a novel or a new product is introduced, advertising concentrates on creation of primary demand for such products. In the introductory stage of new products, this type of advertising is common.

iv. *Competitive advertising* Here, the advertisements emphasize merits of a producer's brand over those of competitors. Minor differences in price, quality, etc. are highlighted.

v. *Comparative advertising* Specific comparisons of cut-throat nature may be made with competing products to gain business at each other's cost. For example, the bitter publicity war between "Nirma" and "Surf" highlights this method.

vi. *Shortage advertising* When a product is in short-supply, appeals may be made for its conservation and avoiding wastage, for example, petroleum products in India.

vii. *Cooperative advertising* If producer, wholesaler or dealers carry on combined advertising, the names of dealers and producers are used in combination, highlighting the distribution outlets. This method is widely practised in automobile selling.

viii. *Commercial advertising* This is also called as business advertising and meant for increasing the sales or business.

Professionals like chartered accountants, lawyers, doctors use this method. Also, selling farm inputs like fertilizers, pesticides, farm implements, etc., and selling for industrial products, this type of advertising is adopted. The commercial advertising is confined to selected segments and can be called as selective advertising.

ix. *Non-commercial advertising* Advertising by charities, educational institutions, etc. falls under this category. They are not meant for business purpose but to collect donations or attract students.

Objections against Advertising

Advertising is a service whose benefits are not fully tangible. It helps people to choose among alternatives which itself is a service to the customers.

i. *Extravagance*   Advertising persuades people to buy goods which are beyond their needs. There is no doubt advertising arouses people's interest in products but every man or woman is the sole judge of what he or she needs. Prudence in expenditure is a personal characteristic and nobody can force a person to buy something.

ii. *Shifting*   Advertising only shifts demand from the products of one producer to those of the other. Effectively it achieves nothing. Advertising creates primary demand and also extends demand for products. So the notion that "total demand for a product is static" is wrong.

iii. *Cost of goods*   Advertising is an additional cost which increases cost and selling price of goods. Expenditure on advertising is not productive. Its cost is added to the product, but it does not increase the quality or utility of the products.

iv. *Monopoly*   Advertising makes people stick to particular brands which give a position of monopoly to those producers. In these days of severe competition, this argument does not hold good.

v. *Wastage*   Advertising constantly makes new products and fashions popular. This forces people to waste their existing goods and go for the new products.

vi. *False claims*   Advertising helps manufacturers to deceive the public through false claims, misrepresentations, etc. about the products to attract the consumers to buy them. But such manufacturers and products cannot survive for long. They are exposed quickly.

v. *Press freedom*   Businessmen can yield great influence over communication media. Most of the newspapers and magazines depend on advertising revenue for their survival.

In these days of numerous competing advertisers, the press is in a commanding position and need not bow to any pressures.

viii. *Ethical objections*   Advertising may glorify habit-forming and unhealthy products which may make consumers to buy them, for example, cigarettes, liquors, etc. Legal restrictions have been imposed on such advertisements.

Advertising kindles desire for glamourous goods among weaker sections. This may turn them towards unlawful activities.

Advertisement Copy

The words used to convey an advertising theme or idea is called as copy. The person who prepares the copy is a copywriter.

The copy should convey the product message and make people act upon it. It should describe the product in such a way that it is convincing to the reader.

The nature of a copy should be descriptive, narrative, argumentative and should lead to exposition of product qualities. It should be imaginative but never misleading. The appeal should be personal in nature.

Preparation of a copy needs artistic, psychological and imaginative skills. The copywriter should have thorough knowledge of the product, of the motivational factors and of the company. The AIDA formula of attention, interest, desire and action should be the goal while preparing advertising copy.

i. *Attention value*   The copy must be able to attract immediate attention of those who look at it. This may be achieved through attractive headlines and slogans or artistic borders, pictures and drawings, contests and reply coupons.

ii. *Suggestive value* A good copy should be able to suggest the benefits of buying a particular product. The suggestion must be in catchy phrases or slogans.

iii. *Memorizing value* The advertisement should be easy to remember and memorize. Symbols, brand names, etc., enhance memorizing value of an advertisement.

iv. *Conviction value* An advertisement should be able to convince a reader. False claims, misleading statements, etc. when exposed, will have negative effect.

v. *Sentimental value* An advertisement should not adversely affect people's sentiments. If possible, sentiments should be positively used. A silk saree may be related to marriage, a ring may be connected to engagement, etc.

vi. *Educational value* An advertisement should be able to convey useful information about the product. A toothpaste advertisement may say how gums are affected due to scraps of food and claim that the toothpaste is a remedy for affected gums as well as for bad breath.

vii. *Instinct value* The instinct to protect children maintaining status, self-preservation, etc. are basic characteristics of human beings. An advertisement should appeal to one of the human instincts to have a strong motivation. For example, protecting children and family is the instinct to which an insurance advertisement can appeal.

Advertising Media

Advertising medium is any object or device which carries the advertising message. There are different types of media which are classified into direct and indirect media. The direct media help to contact the prospective customers directly, for example, direct mailing, where personal letters are posted to each prospective customer. Indirect media involves usage of a hired agency for spreading information, for example, newspaper, television, etc.

Selection of media   The medium should cover the largest number of prospective customers and able to gain the attention of them. It should be comparatively inexpensive.

The following factors influence the selection of media:

i. *Character of the medium*   This includes the geographical coverage of the medium, which may be national or regional or local. A magazine like *India Today* has national coverage whereas *Malayala Manorama* has regional coverage.

ii. *Nature of readers*   The medium may have a particular type of readers. For example, *Women's Era* has housewives as its readers whereas *Chandamama* is read by children.

iii. *Frequency of publication*   The medium may be a daily or a weekly or a monthly.

iv. *Atmosphere of the medium*   Some media have persuasive atmosphere and some others may not have such persuasive effect. A radio broadcast of a commercial may or may not, be listened, but a TV commercial in prime time is automatically viewed by people.

v. *Medium coverage*   The number of people covered by the medium is important in selection.

vi. *Cost of the medium*   The cost must have relation to probable benefit and coverage.

vii. *Size and position of the advertisement*   A small advertisement can be inserted in some corner of a magazine at low cost. A front page advertisement in a national newspaper may be expensive.

viii. *Nature of product*   The product to be advertised has a definite say in the medium to be selected. For example, cosmetics may be advertised in women's magazines.

ix. *Type of buyers*   If buyers to be reached belong to upper class, glossy magazines and television may be more suitable. Middle class buyers may be reached through family weekly magazines like *Sudga, Kumudam, Andhraboomi*, etc.

Kinds of Advertising Media

Different media have their own strengths and weaknesses from the advertising point of view. The following brief discussion of different media can bring out their merits and limitations:

i. *Press publicity* The print media includes newspapers and magazines. Newspapers in English have larger circulation than those in local language.

(a) *Newspapers* They are published daily and enjoy wide readership. They are most suitable for advertising new products and new developments in existing products. Their frequency makes them ideal for repeat advertising.

Merits

○ They reach every nook and corner of a market, thus providing wide coverage.

○ Compared to visual media, this is cheaper.

○ Advertising copy can be tested through local newspapers.

○ Good artists can create visual effects in newspaper advertising.

Limitations

○ Papers are printed on cheap newsprint which sets limitation for visual effects.

○ The lifespan of a newspaper is a single day. So repeated advertisements may be needed.

○ A paper may reach large number of readers who have no interest in the products.

(b) *Magazines* Different magazines in different languages with different periodicity of publication are available in India for advertising. Some of them are general, with mixed readership, like *Illustrated Weekly, India Today*, etc. Some others are specialized with segmented readership for example, *Femina, Commerce, Sports Star*, etc. Some magazines are the best way to reach special segments of customers. For example, sports equipment can be brought to the notice of sporting public through *Sports Week* and *Sports Star*.

Merits

- Better quality paper enables magazines to print better quality advertisements.
- The lifespan of a magazine is usually longer, thus giving longer span for each advertisement.
- Wastage of circulation is avoided because magazines are mostly selective in nature.

Limitations

- Cost of advertising is proportionately high.
- There can be delay in publishing advertisements.

ii. **Direct mailing**   This method has full control over the persons to whom appeal is made. So it is also called as controlled advertising.

In this method, a single sheet of pamphlet, printed on one or both sides, or a booklet or catalogue containing a number of sheets which may be illustrated, can be used.

A mailing list should be prepared which contain lists of past customers, lists provided by salesmen, telephone directory, government records, newspapers, members of trade associations, etc.

Merits

- The targeted prospects are selected. So the response rate can be very high.
- Effective personalized message can be sent to influence prospective customers unlike general message possible in other media.

Limitations

- It is a costly method because of printing and postal charges.
- Time and efforts are needed to prepare mailing lists.

Direct mailing is a method successfully employed in book trade by textbook printers and also publishers of *Readers Digest*, *Dalal street*, etc.

iii. *Outdoor advertising*

Outdoor advertising consists of the following:

- Murals which are pasted on walls, for example, cinema posters.
- Boards which are erected at central spots like road junctions, bus stops and railway stations.
- Neon signs or electric displays which can be seen in front of most of the shops and companies at night time.

Merits

- The attention value of boards and posters is very high.
- They have value of repetition because same people may see and read the same advertisements several times.
- Usually the cost is lower and coverage is greater.

Limitations

- The prestige value of advertisement is low.
- It cannot be used as a sole medium, but only as a supplementary medium.

iv. *Audio–visual methods*

This method includes advertising films shown on TV or cinema, documentary films, sponsored advertisements in radio, etc. These methods have direct impact on the listeners or viewers.

Merits

- Wide coverage, when prospective customers are relaxing and in a receptive mood, is the greatest merit of TV and radio advertising.
- Explanations and demonstrations of product usage are possible.

Limitations

- There may be censor on audio–visual advertisements.
- The cooperation of theatres, radio or TV management is essential.

v. *Point of purchase advertisement* This method includes window display, counter display, special displays and shows, showrooms, etc. mostly at the spot of selling.

Merits

- The methods have longer lifespan because of regularity in their presentation.
- It is possible for prospective customers to clarify doubts and get additional information on the spot. The products can be seen and their merits ascertained.

Limitations

- Only those in the vicinity can approach the dealers or sellers. So its coverage is limited.
- These methods cannot be main advertising techniques, but only supplemental efforts to other major methods.

vi. *Specialty advertising* This includes calendars, gift articles with producer's or distributor's names. These are given to present or prospective customers.

Advertising Budget

The amount set apart by a manufacturer to be spent for advertising during a specific future period is called as advertising appropriation or advertising budget. Usually a predetermined amount that could be spent on advertising is arrived at on the basis of nature of products, analysis of consumers and markets.

The following methods are generally used in determining advertising appropriation:

i. *Market share approach* Advertising budgets are prepared in such a way that a given amount spent would retain a given market share or target share. If a satisfactory market share is obtained by spending a specific amount, the same amount may be budgeted for the next period to retain the same share.

It ignores market dynamics and creativity. For new products, this method is not applicable.

ii. *Arbitrary allocation* A flat amount may be decided as advertising budget without any systematic assessment. This method is followed in autocratic establishments where the owner decides everything as per his whims and fancies.

iii. *Percentage of sales method* Here advertising appropriation is a fixed percentage of previous period's sales or expected future sales. This method may be extended to each product, division, area, etc. Its fundamental assumption is that when sales decrease, advertising expenditure should also decrease and vice versa. But actually the reverse may be more useful and practical. Declining sales may need better support from advertising.

iv. *Task and objective method* Initially advertising objectives are established. Then the different methods of advertising are designed to achieve the objectives. Finally, the cost of the selected methods is computed. Thus, advertising appropriation is related to the objectives to be achieved.

v. *Competitive comparison method* Here advertising budget depends on the competitor's method of advertising. What they did in the past and are likely to do in future is accepted as the basis for computing advertising appropriation.

vi. *Funds available method* From the actual sales of previous period, expenses, dividends are set aside and a portion of the balance is spent for advertising, the balance being savings. This method also presumes that more should be spent when more money is available.

vii. *Incremental method* Here advertising budget is a percentage of investment. Out of the total funds invested in a period, a percentage is set aside. This method is more reasonable than sales percentage method. But here also, need-based advertising is ignored.

viii. *Unit-based method* For every unit expected to be sold, a specific amount is budgeted for advertising. It may be based on past sales also. This method protects the budget from selling price changes.

Advertising Agency

Many small and medium-sized firms who cannot afford to maintain an advertising department find it difficult to cope up with modern advertising arena. This has given birth to a specialized profession called as "advertising agency".

Initially advertising agents used to sell space in media to their clients. But recently they have been rendering advice and creative service to clients. The creative talent and past experience of the agents serve the needs of manufacturers efficiently.

The following are some of the services rendered by modern advertising agents:

- They prepare posters and notices for clients.
- They take charge of direct mailing activities on behalf of clients.
- They manage the job of producing adfilms for clients. They book space and execute advertising programmes for clients in television, radio, cinema, outdoor and press media. They take responsibility of preparing advertising copy and testing the copy.
- They conduct audience research and market research for clients.

Selection of advertising agency

The advertising agency is selected on the basis of the following:

    i.   Facilities and talents available.

   ii.   The size and number of staff of the agency

  iii.   Remuneration generally expected by agent.

  iv.   The products in which they have specialized.

   v.   The rapport the agent has with different media.

Advantages of using an advertising agency

- Small firms and individual businessmen can get benefits of expert services at relatively low cost.

- Rapport with media enables the agents to secure media time and space at lower rates.

- Benefits of the services of artists, researchers and other specialists are available to the advertisers.

- Advice on marketing research, new product introduction may also be available from the agents.

- Advertising agents are better suited to measure the effectiveness of advertising and determining the future course of advertising of a particular firm.

Most of the producers determine promotional mix and prepare advertising copy. Advertising media are carefully selected. The advertising programmes are carefully implemented. All this is only one side of the coin. The other side is measuring or assessing the effects and benefits of the programmes. Measuring of effectiveness is essential for the following reasons:

- Huge amounts are spent on advertising. The return on such expenditure should be sufficient and substantial to continue such investment.

- The media selected for advertising should be effective. For future guidance, effectiveness of each medium should be known.

- Whether advertising was able to achieve the usual objectives like, increase in sales of different market segment establishing brand loyalty and stimulating and arousing interest, demand for the company's products, etc.

Methods of Assessing Effectiveness of Advertising

Pre-tests   The following are some of the pre-campaign tests used:

Readability studies   People from different backgrounds are selected as respondents. They are tested to find out the ease and effectiveness that have been achieved while reading the advertisements. On this basis, any necessary changes may be made in the advertising copy.

Eye-movement analysis   The movements of respondent's eyes are shown to them on a screen. This method reveals any strain in reading or following the advertisements.

Tachisro scope tests   These tests record the time taken for an advertisement to register with an onlooker. Perception questions asked afterwards can reveal the respondent's reaction to the time and message.

Post-tests   These tests strive to measure the sales effectiveness of the advertisements after they are placed in the chosen media.

Recall tests   Some targeted customers may be selected and surveys are conducted to determine the amount of information learnt and recalled by them. This method helps to identify the most acceptable medium.

Recognition tests   These tests are conducted on readers or viewers of media to find out how many of them remember the advertisements and how long they are remembered.

Concurrent tests   These tests are conducted on the spot, like live programmes on TV. When readers finish reading an advertisement in a paper, they may be interviewed immediately to assess its impact. When an advertisement comes through radio or TV, the listeners and viewers may be interviewed on the spot to learn their reactions.

Keying the advertisements Pre and post-test mostly indicate the appropriateness and the effect of advertisements on selected respondents. However, these methods do not exactly reveal the effect of advertisements in the form of benefits and orders quantitatively. Keying is a method which aims at knowing the result of advertising.

Variable addresses Different addresses may be given for responding when advertisements are given in different media. The orders or enquiries received at each address indicate response to that medium.

Attached response forms When advertisements are given in newspapers or magazines, a printed format may be attached for response. This can show the exact response for each advertisement.

Reference method Prospective customers may be asked to refer to the medium from which they got the information for their inquiry. This method covers audio and visual media also.

REVIEW QUESTIONS

I. Short-answer questions:

1. What is promotion?
2. What is sales promotion?
3. What is personal selling?
4. What is salesmanship?
5. What is sales force?
6. What is advertising?
7. What is interview schedule?
8. What is publicity?

9.   Who is a salesman?

10.   What is indoor advertising?

11.   What is media advertising?

12.   What is promotion mix?

13.   What is media?

14.   State the various promotional measures.

15.   What is advertising copy?

16.   What are the sources of recruiting salesman?

17.   What are the steps to select salesman?

18.   What is discount?

19.   What is trade discount?

20.   What is outdoor advertising?

II. Essay-types questions:

1.   What are benefits of personal selling?

2.   Explain the promotional mix elements?

3.   What are the qualities of a good salesman?

4.   What are the merits and demerits of advertising?

5.   Explain the types of advertising?

6.   What are the factors influencing the media selection?

7.   Explain the steps for recuriting the salesman.

8.   Explain the types of media advertising.

9.   What are the functions of personal selling?

10.   What are the sources of recruiting the salesman?

11.   What are types of tests to be conducted to select salesman?

12.   What are benefits of salesmanship?

14

MARKETING OF CONSUMER GOODS

Goods may be defined as any commodity, product or service, which are useful for people and have monetary value. Goods may be tangible or intangible. Tangible goods have the characteristics of tangibility, that is, the goods can be touched, seen, felt etc. For example, car, scooter, soap, fan, cloth etc are tangible goods. Intangible goods are in the form of services, such as repairing, services by banks, insurances companies, etc.

CLASSIFICATION OF GOODS

Goods can be divided into three categories on the basis of consumer needs: They are discussed in detail.

1. Manufactured Goods

American Marketing Association (AMA) committee has defined manufactured goods as products that include all those which are destined for use by ultimate consumers or households in such a form that they can be used without commercial processing.

The manufactured goods may be semi-finished or finished. Semi-finished products are the ones which have undergone some processing, it is further required to undergo some more processing, in order to convert it into finished goods. For instance, flour, cotton, woollen yarn and molasses. Finished goods are those products which have undergone complete processing and they are ready for direct consumption or usage, for example, readymade garments, suits, shirt, pants, electronic goods, soaps, published books etc.

Manufactured goods can be classified into two types namely, consumer goods and industrial goods.

i. *Consumer goods* Goods which can be consumed directly by ultimate consumers and households are called consumer goods. These products are prerequisites for our day-to-day lifestyle, which may be durable and non-durable, for example, car, television, radio, cycle, shoe, toys, furniture etc. Marketing of consumer goods is more complicated when compared to others.

ii. *Industrial goods* Commodities which are prepared in order to use them for the manufacture other products or kept for the purpose of rendering services in the operation of business activities or industrial enterprises are called industrial goods. Examples of such goods are industrial equipments, fabricating material and parts, raw-materials components, parts and operating supplies of machines, computers etc.

The differences between consumer goods and industrial goods are given in Table 14.1.

Table 14.1   Differences between consumer goods and industrial goods

Consumer goods	Industrial goods
Goods bought are meant for consumption.	Goods bought are meant for further processing.
There is a direct demand.	There is a derived demand.
The demand is elastic.	The demand is inelastic.
Purchase is made in small lots.	Purchase is made in bulk.
To make purchases, expert knowledge is not needed.	To make purchases, expert knowledge is needed.

2. Agricultural Goods

Agricultural goods refer to the products that result from cultivation by farmers. These agriculture goods depend more on natural convenience than on human efforts. Here, the nature plays a greater role than human efforts in determining the quality and quantity of the goods. For example, wheat, rice, barley, rye, millets, sugarcane, tobacco, cotton, jute, rubber, fruits, milk, ghee, butter, vegetables, meat etc. are agricultural goods. These agricultural products may be raw materials for industries or may serve as industrial and consumer goods.

3. Natural Raw Materials

Natural raw materials are the gifts of nature, for example, mines, forests etc. and these raw materials need further processing before use.

CHARACTERISTICS OF CONSUMER GOODS

Manufactured consumer goods are sold to the consumers for consumption. Further processing is not required before consumption.

The following are the features of consumer goods:

1. *Customers are numerous* The buyers of consumer goods are scattered and the markets are widespread. Because of the numerous buyers, it is not possible for the manufacturers to deal directly with the buyers individually. Hence, the producers of manufactured goods employ the services of middlemen wholesalers and retailers, through whom the distribution of goods is done.

2. *Purchase in small lots* Generally, the unit cost of consumer goods is low. People buy in small quantities, for instance, paste, brush, soaps, hair-oil etc. This is because:

    i. The goods are available at convenient places.

    ii. Most of the consumers are financially poor.

iii. The goods can be purchased at frequent intervals in any quantity.

iv. Locking up of capital is avoided.

v. Deterioration of quality do not occur.

The manufacturers of consumer goods generally adopt mass method of selling. They advertise their products in radio, newspapers, television etc. They also adopt distribution of free samples, display of the products in various retail shops etc.

3. *Mass production*   The demand for the consumer goods is greater and as such large-scale production is essential.

4. *Primary demand*   The world is progressing. At the same time, human beings are also improving their standard of living. A scooter, which was formerly a luxury item, has now become a comfort item. People earn more and are influenced by more advertising and other promotional methods, which induce them to raise their standard, accepting luxuries as necessities.

5. *Buyers are poorly informed*   Consumers may buy varieties of goods, they are generally not interested in studying their characteristics. Manufacturers also do not inform the buyer about the characteristics of the product. Consumers may not be experts in buying the goods. They depend upon the advice of the seller.

6. *Competition*   When similar consumer goods are marketed, there arises competition. Competition may be with regard to price, quality, substitute products etc. To overcome stiff competitions, manufacturers adopt various methods of branding, packaging etc.

7. *Changes in fashion*   We may generally come across occasions of clearance sales. This is because in fashion change new developments occur and new fashion comes in as a threat to the existing fashion. Many products disappear before they reach the maturity stage.

8. *Personal considerations*   Consumer goods must give satisfaction to the consumer. Conditions of sales, home delivery, repair facility, fitting, guarantee, installation, etc., have influence on the buying decisions.

9. *Manufacturers exercise control over the price*

10. *Buying motives* Consumer goods are bought by consumers because of buying emotional motives. This emotional motive may be pride, imitation, prestige, comfort, social status etc.

CLASSIFICATION OF CONSUMER GOODS

On the basis of buying habits, manufactured consumer goods are classified into three classes. They are

1. Convenience Goods

These are goods that the customers usually purchase frequently, immediately, and with the minimum effort. Low-unit cost, availability at convenient places, at frequent intervals, with minimum effort, etc. are important characteristics of convenience goods. Convenience goods are daily necessities for human beings, for instance, newspapers, soap, bread, sugar, coffee, tea, toothpaste etc.

Features

The features of convenience goods are:

i. Most of the convenience goods are perishable.

ii. Consumers possess full knowledge about the goods.

iii. Shops, dealing in the goods are located at convenient places.

iv. There is a regular and continuous demand for these goods.

v. The goods are purchased frequently in any quantity.

vi. There is a high competition in the market among competitors.

vii. All goods are standardized and duly branded.

viii. To get the goods, minimum effort is required.

ix. Each of these such goods has substitutions, for example, soap, paste, etc.

x. Almost all the goods are needed in day-to-day activities.

Marketing consideration   Since substitute products are available to consumers, there arises a keen competition. Convenience goods are produced by numerous firms in large-scale and in many varieties. Each producer tries to sell the maximum of his products. The following factors are given consideration:

i. *Convenient location*   The consumers prefer to buy these goods at a particular shop which is most convenient in distance, treatment, service etc.

ii. *Aggressive selling*   The manufacturer adopts aggressive selling efforts with a view to drag the attention of the customer immediately and disappears within a short period.

iii. *Display*   Window display and counter display are essential to attract the consumer at the point of purchases.

iv. *Advertising*   Retailers may stock several brands and they may be interested to make a sale but not of a particular brand. Hence, the manufacturers advertise these products in newspapers, television, radio, popular magazines, etc.

v. *Roll of wholesalers and retailers*   Consumers are countless. Direct selling is not practical. The product must be available on almost all retail shops. If the desired product is not available, consumers may go for substitute brands. The services of wholesalers are essential to facilitate the distribution of convenience goods to retailers who stock such goods in sufficient quantities.

2. Shopping Goods

Shopping goods are those wherein the ultimate consumer spend much more time in doing selection of these goods by visiting many shops with a view to compare its quality, quantity, style, price, suitability features, technology, durability and to know how distinct this product is with other available products in the market.

Examples are cloths, furniture, television, radio, jewellery, washing machines, fans, etc. Shopping goods are divided into two, namely, homogeneous and heterogenous. Homogenous are products having similar characteristics where as heterogenous means products having different characteristics.

Features

The features of shopping goods are:
   i. Products are durable and have a longer life.
  ii. The unit price is higher than that of convenience goods.
 iii. Branding is essential.
  iv. Buyers devote time and effort in the selection process.
   v. Generally producers supply goods directly to retailers.

Marketing consideration Shops dealing in shopping goods are located in central places. Manufacturers generally have a few outlets for the sales of goods. Shopkeepers keep the right goods to satisfy the customers. Generally, manufacturers supply goods directly to the retailers. For instance, a shop dealing in electrical goods may stock electrical goods but not other goods.

For example, a television dealer may stock television of the following brands: Hitachi, Samsung, LG, Onida, Panasonic, Sony, Videocon, etc. The consumers can compare the prices, performance, etc. at the time of demonstration.

Advertisements and displays are commonly done by the retailer. The location of the store, reputation of the dealer, salesmanship, price, design, etc., are important factors for the consumers to purchase these goods.

3. Specialty Goods

Speciality goods are those goods, which have unique characteristics for which customers have to pay special efforts, price, while purchasing them.

Specialty goods are those which have some particular attraction for the consumer other than price, for example, ear, house, costly branded items. These are also known as luxurious goods.

Speciality goods have special features which are considered as symbols of status and buyers of such goods make special efforts to visit any store, within or outside the city in which they are sold purchase without bargaining. The price and efforts are not considered important for purchase.

Features

The features of speciality goods are:

 i. Consumers insist on a particular brand.

 ii. Goods are high-priced ones.

 iii. The buyers are well-informed.

 iv. Goods have their own unique attraction.

 v. Consumers are prepared to spend considerable time and effort for the wanted goods.

 vi. Substitute brands are not generally accepted by consumers.

Marketing consideration Specialty goods enjoy brand loyalty. There are a few outlets. Generally manufacturers may run their own retail outlets for the sale of specialty goods. If the preferred brand is unavailable or out of stock, customers prefer to wait until they arrive in stores. Manufacturers and retailers advertise the products extensively. In the marketing of these goods, repair service, installation, etc., are very important. The retailer's reputation also plays an important role. For instance, a buyer purchasing a two-wheeler, "Bajaj Chetak" will make the choice after comparing it with other similar two-wheelers or because of certain unique features or for the brand name or the confidence in the dealer.

Clear distinction between shopping and speciality goods is not always possible.

CHANNELS OF DISTRIBUTION

A channel of distribution or trade channel for products is the route through which goods move from the manufacturers or producers to the ultimate consumers. In brief, the types of distributions or channels for consumer goods are:

1. Manufacturer to consumer.
2. Manufacturer to retailer to consumer.
3. Manufacturer to wholesaler to retailer to consumer.
4. Manufacturer, through an agent, to wholesaler to retailer to consumer.
5. Manufacturer, through an agent middleman, to retailer to consumer.

To conclude, marketing of consumer goods is extremely complex in all respects. Because the present day market is a challenging complex of buyers and sellers of commodities and services acting under different competitive forces, all these naturally affect demand and prices at a given time in a given area, which is a challenging job for marketers of consumer products.

REVIEW QUESTIONS

I. Short-answer questions:

1. What are the features of consumer goods?
2. What are the types of consumer goods?
3. What is consumer goods.

4. What do you mean by shopping goods?

5. Define convenience goods.

6. Distinguish between convenience goods, shopping and speciality goods.

7. Discuss briefly the common channels of distribution for consumer goods.

8. What are the features of speciality goods?

II. Essay-type questions:

1. Explain the various features of consumer goods.

2. What do you mean by shopping goods? Explain their features and marketing considerations.

3. Write a note an buying motives.

4. What are the features of speciality goods?

5. What are the various classes of consumer goods?

6. Discuss briefly the common channels of distribution for consumer goods.

15

MARKETING OF INDUSTRIAL GOODS

Industrial goods are those goods which are destined to be sold primarily for use in producing other goods or rendering services in contrast with goods destined to be sold primarily to the ultimate consumer. Industrial goods are bought by industrial users for the purpose of production.

BUYING MOTIVES OF INDUSTRIAL USERS

Industrial buyers are rational. The buying motives of industrial users can easily be determined when compared to the consumer's buying motives. The following are the motives generally found in industrial buyers:

1. *Reduced price* When a few items are purchased, negligible price change is not considered. But industrial users purchase goods in large quantities and therefore the buyers are rational, that is, price is a major consideration.

2. *Regular supply* Regular supply of goods is preferred for production. The source from where the supply is expected, must be dependable. The supplier must be able to supply required quantity of right quality goods.

3. *Durability* Consumers always prefer durable products even at a higher price. For example, a screw driver we purchase

is used to loosen a screw, but if the tongue of the screw driver bends, we immediately take a decision not to purchase the screw driver of that particular brand again. As such, only durable and quality products can be sold in the market. This fact is always remembered by the manufacturer.

4. *Greater economy* Industrial users prefer to purchase plants and machineries by which they can increase production at less cost. An efficient machine can yield more output of improved quality.

5. *Protection* Purchases of goods are also desired to be protected against risk such as theft, fire, etc., for example, purchasing of steel furniture instead of wooden furniture.

Industrial buyers aim primarily to increase their profits; and thus their buying goal is to have quality items at cheaper rate and to increase saleability of goods having durability.

CHARACTERISTICS OF THE MARKET FOR INDUSTRIAL GOODS

An industrial market consists of manufacturers, government service organizations, industrial distributors, middlemen, etc. All these categories, engaged in business or process of operations in making other products, constitute the market for industrial goods. These categories are explained below:

1. *Geographical Concentration* The market for the industrial goods is generally concentrated in certain geographical areas. This is because industries are located at a particular region. The demand for the goods comes from the area where industries are located, whereas the market for consumer goods is spread over a wide area, as buyers are scattered all over the country. For example, there is a good demand for automobile spare parts from Bangalore, Bombay, etc. because automobile industries are concentrated there.

2. *Limited Buyers* Compared to the number of buyers of consumer goods, there are only a few buyers of industrial goods.

Roughly 10% of the total number of consumers are industrial users, because only a few industries exist. Hence, there is a limited number of buyers of industrial goods.

3. *Derived Demand* The demand for industrial goods depends upon the demand for consumer goods. Industrial goods are used in manufacturing consumer goods. The increase or decrease of demand for industrial goods depends upon the increase or decrease of demand for final products, that is, consumer goods.

4. *Large-scale Individual Purchase* The seller of industrial goods pays maximum attention to please his customer, because the buyer of industrial goods may order for a large quantity and the sales amount is high.

5. *Technical Consideration* The manufacturers or their agents are the professional buyers, who possess thorough knowledge of the industrial goods. For example, a manufacturer of transistor radio may aim to good quality purchase materials and parts, which will go into the final product of transistor radio. If any change in the quality of material or parts occurs, it will create trouble in the final products.

6. *Reciprocal Buying* Reciprocal buying is nowadays common amongst the industrial goods purchasers. For example, a paper manufacturer buys chemicals from a chemical firm that buys considerable amount of paper from the paper manufacturer. Another example is a truck manufacturer purchases tyres from a firm that purchases trucks. The purpose of these types of dealings is that to some extent the demand for the products is assured on mutual understanding.

7. *Leasing Instead of Buying* Heavy, costly equipment of industrial goods are leased instead of purchasing. For example, parcel service agencies may not purchase trucks, but hire trucks; a building contractor may not purchase cement concrete mixer, but he may use a hired mixer; distribution agencies may use hired vehicles for distribution; a farmer may hire tractor to plough his land, etc. Lessor enjoys more income than the lessee in this sales promotion method.

8. Buying Decision Compared to consumer goods, the period of negotiations for the sale of industrial goods is generally longer. This is because many persons are involved in the decision to purchase such as engineers, production managers in charge, cost accountants, etc. All formalities of the purchasing department—calling for quotations, preparing comparative statement, etc.—have to be undergone and finance has to be arranged.

CLASSIFICATION OF INDUSTRIAL GOODS

Industrial goods may be classified based on the broad uses of the product into four categories:

1. Raw Materials

Raw materials are source of industrial goods which become a major part of finished goods, and which do not require any processing other than more economical movements. The raw material are supplied and produced by nature, such as forest products like wood, honey, lac, cashewnut, herbs of medicinal value, etc., mineral products like mica, copper, iron, zinc, coloured pebbles, graphite, gold, diamond, stones, lime, coal, manganese, crude oil, bauxite, aluminum, etc., sea products like fish, snails, prawns, oysters, corals, sand, crabs, pearls, shell etc.

Agricultural raw materials are those which are produced by agriculture activities. They include products such as tobacco, cotton, jute, cane, oil, seeds, etc.

Characteristics of natural raw materials

i. *Limited supply* The supply of natural raw materials is limited. Moreover, such materials cannot be reproduced. The supply is scarce mainly in relation to demand.

ii. *Huge capital* Production of natural raw materials needs huge capital investment. Apart from this, highly skilled personal services are needed. Further the producers of natural raw materials are few in numbers.

iii. *Variation in quality* The quality of the raw materials may differ from place to place.

iv. *Bulk quantity* The materials are bulky in nature. But intrinsic value is low when we compare to size or shape. For example, the paper industries use 1000 kg of bamboo, which may produce 500 kg of paper.

v. *Perishability* Certain types of natural raw materials such as sea products are perishable.

vi. *Controlled production* Overproduction can be controlled and this avoids the expenses of storage.

vii. *Concentrated production* Compared to the farm products, the production of natural raw materials is relatively concentrated and not widely scattered.

Marketing considerations

i. *Channels of distribution* Since the natural raw materials is produced by nature are limited scale, users are also limited. Due to this, industrial users adopt shortest channel of distribution, such as directly from produces to industrial users, in order to have a control over the sources of supply. Agent, middlemen may also be employed.

ii. *Transportation cost* Transportation cost of these bulky materials to a longer distance will be more. At the same time, the intrinsic value is lesser than the transportation cost. The transportation cost will decide whether the materials should be processed before they are carried to the factory. In processing, the waste is removed and thus the materials are thinned, which reduces the transportation cost. For example, sugar mill industries are located near the place where sugar cane is cultivated. If the factory is too far off, the canes are to be transported to the factory and naturally, a greater amount will have to be spent on transporting.

iii. *Need for standardization* The raw materials, which are extracted from nature, are of different qualities. When manufacturers are concerned with materials of specific quality for their finished goods, then grading and standardization are essential. As stated earlier, producers have no control on materials extracted from nature. Therefore, the producers of natural raw materials have to standardize and grade the raw materials.

iv. *Adequate and guaranteed supply* Regular supply of raw materials is to be assured by the supplier. These may be done by either entering into a long period contract with the supplier purchasing from open market at low price or by owning the source of supply.

2. Fabricating Materials and Parts

These goods are part and parcel of the finished goods to be manufactured. They undergo processing. Fabricating materials, which have been processed, will undergo further processing in the course of manufacturing of finished products, for example, flour going into bread, yarn going into cloth, pig iron going into steel, etc. Fabricating parts are also industrial goods that have undergone complete manufacturing process, and generally do not require further processing. They become part of the finished product and can be recognized easily.

Characteristics

i. *Adequate supply* A manufacturer of finished goods needs regular and adequate supply of fabricated materials and parts. For example, without tubes, cycles cannot be produced; without flour, bread cannot be prepared; without yarn, clothes cannot be made, etc.

ii. *Competitive price* These materials must be priced at competitive price so that the manufacturers are facilitated to produce their finished products at competitive price.

iii. *Inspection* Buyers of these goods, generally, possess good knowledge of these products. They are particular about the quality, suitability, price, etc.

iv. *Uniformity* Standard of quality and uniformity in size are of vital importance to the buyers. Buyers have many choices, (even one supplier is unable to supply standard materials and parts).

Marketing considerations

i. *Motives of buyers* Fabricating materials and parts are purchased in large quantities. Buyers need better quality. Brand has little to do with the buying motives. The price also does not have much consideration here.

ii. *Timely supply* The purchase is always based on timely supply and uniform supply. This is because the finished products are manufactured along with the fabricated materials or spares. If these are not supplied regularly and timely, an industrial user cannot produce finished products.

iii. *Dealings* Most of the fabricating materials and parts are sold directly to the industrial users, with orders placed often a year or more in advance. Maximum dealings are direct. Middlemen are used for small quantity. The firm, supplying the materials, has its own salesmen and they call upon the users.

3. Equipment

Equipment refer to both installations and accessories.

Installations

Installations are manufactured industrial products—the long-living, expensive major equipment of an industrial user. Installation consists of building factories and offices; fixed equipments such as power-looms, generators, elevators, boilers, cranes, locomotives, sawmills, lathes, etc. Generally they are bought directly from the producer. Its negotiation period is also long.

Characteristics

i. *Specifications* Specifications are always designed by the purchaser/user. Before making a decision to purchase, suggestions of experts in the line are sought. The installations are manufactured strictly according to the specification laid down by the user.

ii. *Obsolescence* Fashion habit, consumer behaviour, etc. may change often. Because of the development of science and technology, new inventions or economical methods come up. This causes the machineries or installations to become obsolete.

iii. *Durable and costly* Installations are costly and are meant for longer period, for example, installations of locomotives, or a sugar factory can be used for a long period.

Testing Generally it is found that the working of installations cannot be judged exactly. When the installations are put into use, the working or performance can be decided.

Marketing considerations

i. In many cases, pre-sale and post-sales services are needed. As such, the seller makes provision for repairing in order to earn goodwill.

ii. Personal selling is more effective than any other method. Generally, no middlemen are involved and the channel is also direct, from the producer to the user.

iii. Longer negotiations take place before finalizing transaction as these installations are costly or purchased once in a while, and prepared according to the detailed specifications of the purchase order.

iv. Leasing system is widely followed since the price level is very high.

Accessories

The minor machines or machine tools, for example, welding equipment, speed reducers, typewriters, fans, computers, etc., are commonly called accessory equipments. They are used as an aid in the production. They do not enter into final products. Most of the products are standardized with respect to quality, durability, size and price. They do not become obsolete. The cost is very low. Their life is longer than that of operating supplies. The buyers have brand preferences over the buying decision. Generally, industrial users make inquiry from those who are already using them before taking a decision.

Characteristics

i. *Produced against demand* These accessories are standardized in terms of quality and price. They are produced against specific order but are also produced in anticipation of the demand.

ii. *No chance of obsolescence* These accessories will not be rendered obsolete to replacement or change of plant, as these are facilitating equipments, which are meant or specific purpose. Screwdriver will assist to loosen the nuts it would not be obsolete. The machine may be changed but these accessories are still useful. However, installations will become obsolete, due to change in fashion, habits and loss of life.

Short life Life of accessories is very short as they are cheap and easily available in the market.

Not a part of finished goods The accessories do not enter into the final product and is exhausted by repeated usage.

Marketing considerations

i. *Aggressive advertisement* To attract the industrial users, wide publicity is made, apart from sales promotional methods for such as typewriters, fans, hand tools, etc.

ii. *Sales policy* Manufacturers of these products like to sell their products to industrial users through their own salesman and through middlemen by direct selling and indirect selling. When the market is geographically scattered, the services of middlemen are adopted.

iii. *Promptness of supply* In the absence of these items, the scale of operation is not affected. However, the flow of production is affected. As such, timely supply is preferred.

4. Operating Supplies

Goods which are used by the industrial producers with a view to provide facilities for the operation of machine or plant continuously without loss of time, but which will not become a part of the finished product, are called as operating supplies.

Items such as lubricants, oil, grease, petrol, stationery, distilled water etc. are operating supplies. They do not become part of the end product. They are consumed in the operations.

Characteristics

i. *Short life*   The life of operating supplies is short. They are lowpriced. They are used up or lose value immediately.

ii. *Effort to buy*   Almost all such supplies can be purchased with minimum effort. They are readily available in the market, apart from low-unit value.

Marketing considerations

i. *Price competition*   Generally the buyer's decision is based on price. This is because many manufacturers produce similar goods.

ii. *Widespread market*   There is widespread market throughout the country. Sales of these items are in small quantities as they are available anywhere and at any time.

iii. *Effort to sell*   The producers of these products, through extensive wholesaling middlemen, sell their products. Their unit value is less. They are bought in small quantities and they go to many users.

CHANNELS OF DISTRIBUTION

The channels of distribution constitute the extension of the marketer into the markets he plans to supply. The channel of distribution has to be selected by the marketer for distribution of industrial goods in the industrial market.

In the industrial market, there are five channels of distribution. They are discussed below:

1.Sales Branches

Manufacturer's branch houses and branch offices can bring about distribution of product with the help of salesmen having professional and technical competence. Such distribution outlets are part of the internal organization of the manufacturer. There is a direct sale to industrial users without any middlemen.

Direct channel (no independent middlemen) is more common in industrial marketing. It is always preferred due to the following reasons:

i. Very large purchase orders can be handled directly.

ii. Limited number of buyers can be approached directly.

iii. When there is a special demand for close and continuous buyer–seller relationship.

iv. Pre-sales and after-sale services are important.

v. Technical and pricing problems demand direct negotiation between seller and buyer.

2. Sales Agents

Manufacturers may employ sales agents who are also called manufacturer's representatives. They act on their own account on the basis of commission. In reality they are independent salesmen. They handle the products of several, but non-competing manufacturers. They have on-going, long-term relationships with their principals. They are given certain sales territories. They are useful as an alternative to company employed salesmen. They are necessary for small manufacturers, who cannot have their sales branches and sales force, and who lack marketing experience.

There are a few drawbacks of agents against their advantages of low-marketing cost, established contacts and competent selling: (i) Manufacturer has loose control over sales agents, (ii) Sales agents sell at fixed prices determined by the manufacturers and they cannot change prices even though situation demands flexible pricing.

3. Industrial Distributors

Industrial distributors are middlemen who buy and sell industrial products. They are merchant middlemen buying goods, assuming ownership, stocking products, undertaking marketing risks and maintaining close contact with industrial buyers.

There are general line distributors or mill supply houses and full service merchant wholesalers. They carry large number of items.

There are also special distributing firms. They carry limited line of related products. They specialize in a particular line of industrial goods.

A combination house does other forms of wholesaling in addition to industrial distribution. For example, an industrial distributor of electrical goods sells to retailers, institutional buyers as well as to the manufacturers and the construction firms.

There are certain advantages in buying from industrial distributors. They are:

    i.   Buyer can get fast and economical delivery of goods. Buyer can place one order for many goods. Local distributor can give quick delivery, and save paper work in buying. Speed and certainty of delivery are always welcome by industrial buyers.

    ii.   Buyers can get product information. Distributors' catalogues provide a fund of information about the products of many manufacturers.

    iii.   To small buyers, the industrial distributors offer credit.

    iv.   The distributors know buyer's needs and expectations fully. They can offer a wide assortment of products to fulfill the special needs of their customers.

    v.   Distributors perform all marketing functions, such as assorting, financing, storage, sorting, transportation, risk-taking, etc. They can offer these specialized services at a reasonable cost to the manufacturer.

4. Brokers

In industrial marketing, brokers play a minor role. If goods are standardized, sale by description of brand is possible, the marketer can use broker's services for selling the products. Operating supplies and raw materials can be sold through brokers conveniently. In the marketing of raw materials, that is, agricultural products, brokers are helpful, for example, the cotton industry. Brokers are expert buyers in their field.

5. Selling Agents

Manufacturer's agents do not take over the stocks of their principals but sell items for more than one producer. The selling agent is under contract to dispose off the whole output of the factory and to handle no other goods—at least no competing goods. Manufacturer's agent has a certain sale territory. Selling agent sells wherever he can.

PHASES IN INDUSTRIAL BUYING

The following are the steps involved in industrial buying:

1. Recognition of buyer's problem and need.
2. Determination of the quality and characteristics of the needed products.
3. Description of the quality and characteristics of the required product.
4. Search for and qualification of potential sources.
5. Acquisition and analysis of proposals available.
6. Evaluation of proposals and selection of suppliers.
7. Selection and order routine.
8. Performance evaluation and feedback for the goods or services that have been bought.

PURCHASE DECISIONS

The purchase decision is made by the following people.

1. Top management
2. Finance executives
3. Research and Development executives
4. Production and/or engineering staff
5. Industrial engineer and/or production control executives
6. Quality control staff
7. Marketing staff
8. Purchasing staff
9. Department staff of Factory receiving or storing control

In the new purchase decision, technological and economic factors will have to be given special considerations. Industrial buyers want products or services of the right quality, at acceptable prices, in the right quantity, at the right place, at the right time and from the best sources.

REVIEW QUESTIONS

I. Short-answer questions:

1. Discuss the characteristics of industrial goods.
2. What are industrial goods?
3. State the different classes of industrial goods.
4. What do you mean by fabricating materials and parts?
5. What are natural raw materials?
6. State the classes of raw materials.
7. Discuss the features of industrial goods.

II. Essay-type questions:

1. Discuss the characteristics of the market for industrial goods.
2. Discuss the common channels for industrial goods.

3. What are the special features of industrial goods.

4. Explain the types of industrial goods.

5. What are fabricating materials and parts? Explain their features and marketing considerations.

6. Discuss the natural raw materials along with its characteristics and marketing considerations.

7. Explain installations and accessory equipments.

16

MARKETING OF AGRICULTURAL GOODS

Marketing of agricultural goods in India is of no mean significance. Agricultural marketing is one of the manifold problems, which has direct bearing upon the prosperity of the cultivator. Agricultural marketing, in its wide sense, comprises all the operations involved in the movement of goods and raw materials from the field to the final consumer. It includes handling of product at the farm, initial processing, grading and packing in order to maintain and enhance quality and avoid wastage. Unfortunately, the present system of marketing of agricultural goods in India is extremely defective and needs a thorough overhauling.

AGRICULTURAL GOODS

Agricultural goods refer to the products that result from cultivation by farmers. Such goods include the products of dairy farming, pig farming, poultry farming, etc., such as wheat, rice, barley, rye, millets, sugarcane, tobacco, cotton, jute, rubber, fruits, vegetables, milk, ghee, butter, cheese, meat, eggs, leather etc.

CLASSIFICATION OF AGRICULTURAL GOODS

Agricultural goods can be classified as follows:

1. Raw materials for industries, for example, cotton, jute tobacco.

2. Consumer and industrial goods.

Raw materials for industries, for example, cotton, jute, tobacco, etc., are those that are processed. The ultimate consumers use these products after they pass through many manufacturing processes. The process is long in some cases, like conversion of cotton into cloth, sugarcane into sugar, etc.

Consumer and industrial goods are those used by both consumers and industries. When vegetables and fruits are sold to the consumers for consumption purpose, then they are called consumer goods. Consumer goods can be used by the consumers in their natural form without any change by manufacturing process. They are fruits, vegetables, egg, milk, etc. When they are sold to a canning factory for further processing, then they are called industrial goods. Sugarcane and coconuts are some examples.

CHARACTERISTICS OF AGRICULTURAL GOODS

The characteristics of agricultural goods can be studied under three headings. They are: 1) Production characteristics, 2) Product characteristics and 3) Consumption characteristics

Production Characteristics

Small-scale production Farmers have small holdings of land. The production in those lands is also very small, which is sufficient only for their family needs. They do not have the knowledge of efficient marketing methods, such as grading, standardization, storing, warehousing, etc. To be more effective and economical, there must be large quantity of goods. As such they depend upon middlemen or cooperative societies to market their produce. Small-scale agricultural goods are not suitable for demand creation. Advertising is not possible due to the small-scale production. Branding is not possible due to different qualities of goods. Further, subdivision of divided holding, under the law of succession, into many fragmented holdings increases the problem.

Scattered and specialized production Agriculture production depends upon some natural factors, such as, suitability of soil and climatic conditions. If the fertility of the soil is rich and the climatic condition is favourable, then the place will be suitable for agricultural production. Different crops need different types of soil and different climatic conditions.

Seasonal production Agricultural production is seasonal in character. But there is demand for agricultural goods throughout the year, whereas the harvest is seasonal. For smoothening, there must be adequate transport facilities, storage facility, apart from finance.

Product Characteristics

Different quality and quantity In agriculture, man and nature are the two partners. Nature is the important partner. As such, the quality of agricultural products is beyond the control of the producers. Flood, drought, hailstorm, plant diseases, insects and pests, etc. affect the agricultural production very much, even in advanced countries. Grading and standardization become difficult; even the farmer cannot guess the quality and quantity of his products in advance.

Bulky agricultural goods When compared to their value, most of the agricultural goods are bulky. As such, their transportation costs are high, storage of these goods is expensive, when compared to manufactured goods.

Perishability Many agricultural goods are perishable by nature. Perishable products like fruits, vegetables, milk, dairy products, poultry products, meat, etc., need special storage and transport facilities. For these perishable products, cold storage and refrigerators are needed.

Consumption Characteristics

Inelastic demand and supply Agricultural goods are necessary for every human being. Hence, their demand is also inelastic. Price changes do not affect the demand. Demand for food grains is not affected by fall or rise in price. Price fluctuates due to imbalance in supply and demand. The Government is taking necessary steps to stabilize price in order to protect the countless small farmers from the clutches of adverse price change. It procures marketed surplus and releases as and when needed.

AGRICULTURAL GOODS
VERSUS MANUFACTURED GOODS

The Differences between agricultural products and manufactured goods are given below:

1. Manufacturers engage in production continuously and they utilise their capacity to the fullest extent possible. This compels them to be cost conscious and to concentrate equally on production and marketing activities, where as the agriculturalists are purely producer and they cannot utilise themselves to the fullest capacity due to various constraints.

2. A manufacturer have the control over the sale of his products to the middlemen. But this is not so in the case of agricultural producer where middlemen exploit the producer.

3. Manufactured goods are mostly produced on a large-scale and are then broken up into small lots for marketing, where as agricultural products are collected in small quantities.

4. Manufactured goods can be easily controlled, both qualitatively and quantitatively and these can be fixed in advance in almost accurate terms. Both these aspects are beyond the control of an agriculturalist and the entire production is based on natural and climatic conditions.

5. Important characteristic of marketing of manufactured goods is effective demand creation. But these activities are completely absent in case of agricultural marketing.

6. Finally, the manufactured goods can identify themselves completely with their products and customers buy the products based on their quality and reputation of producers also. This is not so in case of agricultural marketing.

PROBLEMS IN THE MARKETING OF AGRICULTURAL GOODS

1. Concentration process is very important for agricultural goods. A long channel of distribution is needed and hence there is a large number of middlemen.
2. There is high demand for transportation and storage facilities in the harvest season in order to protect the produce from deterioration in quality.
3. To finance seasonal requirements, more finance is necessary in a particular period.
4. Grading and standardization are important for agricultural products. But it is very difficult to grade and standardize the products, as there are many agricultural goods and one produce has many qualities.
5. Branding is also not an easy job.
6. There is price fluctuation in agricultural products due to the imbalance in supply and demand.

Channels of Distribution for Agricultural Goods

In spite of developed agricultural marketing with respect to highly sophisticated means of transport facilities, improved form of standardization and grading, advanced communication system, scientific method of storage and warehousing, the Indian agriculture is still for behind. Therefore, it is required that wide and effective distribution channels should be used for different types of marketing, which exercise different functions in the marketing of agricultural goods. The small-scale production of farm products further leads to concentration, equalization and dispersion. As a result, these agricultural goods necessarily move through some important wholesale markets such as jobbing market and secondary market.

KINDS OF MARKETS

The types of wholesale markets found in practice are given below: 1) Local markets, 2) Central markets, 3) Jobbing markets and 4) Secondary markets

Local Markets

Local markets function daily or twice a week. Wholesale markets are located in towns near the production area. They are the major point of concentration. This type of market generally functions along the roadside or centrally situated localities. In this market, the produce of individual farmers is collected into economical lots; grading and packaging are done before moving them to central markets. The middlemen functioning in the market are of many types.

i. *Local resident buyers*   They have a fixed place of business in a market.

ii. *Travelling buyers*   The buyers move from place to place or farm to farm or even open a collection shop at a convenient place and collect produces during seasons and move them to other areas.

iii. *Cooperative societies*   Members can sell their products to the wholesalers through the societies.

iv. *Auction companies*   When the buyers and sellers assemble, produces are sold through open market.

Central Markets

In the local markets, the assembly of agricultural goods is done and from there they move to large central markets or terminal markets. Here, the wholesaler looks after the marketing processes—concentration, equalization and dispersion. The central markets are situated in towns. The produces concentrated in these markets are partly sold for local consumption and the rest, transported to consuming centres.

Features of central markets

i. They have a large number of specialized middlemen.
ii. They have suitable location nearer to the producing and consuming centres.
iii. They have adequate storage, warehouse facility, and facilities of communications, finance, advertisement, etc.

Functions

i. Assembly of goods
ii. Determining fair price
iii. Collection and distribution of marketing information
iv. Financing
v. Facilitating future trading and hedging

Jobbing Markets

Jobbers are similar to mini-wholesalers. These markets are bigger than local markets, but smaller than the central markets. The importance of jobbers is reduced by direct dealing between retailers and central market.

Secondary Markets

In secondary markets, agricultural raw materials are dealt with. They are also called as sub-terminal markets.

DEFECTS OF AGRICULTURAL MARKETING

1. *Lack of organization* There is lack of organization among producers. Producers are small and scattered. They have no collective organization of their own to protect their interests.

2. *Forced sales*

The formers are forced to sell their products due to:

i. poverty and prior indebtedness
ii. lack of storage facilities
iii. time factor, particularly with regard to perishable goods.

3. *Existence of large number of middlemen* There are a large number of intermediaries or middlemen between the producers and the consumers. These middlemen sell the produce to the consumers at a higher price and give lower returns to the producers.

Approximately 50% of the price paid by the consumer goes to middlemen.

4. *Multiplicity of market charges* The producers pay numerous and various marketing charges. They are more than 20% of the income of the produce. They pay market charges at different levels such as commission to the dalal, weighmen charges, brokerage, charges of labourers who help in unloading the cart, etc., apart from the deduction for impurities in the produce by the wholesaler.

5. *Multiplicity of weights and measures* There is lack of standard weights and measures. Weights made of sticks, stones, bits of old iron are commonly used in the villages and markets.

The multiplicity of weights and measures employed has many defects:

    i.   It makes supervision very difficult.

    ii. It gives opportunity to cheat the producers.

6. *Adulteration* Due to adulteration, the quality of the produce is reduced. Even the good produces are subjected to customary inclusion of impurities. The adulterants, such as papaya seeds, are mixed with pepper; chilly powder is mixed with red brick powder supari with sawdust; ghee with vanaspathi; and tea dust with sawdust. Medicines are also adulterated.

7. *Inadequate storage facility* Storage facility is far below the requirements in rural and urban areas. The loss due to inadequate storage has been estimated to be 5–15% in weight and quality. Grains lose weights due to the change of weather. Crops like jowar, pulses and maize are found to be infested with insects even before harvest.

8. *Lack of transport facility* There are bad roads which lead to loss during transportation and cause strain to the animals. The freight policy followed by railways in India is also not satisfactory. Railways do not have the facility for quick and safe transport of perishable products.

9. *Absence of grading and standardization* There is no standard grade for important commodities like rice and wheat in the whole country. The ungraded mixed quality are sold at low prices.

10. *Lack of market information* Most of the farmers are illiterates and they are ignorant of the accurate prices ruling in the market. They depend upon inaccurate information.

11. *Lack of financial facility* Most of the financial needs of the farmers in India are met by village moneylenders; the moneylenders come forward, purchase the produce by paying low prices under the loan agreement, and again issue loans for further cultivation or for their family needs. The loan is advanced on the condition that the produce will be sold to them or through them.

B. Correcting the Defects in Agricultural Marketing

The defects of agricultural marketing can be removed by the following measures:

i. *Establishment of regulated market* Many defects of agricultural marketing and malpractices of middlemen can be removed by the establishment of regulated markets.

ii. *Use of standard weights and measures* Cultivators and purchasers are safeguarded against cheating by false or underweight by the use of standard weights and measures.

iii. *Storage and warehousing facilities* Increase in storage and warehousing facilities is necessary to remove the defects in agricultural marketing. Warehousing is the protector of national wealth.

iv. *Improvement in transport facilities* For proper marketing of agricultural goods, adequate and appropriate transport facilities are very important.

v. *Provision of marketing information* The important providers of market information are: private arrangements for traders, newspapers, government publications, regulated markets, radio and TV and cooperative societies.

vi. *Development of cooperative marketing* The defects of agricultural marketing are removed by the development of cooperative marketing.

REVIEW QUESTIONS

I. Short-answer questions:

1. What do you mean by agricultural goods?
2. State the types of agricultural goods.
3. What is local market?
4. What do you mean by jobbing market?
5. What is central market?
6. State the features of agricultural goods.

II. Essay-type questions:

1. Explain the characteristic features of agricultural products.
2. Differentiate between manufactured and agricultural goods.
3. Discuss briefly the defects of agricultural marketing in India and suggest remedial measures for its improvement.
4. What are the types of agricultural goods?
5. Define agricultural goods and explain its product and production characteristics.
6. Discuss the role of agricultural marketing in India with references.

17

MARKETING OF SERVICES

Unlike a product, a service is intangible—something one cannot see, feel, hear, taste or smell. The American Marketing Association defines services as "activities, benefits or satisfactions which are offered for sale or are provided in connection with the sale of goods."

The definition points out three kinds of services:

1. The activities those are intangible in nature, for example, transportation. Here, some kind of products (car, bus) are used to derive the so-called intangible service.
2. Benefits purely derived from services, for example, medical service, insurance service, etc.
3. The service obtained along with the buying of a product, for example, after-sales service or the services rendered by a retailer.

DIFFERENCES BETWEEN PRODUCTS AND SERVICES

The main problem from the marketing standpoint is to determine when a product becomes a service and vice versa.

Theoretically, a car is a product. But when it is hired by a person to travel from one place to another, it ceases to be a product and becomes a service to the purchaser of the service.

There are many factors that distinguish product from service:

1. The first factor is that a product is identifiable and one can feel its presence in various ways. But a service takes a product and converts it into something that can be purchased but cannot be identified. For example, a car as a product could be identified but not the various services rendered by it.

   On the contrary, services are best marketed by meeting the already established needs of the consumer and by performance. If a service is performed well, the business or profession will prosper. It will flourish simply by "word-of-mouth" advertising. Doctors, lawyers and accountants who follow the ethics of their profession do not advertise at all. Still their practice grows, and this growth is on the basis of their performance.

2. The second distinguishing factor is the variety of ways in which the selling of services is undertaken. There are as many ways of selling services as there are services themselves. The products are sold under different methods but they all have a common service pattern. For example, in the case of banking service, different bankers adopt different methods for attracting various kinds of deposits such as fixed, savings or current.

3. Thirdly, many service businesses are outgrowths of the sales of certain products. For example, when a car is sold, the buyer must have insurance, financial assistance, repair facilities, etc.

4. The fourth factor is that when marketing a product, the primary task of the producer is to create a desire or need for his product in the mind of the consumer. It is also necessary to convince the consumer that a particular

product is better than that of the competitors. Advertising has an inevitable tool in the sale of products.

Finally, the opportunities for offering services are unlimited, unlike products. Flexibility for changing or conversion is also greater in the case of services. For example, a house that is rented out for a family could be converted into a lodge.

CHARACTERISTICS OF SERVICES

1. *Intangibility* Many of the problems faced in the marketing of service are due to the intangible nature of services. The fact that a service cannot appeal to a buyer's sense, places a burden on the marketing organization.

Intangibility has certain obvious advantages also. First, there is no problem about its physical distribution. There is no warehousing problem, as there is practically nothing to store. The losses that may arise on account of decline in inventory values also do not affect services.

2. *Inseparability* In many cases, a service cannot be separated from the person who sells it. Therefore, services are often created and marketed simultaneously.

This inseparability element influences the selection of the channel of distribution. Here, direct sale is the only feasible channel of distribution. The inseparability, very often, limits the scale of operation also.

But some industries have been able to modify the inseparability characteristics, for example, insurance services. Here, the insurance company is the producer of the services and the services are distributed through agents.

3. *Perishability and fluctuating demand* The utility of most services is short-lived. Services cannot be mass-produced ahead of time and stored for periods of peak demand. The perishable nature of services is a challenging feature for the marketing enterprise. Idle seats in a bus or train represent business which is lost forever.

Air travel is highly seasonal and the advertisements offering concessions for air travel are regular features now.

Fluctuations in demand pose another problem. The markets for services fluctuate usually by seasons and often by day or week. For example, telephone department offers concessions for using their services during off-peak periods.

4. *Highly differentiated marketing system* In the case of products, the marketing system that evolved out of past experience would be sufficient. However, in the case of services, no fixed pattern could be adopted. For example, the marketing of banking and other financial services bears no resemblance to the marketing of repair services.

Moreover, it is very difficult to maintain uniform performance standards for services. The basic reason for such variation in quality is that service industries are human-intensive.

5. *Absence of certain marketing functions* Since most service firms do not deal in tangible products, the elimination or reduction of certain marketing functions is possible. For example, functions such as transportation, storage, inventory control, etc. need not be performed at all.

6. *Heterogeneity* Services are numerous and it is impossible to standardize the output. The services of even the same seller are sometimes remarkably dissimilar. For example, Hair-cuts done to two individuals by the same barber are not identical. It is particularly so, in designing the quality beforehand. A music programme is a good example. It cannot definitely satisfy all the listeners equally. A service salesman is better equipped to adapt his services to the individualized needs of his customers. For example, insurance policy conforms to standardized rules, but the agent is still able to choose from alternative options to design an individual policy for each buyer. Secondly, heterogeneity forces a salesman to have a complete knowledge of the entire range of his company's services. Moreover, satisfactory matching of service offerings and customers' needs require him to be a more creative salesman.

7. *Customer relationship* Normally the buyer is more prominent in the marketing and production of services than goods. In many service transactions, a client relationship exists between the buyer and seller as distinguished from a customer relationship, for example, the doctor-patient relationship. It is highly personal and most direct in nature.

8. *Lack of standardization* Another notable feature of services is that they cannot be perfectly standardized as is the case in products. The example of hair-cut mentioned above is apt here also.

KINDS OF SERVICES

A service may be classified into:

1. *Personal services* Many services are of personal nature, for example, house painting and various domestic services.

2. *Facility services* When products are offered to the customers to provide some facilities, the services may be described as facility services, for example, car, theatre, etc.

The above distinction is not perfect as some services are really a mixture of the above two. In some cases, the personal services cannot be offered without extensive physical facilities, for example, hospital, university, etc.

3. *Business services* When services are rendered to business houses, they are called business services. These services include activities such as marketing services, management consultancy services, etc.

4. *Customer services* The services that are offered to ultimate consumers are known as customer services. Such services include laundries, hotels, etc.

SERVICE MARKETING PROBLEMS

The unique service features and the kinds of services pose peculiar problems for marketing managers of services. A summary of this is given in Table 17.1.

Table 17.1   Service marketing problems

Unique service features	Resulting marketing problems
Intangibility	Cannot be stored and protected through patents and cannot be readily displayed or communicated. Prices are difficult to set.
Inseparability	Consumer is involved in production. Centralized mass production is difficult.
Perishability	Services cannot be inventoried.
Heterogeneity	Standardization and quality are difficult to control.

In developing a service marketing strategy, many firms consider the following seven areas:

1. Marketing should occur at all levels, from the marketing department to the point where the service is provided.
2. Wherever possible, establishment of direct contact with the customers.
3. Using only high-quality personnel for marketing job.
4. Creation of loyalty among existing customers.
5. Ensuring quick resolution of problems faced by customers.
6. Provision of improved services at lower cost.
7. Branding of services offered.

MARKETING MIX

Service Mix

Goods can be defined in terms of their physical attributes, but services cannot be because they are intangible. But there are also tangibles (facilities, communications) associated with a service. These tangible elements help to form a part of the product and are often the only aspect of a service that can be viewed prior to purchase, which is why marketers must pay close attention to associated tangibles and make sure that they are consistent with the selected image of the service product.

Price Mix

Pricing of services can help smoothen the fluctuations of demand. Given the perishability of service products, this is an important function. A higher price may be used to reduce demand during peak periods, and a lower price may be used to stimulate demand during slack periods. For example, if a room in a hotel is not rented out or if there are vacant seats in a bus, the potential income is lost permanently. The concessional charge allowed for telephone calls in the night proves the stimulation of demand during off-peak period.

Requirement for advance payment is another feature in pricing of service products. This is also related to the perishability of the services.

Negotiated price In many of the service industries, the prices are settled after negotiations. For example, the price for management consultancy services is negotiated and fixed.

Bids for high-price services Bidding is very common in the case of some specialized high-price services. For example, when a building is to be constructed, tenders are invited or when an individual (consumer) wants to have his house painted, he is likely to ask for bids or quotations.

Physical Distribution Mix

Distribution for services is usually simpler and more direct than channels of distribution for goods.

Channel for services The following kinds of middlemen are found in the channel of distribution of services.

Agents for example, travel agents, employment agents, and insurance agents are at par with agent middlemen who do not take a title.

Wholesalers and retailers   The actual service may not be easily transferable as the products could be transferred. Still, tangible representations of the services are transferable, for example, the transfer of shares. This type of channel is often found in cases where a contract exists as a tangible representation of the service.

The merchant middlemen dealing in services are rare. When an organization contracts for a chartered flight and then sells space to others, it is acting as a merchant middleman because it is now the temporary owner of the services. In India, electricity was bought and distributed by some agencies in the past.

Some service firms may market on a wholesale basis. For example, many transporting agencies undertake to transport goods although they do not own any vehicle. The consumer actually has no contract with the firm that actually produces the services, namely the transport company.

There are certain factors that prevent easy selection of a good channel in the marketing of services. Some of these factors are discussed below:

1. *Geographical area*   The seller of a service can reach only a limited area mainly because of the fact that he could employ only a few agencies. Banking institutions have come to realize the importance of this fact in recent years. Accordingly, they have initiated innovations in the distribution of banking services.

2. *Limited view of marketing*   Because of the nature of their product, many service firms depend mainly on population growth to expand their sales. It is not the increase in the size of population that matters but it is really the expanding needs of a growing population that is important.

3. *Lack of competition*   Many services in the past faced only very little competition. Most of them are monopolies even today. The lack of competition is not conducive to innovative marketing.

However, the scene is changing nowadays, and banks, financial institutions, etc. are facing stiff competition.

4. *Lack of creative management* Most of the services are necessary and "consumer orientation" is still not a powerful ingredient in the marketing of service. This leads to inaction and makes the service firms inert.

5. *No fear for obsolescence* Most services, because of their intangibility are not greatly subject to obsolescence. This is definitely an advantage. But it led many firms to be slow in their approach to marketing.

Promotion Mix

Promotion mix is definitely an important aspect of marketing mix for services. The intangibility makes it difficult to use of different media of advertising. Service advertising should thus emphasize tangible cases that will help consumers to understand and evaluate the service. For example, hotels may stress their physical facilities—clean, hygienic room facilities, etc.

Personal selling is potentially powerful in services because this form of promotion lets consumers and sales people to interact. Sales personnel can be trained to use this opportunity to reduce customer uncertainty, give reassurance, reduce dissonance and promote the reputation of the organization.

Sales promotions, such as contests, are feasible for service firms, but other types of promotions are more difficult to implement. For instance, a service can neither be displayed nor can it give free samples.

Consumers tend to value word-of-mouth communications more than company-sponsored communications.

More stress on consumer benefits In the promotion of tangible goods, it is possible to elaborate the product features. Convincing is easier either by using a brand name or by stressing the deviations from a competing product. This is obviously not possible in the case of services. For example, it is really difficult for two airways to promote the services in terms of same benefits to the buyer.

Importance of personal selling Like the tangible products, a few services can be sold by mail or through vending machines. But in many cases detailed explanations are often necessary. For example, in the case of a doctor or lawyer, detailed explanations to their clients are required. Further, these services develop into a continuing relationship. Very often price negotiations are necessary. Marketing of life insurance services is an apt example in this regard. All these confirm that personal selling is very important in the marketing of services.

Marketing research for service industries The importance of marketing information and marketing research is well recognized in transport services. When a new line is to be opened, the authorities do obtain feasibility report including the details covering how many passengers are likely to use the line, the quantity of goods that would be transported, etc. Without obtaining these details, it is not worthwhile for any service business to enter the field.

The concept of modern marketing was not fully adopted in the field of service marketing in the past. However, there are signs that the marketing concept is beginning to be applied now. The banks, insurance companies and airlines are appointing managers exclusively to look after their marketing problems. New services are appearing fast, and almost continually. The varied services rendered by commercial banks at present testify to this aspect.

REVIEW QUESTIONS

I. Short-answer questions:

1. What do you mean by services marketing?
2. State the characteristics of services.
3. What are called services?
4. Discuss the types of services.

II. Essay-type questions:

1. What is meant by services? How services are important?
2. What are the important characteristics of services?
3. What are the differences between services and products?
4. Write an essay on classification of the services.
5. Explain the marketing strategies for marketing services.

18

RURAL MARKETING

MEANING

Rural marketing involves the process of developing, pricing, promoting, distributing rural specific products and a service leading to exchange between rural and urban market, which satisfies consumer demand and also achieves organizational objectives. It is a two-way marketing process wherein the transaction can be:

1. Urban to rural It involves the selling of products and services by urban marketers in rural areas. These include pesticides, FMCG products, consumer durables, etc.

2. Rural to urban Here, a rural producer sells his produce in the urban market. This may not be direct. There generally are middlemen, agencies, government cooperatives, etc. who sell fruits, vegetables, grains, pulses and others.

3. Rural to rural These include selling of agricultural tools, cattle, carts and others to another village in its proximity.

CHARACTERISTICS OF RURAL MARKETS

The rural market of India consists of about 65 per cent of the population of the country spread over nearly 630000 villages.

Rural markets may be considered as the nerve centres of the economic, social and cultural activities of the rural life of the country. It is scattered and widespread into many villages and unlike the urban market not confined to a handful of metros, cosmopolitan cities and towns. The demand for products including consumer non-durables and durables are seasonal and therefore uneven in a year.

Significance of Rural Markets

1. Increase in population and hence increase in demand.
2. Increase in literacy and educational level and resultant inclination to sophisticated lives by the rural folk.
3. Inflow of foreign remittances and foreign-made goods into rural areas.
4. The general rise in the level of prosperity has appeared to have resulted in two dominant shifts in the rural consuming system. One is the conspicuous consumption of consumer durables by almost all segments of rural consumers. The second is the obvious preference for branded goods than non-branded goods of rural origin.

Features of Indian Rural Markets

- *Large, diverse and scattered market* The rural market in India is large and scattered into a number of regions. There may be less number of shops available to market products.

- *Major income of rural consumers — agriculture* Rural prosperity is tied with agricultural prosperity. In the event of a crop failure, the income of the rural masses is directly affected.

- *Standard of living and rising disposable income of the rural customers* It is known that a majority of the rural population lives below the poverty line and has a low literacy rate, low per capital income, societal backwardness, low savings etc. but the new tax structure, good monsoon, government regulation on pricing has created disposable incomes. Today the rural customer spends money to get value and is aware of the happening around him.

○ *Traditional outlook* Villages develop slowly and have traditional outlook. Change is a continuous process but most rural people accept change gradually. This is gradually changing due to literacy, especially in the youth who have begged to change the outlook in the villages.

○ *Rising literacy levels* It is documented that approximately 45 per cent of the rural Indians are literate. Hence, awareness has increased and the farmers are well-informed about the world around them. They are also educating themselves on the new technology around them and aspiring for a better lifestyle.

○ *Diverse socio-economic background* Due to dispersion of geographical areas and uneven land fertility, rural people have disparate socio-economic background, which ultimately affects the rural market.

○ *Infrastructure facilities* The infrastructure facilities like cemented roads, warehouses, communication system and financial facilities are inadequate in rural areas. Hence, physical distribution is a challenge to marketers who have found innovative ways to market their products. As part of a planned economic development, the government is making continuous efforts towards rural development. In this age of liberalization, privatization and globalization, rural market offers a big attraction to the marketers to explore markets that are untapped.

RURAL MARKET ENVIRONMENT

The rural marketing environment is complex and is changing continuously. The marketing organization should foresee and adopt strategies to changing requirements in the market. An adaptive organization that makes its effective marketing plans and its own strategies or a creative one will prosper and create opportunities in the changing environment. Rural marketing environment changes will be in the area of:

- Social changes
- Economic changes
- Ethical changes
- Political changes
- Physical changes
- Technological changes

Social Changes

The social changes consist of 3 factors:

1. *Sociological factors* Consumer society or the community is important. The consumers' lifestyle is influenced by the social set-up. The social constitution and changes influence customer habits, tastes and lifestyles.

2. *Anthropological factors* The regional cultures and sub-cultures and living patterns influence advertising, sales promotion, selling strategies and packaging. The consumers in East India have different tastes.

3. *Psychological factors* Consumer behaviour, attitudes, personality and mental make-ups are unique. The study of behaviour is vital to evolve marketing mix.

Economic Forces/changes

This force consists of three stages:

1. *Competition* A good and healthy competition brings in good and overall improvement in economic activities. It also brings good quality, quantity and prices.

2. *Consumers* The consumers today are quite knowledgeable and choose. Their progress and well-being should be the aim of any economic activity.

3. *Price*   Pricing is a delicate issue, which should be market-friendly, not too high or too little. The marketer has to keep in mind to get decent returns on investment and efforts of procedures and marketers.

Ethical Changes

Business minus ethical values brings degeneration. In the long run, it brings problems. Non-standardization, adulteration, exploitation and falsification are the main ethical issues in business organizations.

Political Changes

The government policies towards trade and commerce, internal taxation, external levies and preferential treatments have profound influence on the marketing strategies.

Physical Changes

The infrastructure availability for movement and storage of goods play a significant role in the physical distribution of goods and in reaching the consumers.

Technological Changes

The fast changing science technologies give a cutting edge to the marketing products. The change of processes reduces manufacturing, packaging and handling cost of products. The changes warrant changes in marketing, inputs and strategies. The capital is made to work faster and harder. So is the case with the marketer. He has to use these new marketing tools and facilities in designing and implementing his marketing strategies, which are adaptive to the changing environment and ensure success.

PROBLEMS IN RURAL MARKETING

The major problems faced by manufacturing and marketing men in rural areas are described below.

i. *Underdeveloped people and underdeveloped market*   Agricultural technology has tried to develop the people and market in rural areas. Unfortunately the impact of the technology is not felt uniformly throughout the country. In addition, the farmers with small agricultural land holdings have also been unable to take advantage of the new technology. Thus the rural markets by and large are characterized by underdeveloped people and consequently underdeveloped markets.

ii. *Lack of proper physical communication facilities*   Nearly 50 percent of the villages in the country do not have roads. Hence the distribution efforts put in by a manufacturer prove expensive and sometimes of no consequence. To be effective, the products have to be physically moved to the places of consumption or places of purchase.

iii. *Media for rural communication*   Among the mass media at some point of time, say, in the late 1950s or early 1960s, radio was considered to be a potential medium for communication to the rural people. This has been extensively used to diffuse agricultural technology to rural areas.

iv. *Many languages and dialects*   Even assuming that media are available for communication or the company commissions its own media vans, the number of languages and dialects vary widely form state to state, region to region and probably from district to district.

v. *Hierarchy of markets*   The rural consumers have identified marketplaces for different items of their requirements. Thus, depending upon the purchase habits of rural people, the distribution network for different commodities has to be different. The innumerable problems mentioned above can be classified into the following categories:

- Consumer motivation and buying habits
- Location and degree of demand
- Dealer availability, attitude and motivation
- Mass communication media

- Logistics, storage, transport and handling
- Marketing organization and staff

Any strategy for rural marketing should take the above problems into account, so that the investments made are easily recovered.

REVIEW QUESTIONS

I. Short-answer questions:

1. Define rural marketing.
2. State the benefits of rural marketing
3. Why we need rural marketing?
4. What are the characteristics of rural marketing?

II. Essay-type questions:

1. Explain the features of rural marketing.
2. Explain the rural market environment.
3. What are the problems of rural marketing?
4. Explain the significance of rural marketing.

19

RETAILING

Retail marketing involves managing marketing activity in the retail sector. Retailing is where the purchase is intended to be consumed by customers through personal, family or household use, and involves 1) retail stores or 2) non-store retailing. Retail stores include the large mixed retailing department and variety stores: hypermarkets, superstores and supermarkets, discount sheds, traditional speciality shops, etc. Non-store retailing is the selling of goods or services outside the confines of a retail facility through mail order, in-home retailing or increasingly via e-commerce. The growth of the Internet and dot.com businesses has increased the use of direct marketing by retailers, many of which do not require retail stores.

DEFINITION

According to the report of the Definition Committee, America, "Retailing includes all activities incidental to selling to the ultimate consumer".

In the words of William J.Stanton, "A retailer or a retail store is a business enterprise which sells primarily to the ultimate consumers for non-business use".

Retailers purchase products for the purposes of reselling them to consumers in order to make a profit. Mail order and automatic vending are also classified as a part of retailing. Retailers provide 1) place utility, by having products where consumers want to buy them; 2) time utility, by trading at times when consumers want to buy; 3) possession utility, by facilitating transfer of ownership or use of products to consumers; and 4) form utility, retail services such as hairdressers, dry cleaners or restaurants, etc.

Retail stores tend to cluster together in order to attract sufficient customer traffic, in traditional town centres (central business district) locations, suburban shopping centre, edge-of-town, on retail parks or in retail villages. The standard categories of retailing include:

1. Food and grocery
2. Men's and women's wear
3. Children's wear
4. Footwear and leather goods
5. Chemist/druggist
6. Books and greetings cards
7. CTN (confectionery, news and tobacco)
8. Furniture, carpets and soft furnishings
9. Toys
10. Music and computer games
11. Jewellery
12. Off-license beverages
13. Electrical (appliances, brown and white goods)
14. Hardware and DIY (do-it-yourself)
15. Mixed retail business

Also included are:

1. Restaurants, cafes and catering
2. Mail order
3. Hotels

4. In-home retailing
5. Automatic vending
6. Banking and financial services
7. Telemarketing

RETAIL VS WHOLESALE

At this point it is essential to understand the subtle, but critical, difference between retail and wholesale. This is because the differences in buying motives are at the root of market segmentation. We all buy goods and services from different shops for our personal consumption. Thus retailing involves all activities that contribute to selling goods and services to the ultimate consumers for their personal consumption. Thus, unlike in wholesale, the focus is on the individual buyer and the goal of the buyer is either his/her personal or family's satisfaction from the consumption of the purchased item. Typically, the unit of purchase is smaller than is the case in wholesale purchasing. Hence the retailer's task is to focus on understanding the needs of this individual buyer and make the experience of buying and consumption a satisfying one.

The purpose of wholesale sales is just the opposite of retail sale. Here, the wholesaler sells to individuals or organizations for their business use. There are firms that are engaged in both retail and wholesale of the same product. Consider, for example, mobile phone company like Orange or Airtel sells a cell phone connection and airtime to a college student, it is retailing for his/her personal use. But if the same company sell in bulk to a firm for business purpose, then it is wholesaling. This is applicable to products of other categories also.

CHARACTERISTICS OF RETAILING

1. There is direct end-user interaction in retailing.
2. It is the only point in the value chain that provides a platform for promotions.

3. Sales at the retail level are generally in smaller unit sizes.
4. There are a larger number of retail business units to meet the needs of geographical coverage and population density.
5. In most retail businesses, services are as important as core products.

CRITICAL SUCCESS FACTORS FOR RETAILERS

The following are the critical success factors for retailers:

1. Maintaining low cost of operations.
2. Investing in appropriate and cost-effective technology.
3. Focusing on customer service and loyalty.
4. Building a reliable supply chain and logistics systems.
5. Making adequate capital investments.
6. Efficient human resource training and retention.
7. Creating and nurturing private label brands.
8. Reducing shrinkage and pilferage.

RETAIL STORES

1. Speciality Stores

Speciality stores, as the name implies, carry a narrow product line with a deep assortment within that line. Typical examples are jewellery stores like Tanishq Chennai, Mumbai and New Delhi, watch stores and garment or apparel stores like In Style and Chirag Din in Mumbai, sporting goods stores, book stores and so on. These stores can be further sub-classified on the basis of the degree of narrowness in their product lines.

Consider the example of garments. A store like Shopper's Stop that retails readymade garments for the family is called a single-line store. A Raymonds showroom that retails only men's clothing and accessories is known as a limited-line store and stores that retail designer clothes for men like Chirag Din, Louis Phillip and Van Heusen are known as super speciality stores.

According to some marketing theoreticians, the future scenario belongs to super speciality stores as they provide increasing opportunities for market segmentation, focused marketing and creation of brand equity. The trend is already gaining ground in the Indian market, particularly in the clothing and fashion goods industry, be it products for men, women, teenagers or children.

2. Department Stores

A department store carries several product lines, invariably all that is required by a typical household. These lines include food, clothing, appliances and other household goods, home furnishings, gifts and curios. In a typical department store, each product line is managed independently by specialist buyers or merchandisers. In India, these stores are still at the introduction phase and they are mainly located in metros like Mumbai, Delhi and Chennai and other cities like Bangalore and Hyderabad. For example, Reliance outlets.

Department stores are believed to be in the decline phase of the retail life cycle, mainly because of increased rivalry among them. Increasing competition from other types of retail stores like discount stores; and major demographic changes in cities are making shopping less pleasurable. However, these stores are fighting for survival and have accordingly evolved several strategies. Some have regular and weekend discount sales, private brands of their own to enable lowest of operations, changed their interiors, created boutique corners, expanded to new residential areas and added several new services. Cheque encashment, return or exchange without any questions, mail order services and even valet parking are just some of the new services, which a department store offers to its customers.

3. Supermarket

This is a large, low cost, low margin, high volume, self-service operation, designed to serve the customers' need for food, laundry and household maintenance products. Much of the future development is likely to take place in this type of retail outlet. This is largely because customers will have very little time to shop around. With more women being employed, shopping around or even just buying from a corner shop is going to reduce. Another reason is that the customers are more assured of product quality and freshness when they buy for their requirements from a store like FoodLand. Moreover, the wide range of product mix carried by these stores make them their favourite retail outlet.

4. Convenience Stores

These are generally food stores that are much smaller in size than supermarkets. They are conveniently located near residential areas and have long hours of operations, seven days a week, and carry a limited line of high turnover convenience products. In the Indian context, the old and faithful street corner grocery store or cold storage or food stores are called as convenience stores. These stores serve a very useful purpose. Due to a high degree of personalized service and home delivery these stores are very useful especially to housewives. They need not have to carry purchases back home or have to wait at the store. Typically, she hands over her weekly or monthly requirements lists to the owner, who then organizes the delivery. Since these stores are open long hours, around 10 to 12 hours everyday, they occupy a niche position in retail marketing. In India, convenience stores have been in existence for a long time.

5. Discount Stores

As the name implies, discount stores are the ones that sell standard merchandise at lower prices than conventional merchants or stores by accepting lower margins but pushing for higher sales volumes. A true discount store has four characteristics:

i.   It regularly sells its goods at a discounted price.
ii. It carries national or reputed brands to enhance its image.

iii. It keeps its operational costs to the minimum by emphasizing on self-service and "no frills" interiors.

iv. Its location tends to be in low rent areas, and it draws customers from even distant locations.

The best known and the biggest discount store in the US is Wal-Mart. Today Big Bazaar and several other hypermarkets are delivering merchandise to customers.

NON-STORE RETAILERS

Although more than 80 percent of retail marketing is done through retail stores, non-store retailing is also gradually gaining popularity in the Indian market. Some of these non-store retailing options are:

1. Automatic Vending Machines

These are very common in Europe and North America for selling food products, soft drinks, newspaper, candy and cigarettes. These are coin-operated machines and are found in all those areas that have a high density of consumer traffic. An extension of these is automatic tellers in banks, which allow customers to perform any banking transaction, 24 hours a day and seven days a week. Today we see automatic vending machines selling hot beverages, soups, soft drink, chocolates and magazines at major airports and commercial centres in the country. Since automatic vending machines provide freedom to the customer, these are likely to be more commonly used in the future.

2. Direct Selling

Direct selling is another form that is re-emerging. The predecessors to modern direct selling are the itinerant peddlers who sold their goods at the customer's doorstep. Today, direct selling is taking goods like cosmetics and personal hygiene products to homes and offices. In India, the originator of this concept is Eureka Forbes, who was the first to sell its vacuum cleaners on a door-to-door basis. Though this is an expensive alternative, it has been preferred to store retailing primarily because the firm is able to compete more effectively in the market-place without having to give in to the trade's demands.

3. Buying Services

A buying service is a store-less retailer, serving specific client groups, usually employers of large organizations like companies, governments, universities, hospitals etc. The organization's members become members of the buying service and are entitled to buy from a selective list of retailers who have agreed to give discounts to the buying service members. Several consumer durable companies like TVS Whirlpool, Sony Orson, Bajaj Electricals and auto dealers like Auto riders have had such arrangements with major industrial groups and universities.

ISSUES IN RETAILING

1. The use of franchising: Many brands are franchised to other businesses that run stores or retail merchandise carrying the well-known franchised brand.
2. The type of locations: Expensive city centre prime pitches, secondary sites, edge-of-town retail parks or free-standing super stores.
3. Property portfolio ownership: Whether to acquire (own) or rent sites, with the associated financial implications.
4. Product assortment (Mix) decisions: How far to extend or diversify.
5. Retail brand positioning, store image and in-store atmospherics: Retailers devote significant attention and resources to develop differentiated and desirable brand identities.
6. Scrambled merchandising: The addition of unrelated products to the product mix.

7. The use of retail technology: It includes inventory management tools, CRM systems and loyalty schemes and in-store displays.

8. Channel coordination: How to harness the possibilities of e-commerce alongside more traditional channels.

9. Regulation: Increasing government regulation over monopoly ownership.

10. Supply chain power: The balance of power and cooperation between retailers and their suppliers.

11. Global retailing: more and more retail companies are acquiring businesses in other countries or spreading their brands into new territories through organic growth.

REVIEW QUESTIONS

I. Short-answer questions:

1. What do you understand by retailing?
2. What do you understand by retailer?
3. Enumerate the services rendered by retailers?
4. What is a departmental store?
5. What is meant by multiple shops?
6. Discuss the features of mail order houses.
7. Discuss the features of super market.
8. Define retailing.
9. What do you mean by itinerant retailers?
10. What do you mean by fixed shop retailing and give examples?

II. Essay-type questions:

1. Enumerate the services rendered by retailers?
2. Explain the various types of retailers and their functions.
3. What is a departmental store? Discuss the features, merits and demerits?
4. What are the trends in retailing? Discuss.
5. What marketing decisions are faced by retailers?
6. What are the types of small retailing?
7. What are the types of large scale retailing?

20

E-MARKETING

Marketing or electronic marketing refers to the application of marketing principles and techniques via electronic media and more specifically the Internet. The terms e-marketing, Internet marketing and online marketing, are frequently interchanged, and can often be considered synonymous.

MEANING

E-marketing is the process of marketing a brand using the Internet. It includes both direct response marketing and indirect marketing elements and uses a range of technologies to help connect businesses to their customers.

E-marketing encompasses all the activities a business conducts via the worldwide web with the aim of attracting new business, retaining current business and developing its brand identity.

E-marketing can be considered to be equivalent to Internet marketing. E-marketing is sometimes considered to have a broader scope since it refers to digital media such as web, e-mail and wireless media, but also includes management of digital customer data and electronic customer relationship management systems (E-CRM systems).

IMPORTANCE OF E-MARKETING

When implemented correctly, the return on investment (ROI) from e-marketing can far exceed that of traditional marketing strategies.

Whether you're a "bricks and mortar" business or a concern operating purely online, the Internet is a force that cannot be ignored. It can be a means to reach literally millions of people every year. It is at the forefront of a redefinition of way businesses interact with their customers.

The e-marketing has number of benefits over traditional marketing such as reach, scope etc. which are discussed indetail.

Reach

The nature of the internet means businesses now have a truly global reach. While traditional media costs limit this kind of reach to huge multinationals, e-marketing opens up new avenues for smaller businesses, on a much smaller budget, to access potential consumers from all over the world.

Scope

Internet marketing allows the marketer to reach consumers in a wide range of ways and enables them to offer a wide range of products and services. E-marketing includes, among other things, information management, public relations, customer service and sales. With the range of new technologies becoming available all the time, this scope can only grow.

Interactivity

Whereas traditional marketing is largely about getting a brand's message out there, e-marketing facilitates conversations between companies and consumers. With a two-way communication channel, companies can feed off of the responses of their consumers, making them more dynamic and adaptive.

Immediacy

Internet marketing is able to, in ways never before imagined, provide an immediate impact. Imagine you're reading your favourite magazine. You see a double-page advertisement for some new product or service, maybe BMW's latest luxury sedan or Apple's latest iPod offering. With this kind of traditional media, it is not that easy for the consumer, to take the step from hearing about a product to actual acquisition.

With e-marketing, it's easy to make that step as simple as possible, meaning that within a few short clicks you could have booked a test drive or ordered the iPod. And all of this can happen regardless of normal office hours. Effectively, Internet marketing makes business hours 24 hours per day, 7 days per week for every week of the year. By closing the gap between providing information and eliciting a consumer reaction, the consumer's buying cycle is speeded up and advertising spend can go much further in creating immediate leads.

Demographics and Targeting

Generally speaking, the demographics of the Internet are a marketer's dream. Internet users, considered as a group, have greater buying power and could perhaps be considered as a population group skewed towards the middle-classes.

Buying power is not all though. The nature of the Internet is such that its users will tend to organise themselves into far more focused groupings. Savvy marketers who know where to look can quite easily find access to the niche markets they wish to target. Marketing messages are most effective when they are presented directly to the audience most likely to be interested. The Internet creates the perfect environment for niche marketing to targeted groups.

Closed Loop Marketing

Closed Loop Marketing requires the constant measurement and analysis of the results of marketing initiatives. By continuously tracking the response and effectiveness of a campaign, the marketer can be far more dynamic in adapting to consumers' wants and needs.

With e-marketing, responses can be analysed in real-time and campaigns can be tweaked continuously. Combined with the immediacy of the Internet as a medium, this means that there's minimal advertising spend wasted on less than effective campaigns. Maximum marketing efficiency from e-marketing creates new opportunities to seize strategic competitive advantages. The combination of all these factors results in an improved ROI and ultimately, more customers, happier customers and an improved bottom line.

ADVANTAGES OF E-MARKETING

The main advantages of e-marketing are:

1. The physical costs of e-marketing are substantially less than direct marketing.
2. E-marketing encourages click through to a website where the offer can be redeemed immediately this increases the likelihood of an immediate, impulsive response.
3. Lead times for producing creative and the whole campaign lifecycle tends to be shorter than traditional media.
4. It is easier and cheaper to personalize e-marketing than for physical media and also than for a website.
5. It is relatively easy and cost effective to test, analyse and compare through e-marketing.
6. Through combining e-marketing with other direct media which can be personalized such as direct mail,

mobile messaging or web personalisation, campaign response can be increased as the message is reinforced by different media.

DISADVANTAGES OF E-MARKETING

The main disadvantages of E-marketing evident are:

1. Difficulty of getting messages delivered through different internet service providers (ISPs), corporate firewalls and webmail systems.
2. Difficulty of displaying the creative as intended within the in-box of different email reading systems.
3. Email recipients are most responsive when they first subscribe to an email. It is difficult to keep them engaged.
4. Recipients will have different preferences for email offers, content and frequency which affect engagement and response. These have to be managed through communications preferences.
5. Although email offers great opportunities for targeting, personalisation and more frequent communications, additional people and technology resources are required to deliver these.

REVIEW QUESTIONS

I. Short-answer questions:

1. What is e-marketing?
2. What is closed loop marketing?

II. Essay-type questions:

1. What are the benefits of e-marketing?
2. What are the differences between e-marketing and traditional marketing?
3. Why e-marketing is necessary?
4. What are the merits and demerits of e-marketing?

21

MARKETING INFORMATION SYSTEM

"A marketing information system (MIS) consists of people, equipment and procedures to gather, sort, analyse, evaluate and distribute needed, timely and accurate information to marketing decision makers."

MIS begins and ends with marketing managers. First, it interacts with these managers to assess information needs. Next, it develops needed information from internal company data, marketing intelligence activities, marketing research and information analysis. Finally, the MIS distributes information to managers in the right form to help them to make better marketing decisions.

ASSESSING INFORMATION NEEDS

"A good marketing information system provides the managers with the information really they need at the right time.

Some managers will ask for whatever information they can get without thinking carefully about what they really need. Too much information can be as harmful as too little. Other managers may omit things they ought to know or may not know to ask for some types of information they should need.

For example, managers might need to know that a competitor plans to introduce a new product during the coming year. Because they do not know about the new product, they do not think to ask about it.

Sometimes the company cannot provide the needed information either because it is not available or because of MIS limitations. For example, a brand manager might want to know how competitors will change their advertising budgets next year and how these changes will affect industry market shares. The information on planned budgets probably is not available. Even if it is, the company's MIS may not be advanced enough to forecast resulting changes in market shares.

Finally, the company must decide whether the benefits of having additional information are worth the cost of providing it, and both value and cost are often hard to assess.

DEVELOPING INFORMATION

The information needed by marketing managers can be obtained from internal data, marketing intelligence and marketing research. The information analysis system then processes this information to make it more useful for managers.

Internal Data

Many companies build extensive internal databases,— "computerized collection of information obtained from data sources within the company".

Information in the database can come from many sources. The accounting department prepares financial statements and keeps detailed records of sales, costs and cash flows, manufacturing reports on production schedules, shipments and inventories. The sales force reports on retailer reactions and competitor activities. The marketing department furnishes information on customer demographics, psychographics and buying behaviour. Research studies done for one department may provide useful information for several others.

Internal databases also present some problems. Because internal information was collected for other purposes, it may be incomplete or in the wrong form for making marketing decisions. For example, sales and cost data used by the accounting department for preparing financial statements must be adapted for use in evaluating product, sales force or channel performance. In addition, a large company produces mountains of information and keeping track of it all is difficult.

Marketing Intelligence

Marketing intelligence is the systematic collection and analysis of publicly available information about competitors and developments in the marketing environment.

Its goal is to improve strategic decision making, assess and track competitor's actions and provide early warning of opportunities and threats. The marketing intelligence system determines what intelligence system is needed, collects it by searching the environment, and delivers it to the marketing managers.

Marketing intelligence can be gathered from many sources. Much intelligence can be collected from the company's own personnel executives, engineers, purchasing agents and the sales force. The company must make them to realize their importance as intelligence gatherers, train them to spot new developments and interact with them on an ongoing basis, and urge them to report intelligence back to the company.

Competitors themselves may reveal information through their annual reports, business publications, press releases, web pages, etc.

Finally companies buy intelligence information from outside suppliers ranging from marketing research firms to consultants who specialize in competitive intelligence.

Some companies set up an office to collect and circulate marketing intelligence.

Marketing Research

Marketing research system is the third component of the MIS. Marketing research offers special information on request when the marketing executives encounter typical marketing problems demanding unique information for solving those problems. MR studies are project -oriented. Mostly they involve studies relating to buyer behaviour, product or brand preferences, product or brand usage, advertising awareness, sales promotion, physical distribution, dealer behaviour, competition and so on.

Management science or operations research is the latest addition to the marketing information system. OR analysts help marketing executives in decision making in such areas as new product development, marketing mix planning, sales, call time allocation, media selection, queuing problems in retail institutions, location of warehouse, inventory control, and so on.

Marketing information system stands between the marketing environment and marketing decision-makers. Marketing data flows the environment to the marketing information systems. Marketing data is processed by the system and converted into marketing information flow, which goes to the marketers for decision-making. Plans and programmes are based on this information flow. Then we have marketing communication flow back to the environment.

In marketing planning, marketers select, screen, synthesis and combine internal and external information inputs in order to recognize the firm's relation to its customers, its competitors and its environment in general. Marketing decisions influence external and internal environment. The results are compared with objective or standards. Feedback provides corrective actions and offers further information for revising and modifying decisions.

IMPORTANCE OF MIS

In earlier days marketing and sales people just went out, met people and tried to sell something. This was enough in the past because it was a producer's market. Gradually, the problem of distribution became more and more complex.

Today, the producer has to face a lot of problems changing behaviours of consumers and competitors. Moreover to manage a business is to manage its future. Management is an ongoing process. Therefore for better management today, tomorrow and the days after, the management should know the information like:

i. Who are the customers and where do they live?
ii. What are the products needed by consumers?
iii. When do they insist on a particular product?
iv. When do they want the product?
v. How big is the market?
vi. Where the products are made available?

For answering these questions, the manufacturer requires plenty of information. That is why collection and analysis of timely information have become the major management function today. It is one of the facilitating functions, which smoothens marketing activities. In other words, marketing information provides light for a manufacturer to walk into the dark future without trembling legs.

There are a number of reasons for considering marketing information as the lifeblood of marketing they are as follows:

1. *Anticipation of consumer demand* Mass production and mass distribution in ever-expanding markets are based on anticipation of consumer demand. Under customer-oriented marketing approach, every marketer needs up-to-date knowledge about consumer needs and wants. In a dynamic economy, consumer tastes, fashions and liking are constantly changing. Without precise information on the nature, character and size of consumer demands, marketers will be simply groping in the dark. Decisions based upon hunches, guesswork, intuition or tradition cannot give desirable result in the modern economy. They must have the support of facts and figures.

2. *Complexity of marketing* Modern marketing process has become much more complex and elaborate. Ever-expanding markets and multinational's marketing activities require adequate market intelligence services. Hence, there is a systematic approach to organized information system. Marketing communications provide information *cues* in non-price competition through advertising and sales promotion.

3. *Significance of economic indicators* Forces of demand and supply are constantly changing. They determine prices and general market conditions. In a wider and complex economy, fluctuations in demand, supply and prices are tremendous. The marketers must have latest information on the changing trends of supply, demand and prices. For this purpose, they rely on the market reports and other market intelligence services. Economic indicators act as barometer indicating trend of prices and general economic conditions. Intelligent forecasting of the future is based on economic indices such as national income, population, price, money flow, growth rate, etc.

4. *Significance of competition* Modern markets are competitive. A market cannot make decision in a competitive vacuum. Modern business is a many-sided game in which rivals and opponents continuously try to formulate strategies to gain advantage over one another. Predicting the behaviour of one's competitors and outguessing of the competitor will need the services of marketing intelligence. A market cannot survive under keen competition without up-to-date market information particularly regarding the nature, character and size of competition to be met.

5. *Development of science and technology* Ever-expanding markets create conditions that lead to technical progress. In most cases, the market was the mother of inventions. The energy crisis since 1974 has given a great encouragement to discover other alternative sources of energy, e.g. atomic energy, solar energy and so on. Modern marketer must be innovative. "Innovate or perish" is the slogan in the existing marketing environment. But innovations are based on information given by research technological developments. New products, new markets, new processes and new techniques are based on facts and figures.

6. *Consumerism* In an ever-widening market, we do have a communication gap between consumers/users and marketers. This gap is responsible for unrealistic marketing plans and programmes. Many marketers are isolated from day-to-day marketing realities. This has led to consumer dissatisfaction. Consumerism and increasing consumer grievances indicate that products do not match consumer needs and desires and marketers have no up-to-date knowledge of real and precise consumer demand.

7. *Marketing planning* We are living in the age of planning and programming. Our plans and programmes are based upon information supplied by economic research (economic forecasts) and marketing research (marketing forecasts), which provide the requisite information about the future economic and marketing conditions. For instance sales forecast is the base of production plan, marketing plan, financial plan and budgets. Marketing information alone can interrelate and coordinate the product and user/consumer demand so that both supply and demand can travel on the same wavelength.

8. *Information explosion* We live in the midst of information explosion. Management has literally a flood of information knocking at its door. Computer and internet are the most immediate force behind the information explosion. Computer and electronic data processing equipment act as our rescue boats to face successfully the fantastic flow of information. The speed with which the computer can absorb process and reproduce large quantities of information is simply staggering. When a computer is effectively programmed, it can certainly add tremendously to the quality of information flow.

CHARACTERISTICS OF MIS

1. MIS is a consciously developed master plan for information flow. It is an ongoing process. It operates continuously.

2. We have best integration and coordination among the functional departments, executives and specialists such as systems analyst, programmer and computer expert.

3. We have some kind of data processing equipment usually operated electronically. Computer is the modern equipment for MIS.

4. MIS is future-oriented. It anticipates and prevents problems as well as it solves marketing problems. It is both preventive as well as a curative process in marketing.

5. The gathered data is processed with the help of management science or operations research techniques. Modern mathematical tools are available for problem solving in the field of marketing.

6. Systems analyst designs and operates the MIS through computers. Operations research analyst offers solutions to the marketing problem with the help of quantitative decision-making tools.

7. Management gets a steady flow of information on a regular basis—the right information, for the right people, at the right time and cost.

In a company operating under the marketing concept, we must have an organized set of producers, information handling routines and reporting techniques designed specially to meet the need for relevant information for making marketing decision. MIS is the answer to fulfill such a need for coordinated, systematic and continuous information gathering and processing. MIS project involves multi-disciplinary collaboration. Systems analysts have an advisory group made up of marketing, finance and accounts executives as well as operation research analysts, data processing experts, etc.

FUNCTIONS OF MIS

The Marketing Information System performs six functions, viz.,

1. Assembling of marketing data.
2. Processing, i.e., editing, tabulating and summarizing the data.
3. Analysing the data, i.e., filling out percentage, ratios, test of significance, etc.
4. Storage and retrieval, i.e., filing and indexing.
5. Evaluating regarding accuracy and reliability of data.
6. Dissemination or distribution of relevant and wanted information to decision makers.

All the above six functions can be brought down to three main stages, viz. 1) collection of market information 2) interpretation of information 3) dissemination of information

Collection of Market Information

The first stage of market intelligence function is gathering the information adequately, timely and relevant from the angle of marketers. Marketing executive gathers market information in many ways by tapping different sources of information collecting is the process of locating and tapping the sources of information. The different sources of market information can be divided into internal sources, external sources and market research.

i. *Internal sources of information* The internal sources of information are the records maintained by the marketing organization. They are financial records of sales, purchase, cash transactions, returns, etc. This information is helpful for the marketing executives to have sales analysis in terms of product, customer analysis and territorial analysis. The internal sources are:

Product analysis Product analysis is the study of actual position of different products. How they are received by the customers, its speed, i.e., slow or fast and causes of decline or rise over the past period.

Customer analysis Customer analysis helps to get classified information by income, age group preference to a particular brand and price range. This helps the marketer to shift his operating ability to those areas where there is necessity of stress to better the performance.

Territorial analysis Territorial analysis gives the break-up picture relating to an area. This helps to have a control over activities of sales forces (salesmen). Effort can be made to pad up (improve) the position in those areas where sales are declining and efforts can be made to maintain the market and extend the market in new areas.

ii. *External sources of information* The efficiency of a marketing firm can be judged not by comparing the internal records but by comparing the firm with others in the same line. The external sources are:

Trade associations and chambers of commerce Chambers of commerce and trade associations have their own publications. They may be monthlies or quarterlies. Even the regulated markets and cooperative societies have such useful publications.

Competitors The best source perhaps is that provided by rivals. The success of a business is getting the secrets of other business. Business tactics or strategies followed by rivals have got to be mastered. Competitors never let their secrets out. A wise marketer has many ways of getting the required information via the employees.

Government publication Different departments of Government of a Nation may be Central or State publish up-to-date information. In India departments of agriculture, statistics, industries and commerce, foreign trade, etc. have been disseminating the vital data to marketers. The examples are: RBI Bulletin, forward Market Bulletin, and Monthly Bulletin of Statistics, Planning Commission Reports, Reports of Export Promotion Councils, Census Reports and Indian Trade Journal, etc. The information given is up-to-date and authentic that helps the marketer to rely on such intelligence.

iii. *Other sources* There are a number of concerns who have taken it as their business to provide information in the form of articles, reports, facts, opinions, criticisms, etc. The best examples of this kinds are: Eastern Economists, Capital, Southern Economists, Commerce, Yojana, Indian Finance, etc. Even the newspapers like *Economic Times, Financial Express* are taken into account. The University Departments, Colleges and Research Centres are the good sources of rich information.

Interpretation of Information

Interpretation of information is the second stage of marketing information system. Collection of data is comparatively easier. However, interpretation is the crux of market information function. Interpretation of data refers to providing analysis of the information to arrive at certain generalizations. Much depends on the dynamic thinking capacity or creative mind of the marketer to have correct generalizations or arriving at correct and logical conclusions. Decision-making is based on interpreting the critical appraisal of the given facts, opinion or estimates. That is why interpretation of data can be called as crucial yet delicate process of creativity.

Dissemination of Market Information

Flow of information is as important as the flow of goods in the marketing system. Effective management of marketing information means not only systematic analysis but also providing or passing the information at different levels in the organization. The marketing executive who has arrived at certain conclusions in respect of the problems faced must communicate to the men of action. There must be a combination of thinking and doing. Thinking has value only when doing is followed.

KINDS OF MARKETING INFORMATION SYSTEM

There are three kinds of systems namely:

Marketing control system   It provides the management information relating to the trends and problems in the market as also the marketing opportunities. The system is useful for controlling the marketing cost and finding out reasons for poor sales.

Marketing planning system   It furnishes information required for future planning of products in a most convenient and intelligible form. The problems handled by this system are sales forecasting, promotional planning, credit management, etc.

Marketing research system   This is useful for analysing and solving current marketing problems. It measures characteristics of different types of customers and their behaviour. Marketing research handles problems concerning advertising, price, etc.

REVIEW QUESTIONS

I. Short-answer questions:

1. What is marketing information system?
2. What is marketing intelligence?
3. What is product analysis?
4. Name the types of sources of information.
5. Name some internal sources of information
6. What is marketing control system?
7. Name some external sources of information.

II. Essay-type questions:

1. Explain the importance of MIS
2. Explain the need of information in marketing.
3. "Information is the lifeblood of marketing"- explain.
4. What are the characteristics of MIS?
5. Explain the components of MIS.
6. Explain the functions of MIS.
7. What are the kinds of MIS.
8. What are the sources of information.
9. Explain the various sources of information.

22

CUSTOMER RELATIONSHIP MANAGEMENT

Effective marketing not only creates new and bigger markets, but also enables industries to reduce cost, create further demand and eventually achieve economies of scale. It is, therefore, essential that marketers keep a constant watch on the marketing horizon to spot the new challenges thrown up by the staggering pace of technological developments and various other changes in the marketing environment, and convert them into highly profitable marketing opportunities.

Customer Relationship Management (CRM) uses technology-enhanced customer interaction to shape appropriate marketing offers designed to nurture ongoing relationships with individual customers within an organization's target market.

Relationship marketing develops ongoing relationships with customers by focusing on maintaining links between marketing, quality and customer service amongst the "six markets" of relationship marketing—customer markets, influences, referral, employee recruitment, suppliers and internal markets within the business. The concept of CRM has grown out of relationship marketing.

According to Cram, relationship marketing is the consistent application of up-to-date knowledge about individual customers to product and service design, which is communicated interactively in order to develop a continuous and long term relationship between customers and suppliers that is mutually beneficial. The focus is on extracting more sales from existing customers through marketing activity, rather than marketing programmes designed to attract new customers.

The development of customer database, the decreasing costs of collecting, storing and using information, better information systems technology, plus the desire to build on-going relationships with existing customers, have led to the growth of interest in CRM. Database advances have enabled marketers to identify which customers they particularly want to keep and with whom to nurture on-going loyalty.

MEANING AND DEFINITION

CRM, a well-defined business strategy, is a fusion of a series of functions, skills, processes and technologies which together allows companies to more profitably manage (acquire and retain) customers as tangible assets.

CRM is a comprehensive approach for creating, maintaining and expanding customer relationship. It is the process of acquiring, retaining and partnering with selective customers to create superior value for the company and the customer.

Thus, CRM provides information on methodologies and software, and usually the Internet capabilities, which help an enterprise manage customer relationship in an organized way.

CRM is a business strategy that maximizes profitability, revenue and customer satisfaction by organizing around customer segments, fostering behaviour that satisfies customers and implementing customer-centric processes.

CRM is the process of managing all aspects of interaction a company has with its customers, including prospecting, sales and service. CRM applications attempt to provide insight into and improve the company/customer relationship by combining all these views of customer interaction into one picture.

EVOLUTION OF CRM

Initially, marketing was more focused on simple strategies that addressed the needs of all customers in general. This was called as mass marketing, where the concentration was on the total market rather than on a particular group of customers. But due to continuous growth in the markets and various changes occurring on a regular basis because of an increase in competition, the mass marketing strategies (and related products) no longer retained the interest of customers.

Customers started identifying their needs with specific niche products and companies. At this stage, companies started interacting with the customers to find out those specific needs. Later, products were produced accordingly giving rise to an interactive marketing system. But this interaction was mostly restricted to a few profitable and large customers.

Slowly, interactive marketing resulted in developing the products and improving them in the ever-changing market scenario for a limited time. Still, building a continuous relationship and sustaining the same was lacking and this led to continued brand switching by the customers. Again because of increasing globalization and competition, customers today have more options to choose from and companies need to provide more customized products/services on a continuous basis, if they want to retain their customers and survive in the market.

This is where customer relationship management has seen its rise, where an organization seeks to build close relationships with its current and potential customers. This type of marketing will help organizations in improving their customer satisfaction and loyalty, which in turn will help in customer retention, in bringing more profits to the organization.

GUIDELINES FOR SUCCESSFUL IMPLEMENTATION OF CRM

1. *Easing slowly into CRM implementation* The business needs have to be established first. Next companies need to establish a CRM project that has a short delivery period so that the project can be delivered in a short timeframe. It is better to opt for phased implementation of small individual projects than a mammoth one. This will ensure that there is adequate return on investment and that there is considerable cost reduction and efficiency.

2. *CRM package vs. business needs* It is important to ensure that the best balance is obtained between the CRM solution and the actual use of it. At most times, business organizations find that they are adjusting their business processes and goals to the CRM package and vice versa. An effort should be made to make use of the CRM tools to the best of its ability while at the same time accommodating business processes.

3. *Management involvement* CRM executives and the top management should be involved. Their participation is critical to the achievement of CRM goals and objectives. The CRM committee appointed or the CRM manager should actively participate in all aspects of the CRM implementation from its inception to the deployment. Responsibility should be given to the appropriate persons thereby ensuring that all the possible CRM benefits are availed of.

4. *Training* Training should be taken seriously. Since the implementation of CRM is a huge task, it is important to plan for individual training within the organization. Classroom training, expert training, etc. will enable the employees to possess the necessary skills required for the job. This is an important part of CRM implementation. Employees should be encouraged to provide feedback on how well the CRM training has gone and whether or not they need additional help.

5. *Implementing CRM* It should be ensured that the business is affected to the barest minimum. The effects of CRM implementation on the business must be analysed and employees must be prepared for the possible jolts. It is most important to focus on the process and allow the CRM tool to manage the process. It is also important to include the entire business even if the CRM project includes only one business unit.

6. *Future focus* Since the CRM implementation will bring with it new changes and new challenges, it is imperative that the resources at hand be used to deal adequately with possible change. It is important to focus on the possibility that changes will undoubtedly occur in future. Plans should be made keeping this in mind. Room should be provided for modifications and the possibility of plans going awry as well. The business should be well-equipped to deal with these changes.

7. *Getting feedback from users* Obtaining user feedback is essential as this can contribute to the success of the CRM project. It yields valuable information about CRM implementation's requirements, user acceptance, etc. While considering implementing the CRM strategy, the adherence to the above factors will go a long way in ensuring success. Getting CRM right will ensure that customer retention is secured, sales leads are followed and marketing is boosted.

After the execution of CRM the results need to be measured often, based on the methodology developed. It is important to ensure that current metrics are established. Both qualitative and quantitative measures should be adopted, after which the results need to be analysed and finally based on this, a methodology should be implemented.

Advantages of CRM

1. Provide better customer service
2. Increase customer revenues
3. Discover new customers

4. Cross-sell/up-sell products more effectively
5. Help sales staff close deals faster
6. Make call centres more efficient
7. Simplify marketing and sales processes

PROBLEMS WITH CRM

1. *Exorbitant costs* One of the problems with CRM is the huge investment that is needed to maintain a customer database. The additional expense comes because of the money needed for computer hardware, software, personnel, etc. The costs involved are enormous and most often than not, the resultant return on investment (ROI) from the CRM implementation fail to cover the costs involved. This leads to a negative feeling within the company about CRM and its so called successes, and ultimately results in CRM collapse.

2. *Inadequate focus on objectives* When starting off on a CRM strategy the objectives are clearly established and followed. Management and employees know fully well what is needed, to work towards organizational goals. The goals themselves are clearly laid out after meticulous planning. However, midway during the CRM implementation, when hard times hit, the organization loses sight of its goals and ultimately steers away from it. At times goals get interchanged and lose their importance. Companies find themselves work towards goals that are less important, forgetting the most important ones. This is one of the fundamental and most felt problem in CRM.

3. *Insufficient resources* Sometimes, in phased implementation of CRM, if conditions worsen within the company, organizations start lowering their budgets for the current phase. When funds are less, budgets are strained, and CRM starts failing midway. The most important aspect—that of maintaining consistency—is lost. Organizations fail to utilize the necessary resources for success and thus result in failure.

4. *Inappropriate metrics* Organizations have basically failed to use the right metrics. Failure to choose the right method of measurement and implementation is one of the chief reasons for CRM failure. Different metrics have to be employed for the calculation of different goals. Companies seldom pause to analyse which metric is needed for which element and ultimately use the wrong one. This results in faulty measurement and CRM disappointments.

5. *Complex systems* CRM packages can be highly complex, with vast amounts of intricacies. Sufficient training has to be given in order that the employees are able to comprehend and deal with the difficulties easily.

6. *Business needs most important* One of the chief mistakes companies make is to let the technology drive their CRM functionality. Companies that are endeavouring to go to the industry leaders, gain the technology needed and then apply it to the business problems only to find that it isn't solving any of them. Instead they need to analyse their business problems first and then find the appropriate CRM solution for it. This backwards step is responsible for CRM failure.

7. *No customer focus* An organization needs to motivate employees to be absolutely customer-centric. This involves tremendous effort on the part of the company. CRM problems arise because of employee reluctance to be more customer-focused. The result is a highly expensive customer strategy being adopted by the company in an effort to retain customers, with reluctant, unfocused employees implementing it.

8. *Slow returns* Another failure of CRM is its inability to provide quick returns on investment. Organizations have to wait for years before they see actual returns on their investment. Most experts view the low ROI as a major problem with CRM but fail to see that the long wait is just as difficult. Waiting for years to see their investments show results, tests patience and leads to both employees and management, slackening their efforts in the implementation. Most CRM problems can be mitigated, resolved and ultimately obliterated. What is most required is the ability to focus on the business needs, choose a CRM package that works towards it, employ the right resources and assume the right metrics. Adopting these measures would go a long way in alleviating CRM problems.

To ensure that CRM is effective, practices in a company must be assessed. Exponent, Merlin Stone, argues that robust CRM involves:

1. Analysis of the behaviour and value of different customers or customer groups and the development of an appreciation of what really are the customers' experiences of dealing with the company.

2. Planning activity and interactions with the customer in order to maximize the value of the customer base, focusing on retention, efficiency, acquisition and penetration of the customer.

3. Proposition development to ensure the customer's needs are met and new customers are attracted.

4. The use of information and technology to store customer information, facilitate customer engagement and enable CRM practices to flourish.

5. The recruitment, development, motivation and development of bespoke customer management personnel, not just in the company but also amongst suppliers and channel members.

6. Process management to ensure customer management personnel are operating effectively and are harnessed by the rest of the business.

7. Customer management activity, including targeting, enquiry management, welcoming of new or upgrading customers, understanding customer characteristics and issues, development of customers so that customers who require it receive a higher or different level of service, the managing of problems customers may have with the business and win-back activity to redress problems with lost customers.

8. Measurement of the value of the CRM function and personnel. All of the CRM activity should be

benchmarked against customer expectations, competitors' standards and industry best practice.

REVIEW QUESTIONS

I. Short-answer questions:

1. Define CRM.
2. Write short notes on the evolution of CRM.
3. What are the advantages of CRM.

II. Essay-type questions:

1. Write an essay on the process of CRM.
2. Discuss the methods involved in the successful implementation of CRM.
3. Explain the problems involved in the application of CRM.

GLOSSARY

Advertisement Any paid form of non-personal presentation and promotion of goods, services or ideas by an identified sponsor.

Agent middlemen Firms such as broker and manufacturer's representatives that find customers or negotiate contracts but do not take title to the merchandise.

Attitude A person's enduring favourable or. unfavourable cognitive evaluations, emotional feelings, and action tendencies

Behaviour segmentation Dividing buyers into groups on the basis of their knowledge, attitude, use, or response to a product.

Belief A descriptive thought that a person holds about something.

Brand A name, term, sign, symbol, or design, or a combination of them which is intended to identify the goods or services of one seller or group of sellers and to differentiate them from those of companies.

Brand mark A part of a brand which can be recognized but is not utterable, such as a symbol, design, or distinctive colouring or lettering.

Brand name A part of a brand which can be vocalized — the utterable.

Buyer The person who make the actual purchase.

Capital items Goods that enter the finished market partly.

Channels of distribution A distribution channel consists of the set of people and firms involved in the transfer of title to a product as the product moves from producer to ultimate consumer or business user.

Cognitive dissonance Almost every purchase is likely to lead to some post purchase discomfort, and the issues are how much discomfort and what will the consumer do about it.

Company demand The Company's sales resulting from its share of market demand.

Convenience goods Goods that the customer usually purchases frequently, immediately, and with minimum effort in comparison and buying.

Copyright The exclusive legal right to reproduce, publish and sell the matter from a literary, musical, or artistic work.

Cues Minor stimuli that determine when, where, and how the person responds.

Customer loyalty It is the behaviour customers' exhibit when they make frequent purchases of a particular brand.

Decider The person who ultimately determines any part of the entire buying decision; what to buy, how to buy or where to buy.

Decline stage The product life cycle stage in which sales and profits deteriorate.

Demand power People's wants that are backed by purchasing power.

Demographic segmentation Dividing the market into groups on the basis of demographic variables such as age, sex, family size, family cycle, income, occupation, education, religion, race and nationality.

Differentiated marketing The firm decides to operate in several segments of the market and designs separate offers to each.

Distribution channel The set of firms and individuals that take title, or assist in transferring title, to the particular good, or service as it moves from the producer to the consumer.

Drive A strong internal stimulus impelling action. A drive becomes a motive when it is directed towards a particular drive reducing stimulates object.

Drop-error Occurs when the company dismissed an otherwise good product idea.

Durable goods Tangible goods that normally survive many uses.

Enterprise A business undertaking or an entire organization rather than a unit or sub-division.

Entrepreneur A person who is skilled at identifying new

products (or new methods of production), setting up operations, marketing the products and arranging the financing of the operations.

Exchange The act of obtaining a desired object from someone by offering something in return.

Fashion A currently accepted or popular style in a given field. Fashions tend to pass through four stages; distinctiveness, emulation, mass fashion and decline.

Forecasting The art of anticipating what buyers are likely to do under a given set of conditions

Geographic segmentation Units such as nations, states, regions, countries, cities or neighbourhoods.

Growth stage The product life cycle stage that is marked by rapid market acceptance and increasing profits.

Human need A stage of felt deprivation in a person.

Human wants The form that human needs take as shaped by a person's culture and individuality.

Industrial market All the individuals and organizations, who acquire goods and services that enter into the production of other products or services that are sold, rented or supplied to others.

Influencer A person whose views or advice carries some weight in making the final decision.

Initiator The person who first suggests or thinks of the idea of buying the particular product or service.

Introduction stage The product life cycle stage that is marked by slow growth and minimal profits as the product is being introduced in the market.

Inventory Inventory is a detailed list of all the items in the stock.

Learning Changes in an individual's behaviour arising from experience.

Life style The person's pattern of living in the world as expressed in his or her activities, interests and opinions.

Macroenvironment The larger societal forces that affect the marketing environment of a company, namely, technological, political and cultural forces.

Market The set of all actual and potential buyers of a product.

Market demand The term refers to the total volume that would be bought by a defined customer group, in a defined time period in defined marketing environment under a defined marketing programme.

Market development It refers to the company that seek increased sales by taking its current products into new markets.

Marketing orientation Marketing orientation is trying to understand the customer's needs and developing an appropriate product or service and selling the same.

Market penetration More sales to a company's present target group of buyers, without changing the product in any way.

Market positioning Formulating a competitive positioning for the product and a detailed marketing mix.

Market potential The limit approached by market demand as industry marketing expenditure goes to infinity for a given set of competitive prices and a given set of environment.

Market segment Customer who respond in a similar way to a given set of marketing stimuli.

Marketing targeting Evaluating each segment's attractiveness and selecting one or more of the market segments to enter.

Marketing testing The stage where the product and marketing programme are introduced into more realistic market settings.

Marketing Human activity directed at satisfying needs and wants through exchange processes.

Marketing channel Performs the work of selling and bringing goods from producers to consumers.

Marketing concept A management orientation that holds that the key to achieving organizational goals consists of determining the needs and wants of target markets and delivering the desired satisfactions more effectively and efficiently than competitors.

Marketing information system A continuing and interacting structure of people, equipment, and procedures together, sort, analyze, evaluate and distribute pertinent, timely, and accurate information for use by marketing decision-makers to improve their marketing planning, execution and control.

Marketing intermediaries Firms that aid the company in promoting, selling, and distributing its goods to final buyers.

Marketing management The analysis, planning, implementation, and control of programmes designed to create, build, and maintain mutually beneficial exchanges with target buyers for the purpose of achieving organizational objectives.

Marketing management process Consists of (1) organizing the marketing planning process (2) analyzing marketing opportunities, (3) selecting target markets, (4) developing the marketing mix, and (5) managing the marketing effort.

Marketing mix The set of controllable marketing variables that the firm blends to produce the response it wants in the target market.

Marketing research The systematic design, collection, analysis, and reporting of data and findings relevant to a specific marketing situation facing the company.

Marketing strategy The marketing logic by which the business unit hopes to achieve its marketing objectives. Marketing strategy consists of specific strategies bearing on target markets, marketing mix and marketing expenditure level.

Mass marketing A style of marketing in which the seller mass produces, mass distributes, and mass-pro-mote one product to all buyers.

Maturity stage The product life cycle stage in which sales growth slows down and profits stabilize.

Merchant middlemen Firms such as wholesalers and retailers that buy, then resell and merchandise.

Micro environment The actors in the company's immediate environment that affect its ability to serve its customers namely, the company, market channel firms, customer markets, competitors and public.

Motive A need that is sufficiently pressing to direct

the person to seek satisfaction of the need.

New product A good, service, or idea is perceived by some potential customers as new.

Nondurable goods Tangible goods normally consumed in one or a few uses.

Packaging The activities of designing and producing the container or wrapper for a product.

Perception The process by which an individual selects organization and interprets information inputs to create a meaningful picture of the world.

Personal selling Oral presentation in a conversation with one or more prospective purchaser for the purpose of making sales.

Physical distribution The tasks involved in planning, implementing and controlling the physical flows of materials and final goods from points of origin to points of use to meet the needs of customers at a profit.

Price leader A product that is priced below its normal mark-up or even below cost. It is used to attract customers to the store

with the hope that they will buy other things at normal markups.

Pricing strategy The task of defining the rough initial price range and planned price movement through time that the company will use to achieve its marketing objectives in the target market.

Product Anything that can be offered to a market for attention, acquisition, use, or consumption that might satisfy a want or need.

Product concept A management orientation that holds that consumers will favour those products that offer the best quality, performance and features, and therefore the organization should devote its energy to making continuous product improvements.

Product development The term refers to the company's seeking increased sales by developing new or improved products for its current markets.

Product differentiation It means making one's product different in some manner from those of competitors, no matter how small the differentiation may be.

Product idea An idea for a possible product that the

company can see itself offering to the market.

Product image The particular picture consumers acquire of an actual or potential product.

Production concept A management orientation that holds that consumers will favour those products that are available and highly affordable, and therefore management should concentrate on improving production and distribution efficiency.

Product item A distinct unit that is distinguishable by size, price, appearance, or some other attribute. An item is sometimes called a stock keeping unit or product variant.

Product line A group of products that are closely related either because they function in a similar manner, are sold to the same customer groups, are marketed through the same types of outlets, or fall within given price ranges.

Product mix The set of all product lines and items that a particular seller offers for sale to buyers.

Promotion Promotion is essentially a firm's sales efforts and includes the function of informing, persuading and influencing the purchase decision of current and prospective customers with the object of increasing sales and profits.

Psychographic segmentation Dividing the buyers into different groups on the basis of their social class, lifestyle and or personality characteristics.

Publicity Non personal stimulation of demand for a product, services, or business unit by planting commercially significant news about it in a published medium or obtaining favourable presentation of it upon radio, television, or stage that is not paid for by the sponsor.

Public relations The management function that evaluated public attitudes, identifies the policies and procedures of an individual or an organization with the public interest, and plans and executes a programme of action to earn public understanding and acceptance.

Pull strategy A strategy that calls for spending a lot of money on advertising and consumer promotion to build up consumer demand.

Push strategy A strategy that calls for using the sales force and trade promotion to push the product through the channels.

Reference groups Those groups that have a direct (face to face) or indirect influence on the person's attitudes or behaviour.

Reseller market All the individuals and organizations who acquire goods for the purpose of reselling or renting to others at a profit.

Retailing All the activities involved in selling goods or services directly to final consumers for their personal, non-business use.

Role The activities that a person is expected to perform according to the persons around him or her.

Sales analysis The act of determining whether the company's sales are coming from by product, customer, territory and so on.

Sales budget A conservative estimate of the expected volume of sales. It is used primarily for making current purchasing production and cash flow decisions.

Sales potential The limit approached by company demand as company marketing expenditure increases in relation to competition.

Sales promotion Short-term incentives to encourage purchase or sale of a product or service.

Sales quota A sales goal set for a product line, company division, or sales representative. It is primarily a management tool for defining and stimulating sales effort.

Secondary data Information that already exists somewhere having been collected for another purpose.

Selling concept A management orientation that holds that consumers will not buy enough of the organization's products unless the organization undertakes a substantial selling and promotion effort.

Service Any activity or benefit that one party can offer to another that is essentially intangible and does not result in the ownership of anything. Its production may or may not be tied to a physical product.

Shopping goods Goods that the customer, in the process of selection and purchase, characteristically compares on such basis as suitability, quality, price and style.

Social classes Relatively homogeneous and enduring divisions in a society which are hierarchically ordered and whose members share similar values, interests and behaviour.

Societal marketing concept A management orientation that holds that the organization's task is to determine the needs, wants and interest of target markets and to deliver the desired satisfaction more effectively and efficiently than competitors in a way that preserves or enhances the consumer's and the society's well being.

Speciality goods Goods with unique characteristics and or brand identification for which a significant group of buyers are habitually willing to make a special purchasing effort.

Status The general esteem that each role is accorded by society.

Strategic Business Unit (SBU) Any business making up the company.

Strategic planning The managerial process of developing and maintaining a strategic fit between the organization's goals and its changing market opportunities. It relies on developing a clear company mission, supporting objectives and goals, a sound business portfolio, and coordinated functional strategies.

Sub-cultures Groups of people with shared value systems emerging from their common life experience or circumstances.

Suppliers Business firms and individuals that provide the resources needed by the company and its competitors to produce the particular goods and services.

Target market A well defined set of customers whose needs the company plans to satisfy.

Target marketing A style o marketing in which the seller distinguishes between market segments, selects one or more of these segments, and develops products and marketing mixes tailored to each segment.

Test marketing Selecting one or more markets in which to introduce a new product and marketing programme to see how well they perform and what revisions are needed, if any.

Trade mark A brand or part of a brand that is given legal protection because it is capable of exclusive appropriation. A trade mark protects the seller's exclusive rights to use the brand name and/or brand mark.

Undifferentiated marketing The firm decides to ignore marketing differences and go after the whole market with on market offer.

Unique Selling Proposition It is one thing that makes a product different than any other that marketers think consumers will buy the product even though it may seem no different from many others just like it.

User The person(s) who consumer or uses the product or service.

Value analysis An approach to cost reduction in which components are carefully studied to determine id they can be redesigned or standardized or made by cheaper methods of production.

Warehousing It is a place where goods are stored or accumulated for sales.

Wholesaling All the activities involved in selling goods and services to those buying for resale or business use.

REFERENCES

Aaker, D. *Strategic Market Management*, 4th edn. (1995). Wiley.

Abraham, Piyus, Sonal, Vandana. (2005). Marketing Paradigms of emerging economics, Jan 12 & 13; IIM, Ahmedabad.

Adcock, D., Halborg, A. and Ross, C. (2001). *Marketing Principles and Practice*, 4th edition, Prentice Hall.

Booz, Allen & Hamilton. (1982). *New Product Management for the 1980s*. Booz, Allen & Hamilton Inc.

Buckley, A. (1993). *The Essence of Services Marketing*, Prentice Hall.

Chaffey, D. (2003). *Total E-Mail Marketing*, Butterworth Heinemann.

Chavadi Chandan and Ganjali Shilpa Rajesh, (2007). Pricate Labels in retailing, Marketing Mastermind, Vol. VII, No.6, pp.14–17.

Doyle, P. (1994). *Marketing Management and Strategy*, Prentice Hall.

Gronroos, C. (1996). Relationship Marketing; strategic and tactical implications, Management Decision, Vol.43, No.3, pp.5–14.

Hollensen, S, (2002). Marketing Management: A Relationship Approach. Prentice Hall.

Jobber, D. (2001). *Principles and Practices of Marketing*, 3rd edn. McGraw-Hill.

Jobber, D. (2004). *Principles and Practices of Marketing*, 4th edn. McGraw-Hill.

Kapferer, J. (1997). *Strategic Brand Management*, 2nd edn. Kogan page.

Kothari C.R. (2005). *Research Methodology*, 3rd edn. Sultan Chand & Sons, New Delhi.

Kotler, P. (1997). *Marketing Management*, 9th edn. Prentice Hall.

Kotler, P., Armstrong, G., Saunders, J. and Wong, V. (1999). *Principles of Marketing*, 2nd European edn. Prentice Hall.

Lancaster, G. and Massingham, L. (2001). *Marketing Management*, 3rd edn., McGraw-Hill.

McGoldrick, P.J. (1990). *Retail Marketing*, McGraw-Hill, pp.7.

Narver, J.C. and Slater, S.F. (1990). "The effects of marketing orientation on business profitability," *Journal of Marketing*. Vol.54, October, pp.20–35.

O'Connor, J. and Galvin, E. (1997). *Marketing and Information technology*, Pitman.

Periman, R. (1975). *Consumers and social Services*, Wiley, pp.55.

Rust, Roland T. and Anthony J. Zahorik, (1993), "Customer Satisfaction, Customer retention and market share," *Journal of Retailing*, 69(summer), pp. 193–215.

Shapiro, B.P. and Jackson, B.B. (1978). "Industrial pricing to meet customer need." *Harvard Business Review*, Nov.-Dec. pp. 119–127.

Sheth, J.N. (1973). "A model of industrial buyer behaviour," *Journal of marketing*, Vol.37, No.4, pp. 50–56.

Websites

www.iima.ac.in

www.indianmba.com

www.coolavenues.com

www.india-reports.com

www.businessworld.in

www.spark.com (online refereed journal.mht)

www.eretailbiz.com

www.capsind.com

INDEX